D1987097

THE PERPETUAL IMMIGRANT AND THE LIMITS OF ATHENIAN DEMOCRACY

In the fifth and fourth centuries BCE, immigrants called "metics" (*metoikoi*) settled in Athens without a path to citizenship. Galvanized by these political realities, classical thinkers cast a critical eye on the nativism defining democracy's membership rules and explored the city's anxieties over intermingling and passing. Yet readers continue to treat immigration and citizenship as separate phenomena of little interest to theorists writing at the time. In *The Perpetual Immigrant and the Limits of Athenian Democracy,* Demetra Kasimis makes visible the long-overlooked centrality of immigration to the originary practices of democracy and political theory in Athens. She dismantles the interpretive and political assumptions that have led readers to turn away from the metic and reveals the key role this figure plays in such texts as Plato's *Republic*. The result is a series of original readings that boldly reframes urgent questions about how democracies order their noncitizen members.

DEMETRA KASIMIS is Assistant Professor of Political Science at the University of Chicago. Her research on classical Greek thought and democratic theory has been funded by the National Endowment for the Humanities and the American Council for Learned Societies. *The Perpetual Immigrant and the Limits of Athenian Democracy* is her first book.

CLASSICS AFTER ANTIQUITY

Editors

ALASTAIR BLANSHARD
University of Queensland
SHANE BUTLER
Johns Hopkins University
EMILY GREENWOOD
Yale University

Classics after Antiquity presents innovative contributions in the field of Classical Reception Studies. Each volume explores the methods and motives of those who, coming after and going after antiquity, have entered into a contest with and for the legacies of the ancient world. The series aims to unsettle, provoke debate, and stimulate a re-evaluation of assumptions about the relationship between Greek and Roman classical pasts and modern histories.

Other titles in the series

Classical Victorians: Scholars, Scoundrels and Generals in Pursuit of Antiquity
Edmund Richardson ISBN: 978-1-107-02677-3
Modernism and Homer: The Odysseys of H.D., James Joyce, Osip Mandelstam, and Ezra Pound Leah Culligan Flack ISBN: 978-1-107-10803-5
Borges' Classics: Global Encounters with the Graeco-Roman Past
Laura Jansen ISBN: 978-1-108-41840-9

THE PERPETUAL IMMIGRANT AND THE LIMITS OF ATHENIAN DEMOCRACY

DEMETRA KASIMIS

University of Chicago

CAMBRIDGE
UNIVERSITY PRESS

CAMBRIDGE
UNIVERSITY PRESS

University Printing House, Cambridge CB2 8BS, United Kingdom

One Liberty Plaza, 20th Floor, New York, NY 10006, USA

477 Williamstown Road, Port Melbourne, VIC 3207, Australia

314–321, 3rd Floor, Plot 3, Splendor Forum, Jasola District Centre, New Delhi – 110025, India

79 Anson Road, #06–04/06, Singapore 079906

Cambridge University Press is part of the University of Cambridge.

It furthers the University's mission by disseminating knowledge in the pursuit of education, learning, and research at the highest international levels of excellence.

www.cambridge.org
Information on this title: www.cambridge.org/9781107052437
DOI: 10.1017/9781107280571

© Demetra Kasimis 2018

This publication is in copyright. Subject to statutory exception and to the provisions of relevant collective licensing agreements, no reproduction of any part may take place without the written permission of Cambridge University Press.

First published 2018

Printed and bound in Great Britain by Clays Ltd, Elcograf S.p.A.

A catalogue record for this publication is available from the British Library.

Library of Congress Cataloging-in-Publication Data
NAMES: Kasimis, Demetra, 1980– author.
TITLE: The perpetual immigrant and the limits of Athenian democracy / Demetra Kasimis.
DESCRIPTION: Cambridge, United Kingdom ; New York, NY : Cambridge University Press, 2018. | Series: Classics after antiquity | Includes bibliographical references and index.
IDENTIFIERS: LCCN 2018015091 | ISBN 9781107052437 (hardback)
SUBJECTS: LCSH: Citizenship – Greece – Athens. | Democracy – Greece – Athens. | Metics. | Athens (Greece) – Emigration and immigration.
CLASSIFICATION: LCC JC75.C5 K37 2018 | DDC 323.60938/5–dc23
LC record available at https://lccn.loc.gov/2018015091

ISBN 978-1-107-05243-7 Hardback

Cambridge University Press has no responsibility for the persistence or accuracy of URLs for external or third-party internet websites referred to in this publication and does not guarantee that any content on such websites is, or will remain, accurate or appropriate.

To my family

Contents

Acknowledgments

This is a book about the figure of the immigrant. It is also a book about the routes we have taken to discount its vitality in classical Greek thought and the new ones we might now travel to engage it. It is in two senses, then, a book about genealogy. In the first sense, it is a book about the descent criterion Athenians used to deny democratic citizenship to resident foreigners (*metoikoi*) and their children and the ways that some Athenian thinkers critically explored the meanings of this nativist rule. In the second, it is a book about the origins of two practices, political theory and democratic citizenship, and the ways that our views about these quintessentially Athenian activities have been shaped in part by displacing the metic (*metoikos*) from the center of ancient democratic life and thought.

Metoikos is a word from my childhood. Yet as any speaker of Modern Greek will tell you, it is not the usual term for immigrant. How I came to care deeply about this figure does not always seem as deliberate as the years I have spent writing about it. I have come to see my relation to the metic as a sign of the winding paths that ideas (about the past) take and a gentle reminder to embrace one's useful prejudice, the term Gadamer coined to suggest that a reader's situatedness does not so much close down as open up one's understanding of a text.

In 1971, in the middle of Greece's military dictatorship, the singer Giorgos Dalaras recorded a version of "Le Métèque," a song Georges Moustaki had released a few years earlier in French. Although he kept the music the same, Dalaras used Greek lyrics that the poet and antiwar activist Dimitris Christodoulou had written under conditions of censorship. The Greek rendition recast Moustaki's ballad about a wandering Greek Jew as the nebulous story of a life derailed by sudden and forced mobility. The terms evoked but left unspoken the fate of Greece's political exiles. Within four years of the song's release, my father had left Greece. A decade later, we danced on the wood floor of our New York apartment to his Greek records. Among them was *O Metoikos.*

I owe this book to the zigzagging routes that the *metoikos* took to reach me – from Ancient Greek to French to Modern Greek and back again. In his *Untimely Meditations,* Nietzsche wrote that it was only to the extent that he had been a pupil of earlier times, especially the Hellenic, that though a child of the present, he was able to see the urgency of thinking critically and diagnostically about the relations we construct to the past and the matters we strategically leave out of these visions. I tend to think it was only because I was a child of a Hellenic present that, though a student of earlier times, the figure of the metic spoke to me years later in a classroom and I stopped to imagine its critical promise. I offer this anecdote about the reception of ideas in celebration of the different and unsung ways we come to classical Greece. Most of all, I offer it as a testament to my father's unyielding spirit and in gratitude for the energy and love with which he taught me his language.

*****

I have many people to thank for their engagement with the ideas in this book. Let me begin with my teachers. This project started as a dissertation in the Department of Political Science at Northwestern University. I thank S. Sara Monoson, Bonnie Honig, and Mary G. Dietz for encouraging me to take risks, holding me to exacting standards, and exhibiting an unwavering commitment to the merits of the argument. The intellectual ambitions of the present study would have been unthinkable without Sara's shrewd advice that I engage deeply with the discipline of classics while training as a political theorist. Not a week goes by that I do not appreciate the emphasis on critique that characterized the political theory program at Northwestern. I am also thankful to former and current Northwestern faculty for opening my eyes in the classroom: Tad Brennan, Michael Hanchard, Marianne Hopman, Richard Kraut, the late Ernesto Laclau, Michael Loriaux, Lyle Massey, and Linda Zerilli. The undergraduate professors I had in philosophy, comparative literature, and Hellenic Studies at Columbia University – Valentina Izmirlieva, Bonnie Kent, Marina Kotzamani, Neni Panourgia, Wolfgang Mann, Karen Van Dyck, and Nadia Urbinati – have implicitly shaped the interdisciplinary style of this work. I also wish to thank Claude Catapano, Geraldine Woods, and Tom LaFarge, my wonderful high school teachers at the Horace Mann School in the Bronx, for first showing me how to read history and literature critically, ambitiously, and with conviction.

My colleagues in the Department of Political Science at the University of Chicago have been extremely generous with their time and incisive in their readings of this manuscript. I am especially grateful to Adom Getachew, Patchen Markell, John McCormick, Jennifer Pitts, Lisa Wedeen, and Linda Zerilli for giving me comments on chapters and cheering me on with verve. The final throes of writing were eased by the kindness of four people who sat down to read the entire manuscript: I thank Karuna Mantena for seeing connections among chapters and, most happily, for telling me I was done; Nancy Worman for noticing where I was selling my claims short and meeting me up and down MacDougal Street to talk about it; Lisa Wedeen for providing page-by-page notes and sharpening the book's vision; and Mary G. Dietz for reading with characteristic depth, dedication, and wit – the marks of our conversations about hermeneutics and political theory are all over this book. For many years, my dear friend Ella Myers has read drafts of my work with a razor-sharp critical eye and the lively, loving voice of encouragement only she possesses. Christopher Skeaff has also discussed this manuscript with subtlety and perspicacity since graduate school. To Samuel Chambers, I owe a large measure of thanks not only for his feedback but also for the wise counsel he provides with a rare kindness.

For their helpful thoughts on the book at different stages and in various forms, I warmly thank Clifford Ando, Larissa Atkison, Ryan Balot, Shadi Bartsch-Zimmer, Mark Bauer, Susan Bickford, Andrés Fabian Henao Castro, Chiara Cordelli, Giuseppe Cumella, Joshua Dienstag, Lisa Disch, Linda Edelstein, Jay Elliott, Michaele Ferguson, Jill Frank, Bryan Garsten, Larry George, James Glisson, Ayten Gündoğdu, Emily Greenwood, Verity Harte, Elizabeth Irwin, Patrick Jagoda, Heather Keenleyside, Zoë Kontes, Rachel Kravetz, Michèle Lowrie, Matthew Landauer, Hélène Landemore, Melissa Lane, Robyn Marasco, Andrew March, James Martel, Jake Matatyaou, Lida Maxwell, Kirstie McClure, Sara Monoson, Sankar Mutthu, Sarah Nooter, Paul North, Paulina Ochoa Espejo, Mark Payne, Maggie Penn, Tracey Rosen, Michael Rossi, Arlene Saxonhouse, Kristen Schilt, Joel Schlosser, Kathryn Slanski, Agatha Slupek, Adam Sonderberg, Jeff Spinner-Halev, Simon Stow, Nathan Tarcov, Chris Trinacty, Joan Tronto, and John Wallach. I am grateful to Claudio Sansone and Agatha Slupek for their helpful research assistance; Madeleine Johnson and Rona Johnston Gordon for their work preparing the final manuscript; and Pam Scholefield for her quick and careful indexing. Earlier versions of Chapters 2 and 4 were published, respectively, as "The Tragedy of Blood-Based Membership: Secrecy and the Politics of Immigration in Euripides' *Ion*" in *Political Theory* 41/2 (April 2013): 231–256 and "Plato's Open Secret," *Contemporary Political Theory* 15/4 (November 2016): 339–357.

For their tough questions and thoughtful remarks, I thank audiences at Columbia, CUNY, Georgetown, Kenyon, King's College London, Northwestern, Princeton, the Remarque Institute (NYU) Kandersteg Seminar, UCLA, UNC–Chapel Hill, the University of Chicago, the University of South Carolina, the University of Toronto, and Yale. I am particularly indebted to the interdisciplinary group of humanists and social scientists at UC Irvine for encouraging me to own the metic's difference from the immigrant. On many occasions, political theorists at the annual conventions of the American Political Science Association, the Western Political Science Association, and the Association for Political Theory have been a source of steady support and friendly criticism.

I am also deeply appreciative to several institutions for funding my writing over the years. My first thanks go to the Alumnae Association of Northwestern University, which awarded me a dissertation fellowship when I began writing. The American Council for Learned Societies gave me a Mellon Early Career Award that supported my last year of dissertating. During book revisions, the National Endowment for the Humanities awarded me a fellowship that supported the research and composition of several new chapters and changed my life. I thank the faculty and administrators at the Whitney Humanities Center at Yale for providing me with a postdoctoral position after graduate school and welcoming me back two years later to carry out the NEH: Mark Bauer, Bryan Garsten, Emily Greenwood, the late Maria Rosa Menocal, Norma Thompson, and Gary Tomlinson. Between my two stays in New Haven, the Political Science Department at California State, Long Beach, gave me my first faculty position and showed me what collegiality and politically engaged teaching mean. I am indebted to my former colleagues at CSULB, in particular Larry George, Terri Wright, Amy Cabrera Rasmussen, Cora Goldstein, and Kevin Wallsten, for their belief in this project.

It has not been easy to reach across disciplinary lines, and I thank my editors at Cambridge University Press for their early and sustained interest in helping me do so. Emily Greenwood has been a steadfast advocate of this book and, in her capacity as a series editor, helped on numerous occasions to strengthen it. I am also grateful to Michael Sharp, Alastair Blanshard, and Shane Butler for guiding the manuscript through the publication process. For his advice at a crucial moment, I thank Robert Dreesen.

My extended family in Corinth and Athens has provided the nourishing conditions for my writing nearly every summer and sometimes for months at a time. I thank my grandmother Dimitra Kasimis, my aunt Sofia, my cousin Chryssa, and in particular, my uncle Charalambos for their humor, affection, and support. In New York, my late maternal grandparents Harry and Gussie Pulin and my late uncle Chuck showed me that there is grace in craft, power in artistry, and mischief in language. I hope that they would have recognized their imprint on this book. I am, as always, deeply appreciative of my oldest friends Adi Segal, Jonathan Ferrantelli, Anya Sawyer, and Carmina Ocampo. Their abiding interest in my work is fortunately surpassed by their excitement to talk about everything else.

This book is dedicated to my brother Nicholas Kasimis, a fierce and loving champion of all my efforts, and to my parents, Janet and Petros, the bravest and most creative people I know. For showing me the pleasure of finding meaning in (nearly!) everything, I especially thank my mother, whose analytic mind is matched in strength only by the intensity of her affection for us all. Philip Baker's brilliant imagination, warmth, playfulness, and love have sustained me throughout the writing of this book. I cannot believe the attention and insight with which he has read every line, but I am certain that he deserves all the credit in the world for reminding me to make this manuscript my very own.

Series Editors' Preface

Among students and scholars of ancient Athenian political thought, it has long been a refrain that Athenian democracy did not produce a systematic theory of democracy. For that we have had to rely on its critics – notably Thucydides, Xenophon, Plato, and Aristotle. In *The Perpetual Immigrant and the Limits of Athenian Democracy*, Demetra Kasimis revolutionizes the terms of this discussion by showing how theories of democracy and citizenship were sustained through the invocation across multiple genres of certain key figures and concepts of exclusion. Athens practiced its political theory in multiple sites through religious rites, dramatic performance, assembly discussions, legal proceedings, and other civic rituals, and we misunderstand how Athenian political theory operated if we fail to recognize this. Within these civic conversations, one figure stands out in particular – the metic, the immigrant. Defining, regulating, and supervising metics became central to the project of Athenian citizenship.

Athens built up its notions of citizenship around a fantasy of blood descent and Athenian exceptionalism. Yet the metic constantly threatened to expose this fantasy and the implications of the possibility that a metic might successfully pass as a citizen were deeply troubling to its democracy. Metics' insider-yet-always-outsider status made them crucial figures for mediating Athenian reflections on the conditions of citizenship. In a series of incisive readings of Euripides, Plato, and Demosthenes, Kasimis reveals the contours of an Athenian debate in which supposedly natural differences between Athenian citizens and noncitizens were fabricated through performance, resulting in the fatal condition that citizen status would always be vulnerable to the quality of that performance. In this civic drama, the metic plays a crucial role as an almost-citizen, a limit-case, who lacks the ultimate blood qualification to act the part of citizens but whose performance is otherwise perilously indistinguishable from that of Athenian citizens. And, as we know, sometimes their civic performance did enable metics to qualify for citizenship, a fact that only exacerbated concerns about the stability of a secure, pure conception of native Athenian citizenship.

In Kasimis's argument, Plato, one of Athenian democracy's arch critics, emerges as the theorist who, in holding up a "metic lens" to Athenian democracy, exposes the aporias of the civic drama of membership performance. Instead of Plato's attack on democracy's "open society," as Karl Popper saw it, *The Perpetual Immigrant* finds Plato in Book VIII of the *Republic* critical of the fundamental hypocrisy of natural differences and the climate of political exclusion that they engender. This hypocrisy means that the equality between citizens is compromised by the suspicion that, while all may act like citizens, not all may qualify equally for citizenship, with the presence of the metic nibbling away at the fiction of the autochthonous Athenian, born not made.

Throughout this book, Kasimis explores multiple forms of reception. She lays bare the different ways in which interpretations of Athenian democratic theory are mediated by the disciplines and schools in which scholars have been trained. For its part, *The Perpetual Immigrant* weaves a rich interpretative web. In its deployment of the critical tools that characterize modernity and postmodernity, this is a work that could only emerge "after Antiquity"; this is a work that both informs and is informed by contemporary theory. In Chapter 2, Euripides' drama of citizenship identity in the *Ion*, in which citizen descent is paradoxically suppressed, is paired with Eve Kosofsky Sedgwick's theory of closeting. In the discussion of Plato in Chapter 5, another theoretical axis points to Homi Bhabha's theorization of colonial mimesis, which exposes, through a regression of mimicry, the play-acting at the heart of the putative "original." Similarly, in Kasimis' wry summary of Plato's critique, "remove a citizen's mask and you will find a metic lurking underneath" (p. 106), we are reminded of Ralph Ellison's exposition of the mask at the heart of American cultural identity, in the essay "Change the Joke and Slip the Yoke" (first published in *Partisan Review* in 1958). There Ellison dissected the constitutive work that masks do in shoring up the myth of Americanness in an elaborate cultural masquerade: "when American life is most American it is apt to be most theatrical."[1] Metics stand in the wings of the *polis*, as understudies of citizen actors, showing up the stagecraft of Athenian, democratic citizen identity.

[1] Ralph Ellison, "Change the Joke and Slip the Yoke," in *The Collected Essays of Ralph Ellison*, edited by John F. Callahan; preface by Saul Bellow. New York: Random House, 1995: 100–112 (quoting from p. 108).

Demetra Kasimis leaves us with the question, "What if the metic is the critical figure of our time?" This is a timely suggestion as scholars of ancient Greek political theory attempt to find lessons for contemporary immigration debates in ancient Greek texts and vice versa. By exposing the deep entanglement of the metic in Athenian democratic identity, *The Perpetual Immigrant* delves deeper, offering a bold theoretical provocation for future studies. In Kasimis's persuasive analysis, the metic presence leads to a "perpetual" aporia that defines not only Athenian thinking about citizenship but also our own.

PART I

Autochthony Trouble

CHAPTER 1

The Metic in and out of Theory

> *The doubt in these cases is, not who is, but whether he who is a citizen ought to be one; and there will still be a further doubt, whether he who ought not to be a citizen, is one in fact, for what ought not to be is what is false.*
>
> – Aristotle, *Politics* 1275b38–1276a2[1]

The desire to reframe the familiar dilemmas of democratic life has often led modern readers to seek inspiration in the politics and thought of classical Athens. Political theorists in particular have found conceptual resources in Athenian texts for opening new spaces of argumentation and unsettling staid lines of criticism. The practice of treating works of Athenian philosophy and literature as investigations into various orders of democratic rule – institutions, activity, discourse – and proposing that these texts speak, at least allegorically, to problems of modern democratic politics is so commonplace as to raise suspicions about the difficult questions that remain assiduously overlooked in this varied enterprise. How democracy orders its immigrants is one of these questions. The significance of this hierarchical relation to some Athenian thinkers and the curious reluctance by theoretically minded critics to see this dynamic as a preoccupation for classical theorists of democracy are the provocations for this book. Historians have long acknowledged the ubiquity of resident foreigners in the life of the Athenian polis. Yet critics have been reluctant to recognize, let alone analyze, the immigrant as an object of political or theoretical concern for Athenian thought.

This book argues that immigration (*metoikia*) is a critical matter of inquiry in the political thought of classical Athens. My objective is not to replicate historical research on metics (*metoikoi*) – although that scholarship informs the following discussion – but to engage the figure of the metic as a site of discursive and political theoretical meaning. I contend

[1] Translations of Aristotle's *Politics* are by Benjamin Jowett (Aristotle 1996) unless otherwise noted.

that the metic dimension of Athenian membership politics is a persistently overlooked interpretive field for reading Athenian texts and their arguments about the meanings and practices of democratic citizenship. My view is that the restoration of the metic as an interpretive lens unleashes new and unexpected critical energy from Athenian political thought: the recovery of the metic animates a strain of criticism in which Athenian thinkers are wrestling deeply with democracy's relation to nativism and its ambiguous, even paradoxical effects.

It is puzzling that narratives of the history of political thought tend to render Athenian texts irrelevant to matters of immigration even in their own space and time. For decades, scholars have been returning to the thought of classical Athens to analyze its engagements with political exclusion. Figurations of the marginal, in particular women, slaves, and barbarians, many have argued, are central to the construction of meaning in Athenian texts, where they function not simply to underscore the democracy's hierarchical order of inclusion but also to call into question that order's naturalness and inevitability.[2] The metic represents a striking exception to this way of reading: from Socrates' hosts in the *Republic* to Aristotle himself, the general presumption is that this frontier figure is somehow uninteresting or uncontroversial to the otherwise wide-ranging examinations of political difference readers find in Athenian texts.[3] Unlike other categories (woman, slave, foreigner), the metic appears to function simply empirically to affirm a reality about the city's political hierarchies rather than (also) symbolically to generate new insights into them.

What might it mean that in spite of a long-standing turn to alterity across the humanities and social sciences, one figure of particular and utmost significance for the definition of Athenian citizenship has generally failed to incite political theoretical interest in its own right? This question guides much of the proceeding study. I wager that the metic's unique and precarious proximity to the citizen makes its signification easy, if not strategically useful, to overlook and all the more crucial to animate. To attend to figurations of *metoikia* in texts by Euripides, Plato, and Demosthenes, my primary interlocutors in this book, is to examine not only the unstable place of the metic in polis life but also the fraught and shifting meaning of the democratic citizen itself.

[2] Vidal-Naquet 1986: 159–224; E. Hall 1989; Saxonhouse 1992; Loraux 1993; Zeitlin 1996; Foley 2001; duBois 2003.

[3] See, for example, Ober (1998: 303), who concludes, "Despite whatever discomforts Aristotle may have felt regarding his own metic status in Athens, this category of persons was not particularly troublesome from the point of view of his political theory."

After the Persian Wars, thousands of people from other parts of Greece and the Mediterranean sought residence in Athens.[4] Migrants had been settling in the polis for years, but in the first half of the fifth century BCE, the city's economic growth, enabled by its expansion of the port of Piraeus, spurred unprecedented immigration to Attica not only from other Hellenic cities but also from places like Syria, Lydia, and Thrace.[5] Sometime in this period, the polis established *metoikia* as a formal institution for regulating immigrant membership and restricting the participation of immigrants in civic life.[6] The polis classified resident foreigners, manumitted slaves, and their Athenian-born children as *metoikoi*,[7] meaning that, as a category of standing, the metic was not coterminous with the immigrant, as I elaborate.[8] Athens disqualified persons from acquiring citizen status, generation after generation, on the basis of

[4] Given the increase in the citizen population in this period, some historians have argued that many immigrants were made citizens. On the "nonnatural" growth of the citizenry, see Patterson 1981: 70. Watson (2010: 260–264) provides an overview of the historical debates on the issue.

[5] Bakewell (2013: 19) relays that "the expansion" of Piraeus encouraged immigration. Xenophon (*Por.* 2.3) refers to metics as Lydians, Phrygians, and Syrians and other "*barbaroi.*" The Athenian cult of Bendis, a Thracian goddess, discussed in Chapter 3, attests to the presence of Thracian metics.

[6] Inscriptions make earlier (sixth-century) reference to metics but invoke the term in a nontechnical sense, according to Whitehead (1977: 27–68, esp. 64n44). It is difficult to say precisely when *metoikia* emerged as a juridical status, but most historians believe it was before 460 BCE. Bakewell (2013: 20) wagers that the metic emerged as a legal category sometime between the mid-470s and 460. By contrast, Watson argues that Athenians were concerned about immigrants in those years but did not create a formal metic status until around 450, when the polis "first took an interest in restricting who might become a citizen" (2010: 271, 260). The emergence of the metic as a distinct formal status would, on Watson's view, coincide roughly with the passage of Pericles' Citizenship Law, which I discuss later on in the chapter. This claim would also fit with the view of Patterson (1981: 134), who sees the hardening of a metic membership category as one of the city's efforts to sharpen the citizen's definition. For an exploration of how Athens encouraged immigration while passing legislation to make citizenship more exclusive, see Irwin 2016.

[7] Whitehead (1986: 81) argues that individual demes were "required to take formal note of any immigrants who chose to settle within their particular bailiwicks – just as the polis itself had now resolved to monitor the immigrant community as a whole – and to *begin* to devise a broad balance between rights for them and obligations upon them." Each deme, he adds, would have been free to decide the extent to which it would note its metic residents. "Within each deme," he adds, "the position of metics may well have varied tremendously" (Whitehead 1986: 84).

[8] Whitehead (1977: 109) points out that many non-Hellenic metics were freed slaves but argues that the precise breakdown of the metic population into freeborn and freed is impossible to know with certainty. "On present *data* and methods," he adds, "we cannot proceed much beyond the painfully obvious statement that metics of non-Hellenic origin were living in Athens throughout the classical period. At no time can proportions be accurately estimated" because *metoikia* status was applied to Hellenic and "barbarian" metics alike (1977: 112, 116). Akrigg (2015: 164–165), however, argues that many metics were former slaves; he criticizes Whitehead's account for suggesting that most metics were economic migrants and downplaying the association of metics with servility. Whether many or most metics were former slaves, the possibility that a metic could fall (back) into slavery made it easy to code *metoikia*, or some metic ways of living and working, as servile. On the last point, see Chapter 6.

blood, not place of birth.[9] While Athenians could naturalize metics or grant them such special privileges as the freedom to own land or buildings in Attica (*enktesis*) or an exemption from the metic tax (*metoikion*), cases of metic enfranchisement were rare because strictly honorific. As David Whitehead observes, "the history of naturalization in classical Athens excludes almost completely the ordinary *metoikos*."[10] Only a decree by the polis could turn a metic into a citizen, usually as a reward for an especially meritorious act, such as giving generous financial support to the city's institutions.[11]

Yet in spite of the legal limits on their political participation, metics enjoyed a practice of freedom and engaged in Athenian civic life in ways that not only distinguished them from slaves but also linked them to aspects of citizen activity that enabled their integration, potential prosperity, political influence, and material benefits to the city.[12] At the start of the Peloponnesian War, metics may have constituted 40 percent of the Athenian hoplite force.[13] Around a century later, Xenophon (*Por.* 2.1) argued that metics were an excellent but underutilized source of revenue for the newly restored democracy. Improving metics' social conditions, he insisted, would encourage more metic settlement and revitalize the Athenian economy.[14]

[9] The earliest extant definition of the metic belongs to Aristophanes of Byzantium (fr. 38), a Hellenistic fragment that is therefore a retrodiction. For a thorough discussion of the lived experience and privileges, restrictions, and responsibilities of the metic, see Clerc 1893 and Whitehead 1977: ch. 3, which also provides a critical overview of earlier scholarship on the metic. See also Kamen 2013: ch. 4, and Adak 2003. Kennedy 2014 provides an historical study of metic women in particular.

[10] Whitehead 1977: 153.

[11] On citizenship decrees, see Whitehead (1977: 69, 153–159) and Rhodes and Osborne 2003. In one widely discussed case, the freed slave Pasion, who grew rich as a metic from the shield factory he owned, eventually acquired citizenship in the late fourth century because he had made a large donation to the city's public institutions. For details on Pasion, see Trevett 1992: 1–49. Aspects of Pasion's life are discussed in Isoc. 17 and Dem. 36 in particular.

[12] There was therefore great heterogeneity within the metic population. Immigrants belonged to every socioeconomic stratum and possessed a range of reasons for coming to or staying (to work) in the city (Whitehead 1977: 18). Nevertheless, Whitehead (1977: 6–7) makes a persuasive case for concluding that the predominant connotation of *metoikos* is "home-changer" and suggests that, whatever the metic's eventual technical scope, the act of immigrating is crucial to the term's original meaning. Foreigners who did not intend to stay in Athens for a long period of time, however, could still be classed as metics. This was probably especially true in the fourth century BCE, he explains, for in the fifth "there are signs that the machinery was less rigorous, so that, on average, metics may have constituted a more settled population *de facto* than they did later, when a *metoikos* might be someone merely completing his *emporia* before sailing home" (Whitehead 1977: 9–10).

[13] Duncan-Jones bases the claim that, among the 29,000 Athenian hoplites, there existed "a force of some 12,000 metic hoplites . . . in 431" on a reading of Thucydides, which he takes to suggest a "massive metic component in the population of hoplite census at Athens" (1980: 101, 106).

[14] Akrigg (2015: 163) reads the *Poroi* to suggest that Xenophon is "bothered not by a shortage of metics – but by a shortage of a particular kind, the ones who brought economic benefits to Athens."

When Athenian texts draw on metic characters, spaces, and activities, they are exploring the meanings and effects of these strategies of inclusion and exclusion. The works I read closely here – Euripides' *Ion*, Plato's *Republic*, Demosthenes' *Against Euboulides* – stage a conflict between metics' formal disenfranchisement and their social and economic integration as a way of exploring a deeper tension in the Athenian conception of membership: is citizenship a particular way of acting made possible by living in the polis or simply the possession of a legal status inherited by blood? If the latter, what political significance does the much-celebrated practice of Athenian citizenship actually carry in the polis?

I argue throughout the book that an exploration of the meaning of the citizen (*politēs*) in Athenian political thought must include an interrogation of the place of the metic. The blood-based distinction the polis used to distinguish citizen from metic insinuates that an unbridgeable, constitutive gap separates these two relatively free and approximate figures. Athenian thinkers draw on the metic in my view not to resecure this assertion of naturalized difference but to reveal its fragility and accentuate the political theoretical stakes that are raised by this sort of distinction. I read their engagements with the metic to suggest that in a heterogeneous, inclusive, yet hierarchal polis, the democratic demand to distinguish the citizen according to a seemingly pregiven difference like blood can generate a need for and an acute anxiety around the deciphering of membership activity as either the authentic expression or the disingenuous performance of a "natural" difference.[15] Within this frame, the verifying, exposing, and proving of consanguinity risk becoming preeminent democratic activities. Thus it is to the possibility of a metic's passing as a citizen that the recently enfranchised speaker in *Against Neaera* turns, in an ironic attempt to save himself from falling back into *metoikia* (if not slavery): within the Athenian legal system, Apollodorus strategizes, the best way to protect one's newfound citizen status from further instability is actually to exploit the ambiguity around membership claims and portray the wife of his enemy accuser as a foreigner fraudulently exercising her own citizen privileges.

Alert to these democratic anxieties about citizen illegibility and status flux, the texts I focus on depict metics passing as citizens and citizens

[15] Consider that population estimates for the middle of the fifth century suggest metics made up anywhere between 20 and 50 percent of the entire free population of Athens and in some demes may have outnumbered citizens (Stewart 1995: 588; Bakewell 2013: ch. 1).

passing as metics through acts of imitation or mimesis. I view this concern with instability not as a lament about democratic egalitarianism run amok but as the more critical insight that the possession of Athenian blood is not necessarily an adequate prerequisite for a practice of membership characterized by freedom and equality. Contrary to what the polis promises its natives, Athenian parentage neither determines nor secures a lived experience of democratic citizenship. Whether citizen or metic, political status emerges in my readings as the uncertain and precarious performance of a naturalized distinction.

In these ways, the book complicates the standard view that sees Athenian political thought as an elite tradition of writing invested primarily in criticizing the egalitarianism of the polis.[16] What concerns critics of democracy is not only the polis's (wishful) erasure of socioeconomic barriers to citizen rule but also its simultaneous dependence on creating new forms of exclusion through a logic of blood. When political theorists invoke Athens as an instructive model of egalitarianism, however, they typically leave this part of the democratic picture undertheorized.[17] To insinuate that the polis was, with the advent of democracy, moving progressively away from a kinship order – that its forward-looking core was inclusive and de-essentializing – is not wrong, but it is misleading. The common portrayal fails to capture the extent to which the Athenian demos was, like most contemporary democratic citizenries, still a descent-based order.[18] What is more, the progressive account distracts us from appreciating that Athenian thinkers do not take for granted the idealized self-conception this order presupposed. Rather than treat the exclusionary dimensions of Athenian democracy as incidental or unimportant to its symbolic politics, self-definition, and cultural power as a critical-historical example of democratic politics, this book asks readers to think about democratic inclusion and exclusion together. It presents Athenian texts as provocations for theorizing the pull of nativism in democracy, a matter of critical importance for contemporary political theory that I explore in the conclusion. The interpretations advanced in what follows suggest that nativism is not simply at odds with democracy's explicit commitments to political

[16] Ober (1998: 5), for example, advances the influential argument that "formal political theorizing originated in the work of an informal, intellectual, and aristocratic community of Athenian readers and writers" who sought to show "what was wrong with 'the power of the people.'"

[17] See Chapter 5.

[18] On the continued and widespread use of a blood-based criterion for contemporary membership, see Stevens 1999.

equality and active participation but also working, paradoxically, to maintain them.

****

I am by training a political theorist, and this disciplinary orientation inspires the book's concerns with criticizing, diagnosing, and theorizing not only practices of political action as they are figured in Athenian texts but also modes of interpretation that have until now stood in the way of our seeing the metic as a live issue in Athenian political thought. In a sense I follow the historian Michel Clerc, who argued more than a century ago that "the history of Athens in the fifth and fourth centuries BCE can only be completely explained if one pays the greatest attention to the foreign population that was incorporated into the city" – but with an important exception.[19] Unlike Clerc and the vast majority of scholars who have written on metics, I do not attempt a historical study in these pages. The book engages carefully with scholarship in ancient history and classical studies, but it does so for purposes of reading Athenian political thought anew. Indeed, one of the book's aims is to liberate the metic from its hitherto primary function as an object of historical evidence and explore its signification and political theoretical meanings in democratic Athens, in some of the city's critical tradition, and on behalf of contemporary democratic theory. My approach thus shares some of the interpretive commitments of Cornelius Castoriadis, Nicole Loraux, S. Sara Monoson, and Josiah Ober, who have variously argued that a political and theoretical analysis of Athenian democracy and its figurations in contemporaneous texts ought to attend to "the patterns of life and ideology"[20] – the wide range of cultural practices, discourses, and ritualized performances – that, along with the city's administrative institutions and procedures, constitute the shifting meaning of democracy for Athenians and in Athenian texts.

I engage the metic, then, primarily as a discursive site, not exclusively as a historical referent within a juridical order, to show that Athenian thinkers do not take the naturalized difference between citizens and their menacing counterparts at face value and to argue that this way of reading opens Athenian texts and some of their most established concepts to new and sometimes dramatically different political and theoretical conclusions. I pay attention not only to the metic *qua* metic in these texts but also, if not chiefly, to the dynamics, myths, idioms, and institutional practices of which this in-between figure is uniquely indicative and generative. There is

[19] This is Bakewell's (2013: 7) translation of Clerc (1893: 2).
[20] Monoson 2000: 7. See also Goldhill 1987; Castoriadis 1997; Connor 1989; Ober 1998.

a reason for this. The politics of *metoikia* are produced symbolically and used rhetorically in ways that demand careful attention to the rhetorical dimensions of political theory as well as to the practices of law and myth making that helped make citizenship appear as an antecedent, expressive status in Athens. Textual engagements with *metoikia* frequently take the form of characterization, setting, or a way of living in the polis, where the metic may not even be mentioned as such.[21] At times, the symbolic politics of *metoikia* circulates under the sign of exceptionalist Athenian idioms, like autochthony or good birth (*eugeneia*), or less obvious ones like mimesis, all of which, in my view, can work in contemporaneous discourse to insinuate that the metic is the naturally undeserving, inadequate, but dangerously good copy of the citizen.

When Athenian thinkers deploy these tropes, I contend, they are both calling on their established meanings and reappropriating them in ways that expose the quotidian political practices – from deme registration to kinship testimonies to accusations of fraudulent citizen activity – that conspire to maintain the artifice of "natural" democratic differences. That *metoikia* is not always named in texts that otherwise implicate or evoke metics does not restrict the power of these works to generate political theoretical meaning about this democratic dimension, nor should it hinder our ability to read for them. Engagements with the city's membership hierarchies need not take overt, doctrinal, or prescriptive forms for us to treat them as theoretical responses to these political realities. The works of tragedy, philosophy, and oratory I read in this book may not endorse citizenship for metics or adumbrate a set of solutions to a metic "problem." They do, however, make political theoretical arguments by rhetorical means. The potential for the metic to provoke new thought about the familiar meanings of democratic citizenship thus depends on animating this figure's shifting, at times contradictory, and seemingly unmarked historical and discursive meanings.

It may come as little surprise, then, that the foregoing analyses of kinship, blood, and citizen performance in Athenian texts are subtly

[21] According to Akrigg (2015: 155), sometimes individual metics "are not explicitly identified as such" in Athenian thought but, if not because, they are "attested throughout the written record, literary and epigraphic, with rarely any indication that their presence is anything but routine in all kinds of contexts." Chapter 3's reading of the *Republic* argues that the tendency for metics to become assimilated within the dramatic worlds of the texts they inhabit leads readers to assume mistakenly that their juridical and political difference is insignificant to the arguments at hand. Relatedly, that Euripides does not use the word *metoikos* or its cognates in the *Ion* ought not inhibit us from engaging the tragedy's preoccupations with living as a metic in Athens. To overlook such textual concerns with *metoikia* is to discount the allegorical dimensions of Athenian political thought in favor of an interpretive strategy of literalness.

informed by arguments in the study of gender and sexuality. Gender does not function as a central category of analysis in this book, though occasionally I consider how a text troubles the meaning of citizen or metic when it figures socially feminine modes of behavior or represents female characters.[22] Rather, what chiefly concerns me is the more general political conceit that a natural substratum precedes and determines one's (political) activity. There may be no more influential set of literatures for criticizing the concept of naturalness, for exploring the pregivenness of membership lines as a taxonomist regulatory fiction, or for investigating that fiction's construction, maintenance, and political utility than certain theories of gender and sexuality, which for some time have argued that gender is enacted and that natural "facts" like sex are also produced discursively, culturally, and politically.[23] This study frequently uses the vocabulary of difference, performance, and expressiveness to give voice to previously unnoticed Athenian arguments about democratic citizenship, nativism, and exclusion.[24]

And yet the use of such contemporary idioms illuminates questions of democratic membership not only because the Athenian citizen was constituted through the political exclusion of woman (as well as metic and slave) or because the theatricality of citizenship and gender roles, the plasticity of nature, and the reifying effects of acting "like" are widely discussed matters in Athenian political thought. Historically and politically sensitive readings, like the ones I attempt, can never wholly transcend the theoretical frames or "fore-meanings" that constitute our "customary usage," to borrow Hans-Georg Gadamer's words.[25] Idioms of difference, in other words, belong to a shared inheritance of critique that has itself been forged through recurring engagements with classical Greek thought. Athenian texts are "already" a privileged site for feminist theory, just as feminist criticism is a privileged site for denaturalizing citizenship categories. Plato's oeuvre, to take one example, constitutes an originary text for such theorists as Luce Irigaray and Judith Butler, who have differently

[22] I discuss questions of gender in a reading of the *Menexenus* in Chapter 5 and in my remarks on women's work in Chapter 6.

[23] Haraway (1991: 135) uses the term "regulatory fiction" in this context. Dietz (2006) provides an overview of the debates around difference and deconstruction feminisms. Since the mid-1970s, she writes, feminist theory has been concerned with "the articulation of gender as a phenomenon separate from but related to biological claims of natural sex difference between men and women" (Dietz 2006: 401).

[24] The language of expressive and performative attributes comes from Butler 2003. See also Butler 1999.

[25] Gadamer 2013: 281, 280.

located in his dialogues the foundations of a patriarchal, essentialist, or materialist impulse. And yet to imply that some modes or languages of feminist theorizing might help us articulate an account of performative citizenship in a text like the *Republic* is also to diverge emphatically from, and therefore to counter, the conclusions that feminists have typically drawn from Plato's thought while at the same time interpreting and criticizing in their spirit: feminist theorists have long questioned calcified reading practices, exhibited a fidelity to the polyvalence of texts, and argued that tropes have the power to generate political and theoretical meaning.[26] The proceeding study shares these commitments. It rejects the notion that readers can or should aspire to gain unmediated access to a text even as they remain alert to its historical particularity. Indeed, I try to be "sensitive to the text's alterity," as Gadamer put it, while acknowledging that "this kind of sensitivity involves neither 'neutrality' with respect to content nor the extinction of one's self but the foregrounding and appropriation of one's own fore-meanings and prejudices."[27] Understanding, in Gadamer's view, "inevitably involves some prejudice" that cannot be transcended but can be foregrounded and made useful.[28]

This leads me back to one of the book's major claims. Making room for Athenian critiques of democratic difference entails reflecting critically on the interpretive habits that have militated against a sustained political theoretical analysis of the metic until now.[29] I suggested earlier that one obstacle to this analysis has been the scholarly habit of overlooking the figural and seemingly unmarked deployment of the metic. Two others deserve mention. One concerns the oppositional frames that govern the study of membership in Athenian thought and politics. Scholars typically map figurations of Athenian identity along the familiar axes of free/slave; citizen/foreigner; native/barbarian; mass/elite; male/female.[30] But the metic classification cuts across or drops out of these binaries because it included free, economically diverse men and women immigrants and their native-born children. However useful, then, the standard membership dyads have the additional

[26] Examples in political theory include Pateman 1988 and Zerilli 1994. [27] Gadamer 2013: 282.

[28] Gadamer 2013: 283.

[29] A recent exception to this tendency is Bakewell 2013, whose reading of Aeschylus' *Suppliants* as a tragedy about metics exemplifies a way of reading for *metoikia* that is historical, literary, politically engaged, and concerned with the figure's particularity. Attentiveness to the metic's symbolic politics is apparent in the work of Loraux (2000: 125–142) and to a lesser extent in Vidal-Naquet (1988: 329–359).

[30] Against the standard oppositions, Kamen (2013: 7) contends that despite the three major categories of standing in Athens (citizen, metic, slave), there were also degrees (e.g., privileged metics) between them. She argues that Athens had a spectrum of statuses.

effect of rendering the metic unintelligible: they fail to generate a conceptual space adequate for articulating the liminal position of a figure who stands on, which is to say not outside of, the margins of these oppositions or for taking stock of the particular tensions this insider-outsider exclusively or especially brings out in democratic life. As free noncitizens, metics had the ability to exert unaccountable political influence in public life and to achieve social mobility and status at the same time that they lacked the legal equality and full protections afforded citizens.[31]

Another reason for the dearth of theoretical interest in the metic has to do with the tendency by political theorists to align citizenship with freedom and underappreciate the fact that Athenians "did not simply separate the free from the unfree but distinguished between a variety of statuses 'between freedom and slavery.'"[32] In the second half of the fifth century, "when democracy was fully developed," Kurt Raaflaub explains,

> merely free status was seen as the crucial condition for the enjoyment of all rights, including political participation – but, of course, from 450/1, only the citizens who narrowly defined themselves as a closed descent group met this requirement. As a criterion for determining citizenship and delimiting the citizen body, freedom was an obvious and necessary but not a sufficient condition.[33]

To overlook the specific meanings of the metic as a free noncitizen is therefore to obscure the role that blood, not freedom, ultimately played in defining the citizen against the metic, not the slave.[34] The metic's free but deprivileged integration into the civic life of the polis does not mean that freedom ceases to function as an indicator of citizen activity but, more interestingly, that it operates as an indicator of the noncitizen's as well. If Athenian membership rules make free participation in some spaces of civic life an indeterminate index, they make possible the conditions for (fearing) the passing of metics into the deliberative spaces of political life, most

[31] I explore these issues in more detail in Chapters 3 and 6.

[32] Raaflaub 2004: 16, 14. The strict citizen/noncitizen dichotomy is variously called into question by Vlassopoulos 2007, Osborne 2011, and Taylor 2015.

[33] Raaflaub 2004: 50. Cohen's argument (2000: 48) that in the fourth century the difference between locals and foreigners was the most meaningful polarity might be another way of challenging the dominance of the free/unfree binary. Cohen (2000: 61) sees the distinction between *xenoi* and *astoi* (free local persons "including but not identical with the *politai* and including some but far from all the metics") in a large number of legal provisions.

[34] In her book on the importance of "racial identity" in Athens, Lape (2010) makes a similar but historical point about the centrality of blood to the conceptualization and practice of Athenian membership and offers an important corrective to the tendency I am drawing attention to here. Unlike Lape, I refrain from using the term "race" when discussing matters of Athenian descent.

notably into the assembling of the demos. This is one reason that in the texts I analyze, mimesis constitutes a powerful idiom for expressing anxieties about infiltration, impersonation, and noncitizen political capacity.

When readers bypass the metic–citizen relation or assimilate it to the free–slave, however, they unwittingly reinforce the interrelated presumptions that the citizen/slave opposition is not only the most illuminating for thinking about Athenian citizenship but also the most instructive binary for posing complicated questions of democratic citizenship up to and including our own time. Two seemingly opposed strands of contemporary political theory, for example, the Roman-derived republican view of freedom as nondomination and the Greek-inspired view of freedom as participation, converge in making freedom (no matter its definition) appear as the paradigmatic condition for theorizing citizenship.[35] Whatever the extent of their engagements with Athens, these efforts make it difficult for us to see the specific political and theoretical significance of a condition of free noncitizenship like *metoikia*. Too often, in other words, critics elide the metic by absorbing the figure into the dominant poles of political theoretical analysis (e.g., freedom/citizenship; unfreedom/noncitizenship; native/foreigner) that capture neither the metic's specificity nor its import and, more crucially, fail to recognize as political, precarious, or threatening the activity of residents who live in democracies without full membership status.[36]

The fact that it is hard to translate *metoikos* into English without losing its theoretical complexity further attests to the figure's susceptibility to elision. The words "immigrant" and "resident foreigner," while evocative and partially right, ultimately do not encapsulate the inheritability and nativity that a metic classification could designate in Athens. This complexity need not signal the metic's contemporary irrelevance. In the conclusion to the book, I suggest that the metic's resistance to easy translation is a provocation to consider what analogous forms of intergenerational democratic exclusion persist today.[37] If the "metic" refers to both an

[35] The tendency to theorize Athenian citizenship as a practice of "positive freedom" is evident, for example, in Ober (1998: 6), who locates "the culmination of Greek republicanism in Athenian democracy."

[36] A different version of the metic's elision is evident in work that theorizes foreignness and casts the metic as a foreigner or a visitor (Derrida 2000: 5; Honig 2001: 3). The tendency to conflate the metic with the *xenos* makes it difficult to ascertain how the metic's status as an insider-outsider might be consequential to its figuration in Plato, for example. The focus on the metic as a foreigner also occludes many aspects of the resident foreigner's experience as an internal, assimilated outsider.

[37] A few years ago, for example, a high court in the Dominican Republic barred Dominican-born children of undocumented Haitian immigrants from citizenship, rendering them stateless. See Archibald 2013.

immigrant and the Athens-born child of an immigrant, its contours make the term a unique conceptual category for thinking about the racial and genealogical dimensions that democratic exclusion still takes, however informally, in the form of "second-class citizenship". The metic prompts us to consider the sense in which this dynamic may in fact be constitutive of democracy as a political arrangement and invites us to unsettle familiar oppositions between natives and foreigners, insiders and outsiders, and citizens and aliens. For all these reasons, I resist equating the metic with the immigrant from here on out. My aim on this score is to bring out the specificity of the metic and establish it as a distinct political theoretical concept.

As is hopefully clear by now, *metoikia* does not signify a clear-cut form of noncitizenship. For although metics were restricted from holding office and participating in the formal institutions of the assembly and law courts, they were able and expected to engage in civic practices that Athenians tied deeply to membership (e.g., religious worship, military service, tax payment for civic festivals) and regarded as socially, economically, and politically influential (e.g., speech writing, trade, sophistry). Indeed, some historians have argued that classical Athenians understood citizenship as a practice of sharing in the polis, not as the possession of a juridical right.[38] In emphasizing the value of citizenship practice, however, we ought to stay attentive to the ways in which this practice was fundamentally entwined with and constrained by (additional) practices of claiming and bestowing status. Democracy makes a "prior" distinction about who is eligible to act like a citizen. The polis delineates the boundaries of the demos according to Athenian parentage and suggests that a kinship distinction exists in advance of, in spite of, and in determination of citizen performance. I am not suggesting that participation in the city's civic institutions is unimportant in classical Athens. I am claiming that the meaning of this participation is contingent and unstable: it turns on and may be revised according to what the city claims to know about the concomitant kinship status of its practitioner. As later chapters will make evident, the potential to query and contest citizen eligibility emerges in densely charged contexts of migration and integration. The fact that citizenship is defined first and foremost as a matter of inherited status suggests that in a diverse city with differing statuses, membership politics can always generate an additional question about the authenticity of citizenship practice. As one classicist observes, in Athens "it was always possible to question who deserved to be

[38] See Manville 1994 and Connor 1994.

counted as a citizen."[39] That Athenians in the second half of the fifth century and throughout the fourth increasingly ground citizen status in claims of birth and ancestry only reconfigures – it does not resolve – the problem of how to make the boundaries of the demos look pregiven. The following pages examine the conditions (political, rhetorical, social) under which citizen identity becomes an aporia for democratic life.

The court speech I read in Chapter 6 (Dem. 57), for example, suggests that no amount of participation in citizen institutions can necessarily (re-) constitute citizenship once a citizen is accused of falsely claiming Athenian ancestry, because what were previously seen as citizen acts can always be recast as metic acts of passing.[40] Passing in my usage does not stand for the salutary admission that a passer possesses the capacity to be a citizen and has been (wrongfully) disqualified from actualizing it. Passing does not necessarily mean that a deprivileged citizen-in-waiting deserves a status change, as the *Republic*'s myth of the metals will allow on my reading. Rather, passing, as I deploy it here, designates a hegemon's anxious coding of a certain practice as the fraudulent and necessarily inadequate political activity of a "naturally" second-rate copy. When figured in Athenian texts, however, passing suggests that the political distinction that the city draws between citizens and metics or authentic and fraudulent is inherently insecure.

****

In 451/0, BCE Pericles' Citizenship Law turned "Athens into a great *genos*" when it required double Athenian parentage for citizen status.[41] Historical scholarship on Pericles' Citizenship Law has tended to focus on the plausible reasons for its establishment (e.g., competition for resources). Conversely, my interest lies in its political and symbolic effects. In Josine Blok's view, Pericles' restrictive conception of membership may be "the first definition of citizen status by polis consensus."[42] The law established

[39] Lape 2010: 2.

[40] This difficulty is evident in *Against Neaera* (Dem. 59) as well. Apollodorus presents Phano's participation in the city's religious rites and her marriage to an Athenian as signifiers not of citizenship, as they had been understood until then, but rather of fraud and passing. The accusation here (and in Dem. 57) intimates the inherent insecurity in political status. The inscrutability of blood ties ensures that the meaning of one's activities might always be contested.

[41] Blok 2009b: 165; Patterson 1981; Davies 1977–1978. The major source for Pericles' Citizenship Law is Aristotle's *Constitution of the Athenians* (26.4), which reports that anyone not born to two *astoi* was blocked from participating in the polis. Aristotle wagers that Pericles issued the law on account of the large number of citizens. (See also Plutarch, *Pericles* 37.2–5.) On possible differences between Aristotle's version and the original, see Blok 2009b. The naturalization of noncitizens was possible but a rare honor decreed by the Council (M. J. Osborne 1982).

[42] Blok 2009b: 141. This does not mean that lineage was not a criterion for citizenship prior to Pericles' Citizenship Law.

an inheritable Athenianness as the precondition for citizenship. It excluded "non-Athenians from the deliberative bodies of the assembly and jury," as Elizabeth Irwin explains, and "'othered' a part of its own native population" that would have been formerly eligible for citizen status.[43] An already-circulating origins story reinforced the policy.[44] Although the term *autochthōn* originally described Athenians as a people who had always lived in their land,[45] over time it fused with other rhetorical inventions to suggest that Athenians were also distinguished by a purity of blood that could be traced back to an earth-born mythical ancestor named Erechtheus.[46] By this logic, Athenians could attribute the circumstances of Erechtheus' birth to themselves, a mythical claim that made them exceptional not only for residing in their land without interruption (the earlier meaning of *autochthōn*) but also for being "born *en masse* from the earth," a condition that politically, at least, could only be inherited.[47] What matters for my purposes is not whether the Periclean law's "prime function" was "the preservation of [Athenians as] the pure 'autochthonous' descent group"[48] but that it conspired with a discourse of autochthony to ensure that the purity and scrutiny of blood became a legal and political necessity and to stimulate anxieties over fraudulent citizenship made manifest in the texts I analyze.

Autochthony rhetoric "forged strong ideological support for the democracy"[49] because it aspired to establish the citizenry's common origins above and beyond differences in wealth and family background and naturalized the legal equality between citizens.[50] But the logic that unified the demos was also an index of political difference. So long as inherited nativity provided for citizen standing, the criterion was a way of keeping the category of citizen safe from contamination by those non-Athenians born inside the polis and on its peripheries whose exclusion was now

[43] Irwin 2016: 85.

[44] Irwin (2016: 89) argues that "the autochthony myth purporting all Athenians to be equal as offspring of the Athenian soil" expresses "an ideology that thrived concomitantly with, and more intensively under, the adoption of [Pericles' Citizenship Law]."

[45] Rosivach 1987: 294–306.

[46] Ogden 1996: 167. J. Hall (2002: 204) questions the common view that "the myth of autochthony was given a concrete reality by means of Perikles' citizenship law of 451/450 BCE, whereby the Athenian citizen body was effectively transformed into a closed, endogamous descent group." We can claim with J. Hall that "a direct association with the territory of Attika takes precedence over issues of descent within the Athenian myth of autochthony" while still appreciating, however, that descent can be used to imagine and secure the territorial tie (2002: 205). Even if it was not "necessary," claiming descent from an earth-born progenitor was a way of sharing collectively and exclusively in that ancestor's direct association to the territory (J. Hall 2002: 204–205).

[47] Ogden 1996: 167; see also Rosivach 1987; Roy 2014.

[48] Ogden 1996: 166, 167.

[49] Blok 2009b: 154, 169.

[50] J. Hall 2002: 204–205.

inevitable and pregiven. Among the disenfranchised, then, were people with one Athenian parent: membership rules now effectively rendered persons born to "mixed" unions bastards (*nothoi*), a term that had previously denoted only the illegitimate offspring of two *unmarried* Athenians, and made their citizenship impossible.[51] The predicament of these various "bastard" Athenians powerfully underscores the point that citizenship eligibility in the polis turns on a prior political judgment about kinship, that is, on another shifting and constructed distinction between pure (*gnēsioi*) and impure births that does not map neatly onto ethnic lines. The pure/impure distinction articulated here thus gives definition to the ethnic Athenian/non-Athenian opposition that governs admission to membership:[52] the policing of kinship lines makes *metoikoi* out of immigrants, indigenous persons who lack dual Athenian parentage, and, however infrequently, the (bastard) children of two unmarried Athenian citizens.[53] In this sense, autochthony politics could be said to unify more than the demos, for it also functions to mark a heterogeneous group of persons as impossible citizens and assign them to *metoikia*.

The exclusion of the metic from citizenship was therefore inheritable. Yet as free people, metics also enjoyed a proximity to citizens that made their passing and illegal enfranchisement a source of social, political, and theoretical concern.[54] The possibility for metics' social, economic, and political mobility meant that public trials for adjudicating questions of genealogy could become particularly charged. Paradoxically, then, it was the very idea of a permanent, inviolable, and internal difference between people, assumed to decide membership practice in advance, that made an act like passing conceivable in the first place. It is to this dynamic that Plato's *Menexenus* will emerge in my reading as a specific critical response.[55] In a postscript to Chapter 5, I ask what it means that Socrates not only attributes an oration that stresses the inherited exceptionalism of Athenians to Aspasia, a metic, but also recounts this oration and its claims entirely in her voice. In order to assert that citizen equality in birth (*genos*) necessitates citizen equality in law (*isonomia*) – that nature determines political difference – Socrates undertakes a mimetic metic performance (239a). Thus we

[51] Irwin 2016: 75. See also Ogden, who maintains that the term *nothos* (bastard) did not necessarily refer exclusively to the offspring of unmarried people after Pericles' Citizenship Law. Ogden (1996: 156) writes, "If the *nothoi* of two Athenian parents could not be citizens, they must by default have belonged to the category of aliens."

[52] Plutarch 1916: 37.2–5.

[53] Ogden argues that the population of *nothoi* born to two Athenians "would have been extremely tiny, and possibly non-existent" (1996: 151).

[54] Davies 1977–1978. [55] I discuss the *Menexenus* in a postscript to Chapter 5.

cannot say that Aspasia is absent from this text: her invocation provides the enabling condition and premise for democracy's founding fiction. The term "citizen" acquires its meaning in Plato's dialogue from her inclusion-exclusion. His dramaturgy enacts the idea that the demos is constituted by the double exclusion of metic and woman.

The Athenian practice of grounding citizenship eligibility in claims of nature is one reason I have chosen to use shorthand expressions like "autochthonous regime" to describe Athenian democracy or "autochthonous difference" to invoke Athenianness. I draw on these terms throughout the study not because I think the myth of autochthony was the only way Athenians talked about their origins or conjured an exceptionalist self-conception. Rather, with autochthony, I try to figure a complex symbolic and juridical membership order characterized by mobility, interaction, and a related preoccupation with distinction. The language of autochthony works, in my view, to signify an Athenian preoccupation with citizen equality and metic exclusion. I use it to keep the tensions between egalitarianism and hierarchy alive and to militate against the reader's desire to resolve them.

The Periclean world I conjured briefly constitutes the political horizon of my readings of the *Ion*, *Republic*, and *Against Euboulides*. But the production dates of these works span a long period, and their relations to these realities require some clarification.[56] Euripides staged the *Ion* sometime around 412 BCE, during the Peloponnesian War, but the action in the tragedy takes place at an earlier mythical moment, which I treat as a critical meditation on the contexts of its production, that is, on the Athenian world the events of the drama are helping to found. The *Republic*, by contrast, is a postfiguration of this fifth-century moment. Plato wrote the dialogue sometime early in or midway through the fourth century but set it in the period of the *Ion*'s fifth-century production. In other words, the *Republic* centers on historical characters that were Euripides' contemporaries, meaning that the dramatic setting of the *Republic* shares the general political climate in which Euripides staged the *Ion*. By contrast, Demosthenes' client defends his citizenship in a court speech written around six decades after Plato composed the *Republic* and some 100 years after Pericles' Citizenship Law. By this point, Aristotle is teaching and Athens is coming to terms with a fading empire. Philip II of Macedon is posing an increasing threat to Athenian independence and expelling some peoples of Athenian descent who find their claims to join the Athenian

[56] For more details, see the appendix, "A Metic Timeline."

demos in question. In this context, the threat of citizen masquerade appears just as urgent as it is in the earlier world of Plato's imagination and Euripides' staging.

****

In short, the argument of this book is that the figuration of the metic – as a character, a space, a legal status, a way of living, an inherited exclusion – intervenes critically in the political practices and discursive spaces that are working in Athens to secure democratic citizenship as a status predetermined by blood. In these texts, blood appears inadequate to accomplish what it is tasked to do. Ties of kinship cannot decide the democratic practice of citizenship. And so the city's membership criterion works to betray its own civic promise to the "earth-born" Athenians and to expose the fragility of its own noble lie. At issue here is not simply that the metic's proximity to the citizen risks revealing the "natural" citizen/metic opposition as a political artifice. The closeness between these figures also jeopardizes the inviolability of the Athenian citizen. Metics are therefore consummate signifiers of democratic difference in my view because they illustrate both the promise and the risk of democracy's citizenship rules. Their juridical exclusion gives meaning to the autochthonous guarantee that only Athenians by blood enjoy a practice of membership at the same time that their freedom, incorporation, and membership activity perpetually threaten the city's ability to make good on that democratic promise. The city's autarky depends on a mimetic metic, and it is here that the trouble begins.

The rest of the book unfolds as follows. I begin Chapter 2 with an origins story courtesy of Euripides. The *Ion*, however, is no ordinary founding myth of autochthony. In this unyielding drama about an early group of Athenian descendants grappling with the demands of an exceptionalist blood-based order, it can be difficult to tell or maintain the difference between insiders and outsiders. Kinship statuses are gained and shed. Misrecognitions abound. Central to the action is a young man who realizes late in the story that he is autochthonous, having been separated from his Athenian mother at birth. The blood knowledge that should send this Athenian progenitor back to Athens in order to secure the pure reproduction of the demos ends in a curious twist, however, when Ion is told he must keep the fortunate news of his autochthonous descent a secret as the condition for his return to Athens and its future as an autochthonous and colonizing regime. In the end, I argue, Ion does not go to Athens as an Athenian: Euripides' autochthony myth turns this native son into a passing metic. The central question the chapter poses is why this particular secret is used to refound Athens. What does Ion's *metoikia* help us see about the future democracy and its membership politics?

Ion's departure as a metic suggests that the possession of Athenian blood need not entail a lived practice of citizenship (blood is indeterminate of his membership activity), and yet in the frustrating world of Euripides' tragedy, the secret that turns an autochthonous Athenian into a metic, that suggests the city does not have to deliver on its civic guarantee to the earth-born, is the only act that can safeguard the future of the demos as an autochthonous *genos*. Why should the secret that makes citizen-metic passing possible actually serve the regime that insists on distinguishing between citizens and metics?

I argue that Ion's foundational act of passing works to establish and therefore to explain (retroactively) a fifth-century democratic reality in which a person's membership could be coded as the wrong (or right) performance. By placing an act of masquerade at the origins of Athenian democracy, the *Ion* suggests this instability is actually the effect of the city's own efforts to turn citizenship into a purportedly expressive, internal attribute like blood. The *Ion* thus provides a critical and originary account – what we might call an etiology – of a democratic predicament in which the suspecting and detecting of autochthonous difference is a pressing political preoccupation aimed at reassuring Athenians of citizenship's pregiven character. Euripides shows us that democracy and autochthony work together to produce a performance-based conception of citizenship that, because founded in claims of nature, aspires to secure citizen equality for the "earth-born" at the same time that it cannot *but* threaten it.

This Euripidean myth sets the terms for the Athenian world I examine in Plato's *Republic*, a dialogue set around the time the *Ion* was written. I devote three chapters to Plato's dialogue in a section of the book called "A Metic *Republic* in Three Acts." This deserves some explanation. Each chapter on the *Republic* treats in depth a significant aspect of the text as a critical interrogation of the democratic politics of its setting. When taken together, the chapters show that a metic perceptual field dislodges some of the most familiar, controversial, and seemingly essentializing arguments in Plato's political thought. From the dialogue's setting in a metic home in Piraeus to its discursive and critical uses of "good birth," autochthony, and mimesis, I find resources in the *Republic* for enabling a formerly unappreciated set of democratic self-criticisms. Plato's dialogue is certainly disparaging of democracy's inclusive criteria for rule, but its critique of democracy also extends to the nativist and exclusionary practices that enabled the expansion of rule to native Athenian men of different economic backgrounds. And it is this dimension of Plato's political thought, I argue, that the metic's recovery brings to the fore.

Chapter 3 reads the *Republic* as a "metic space." I argue that not only do metics provide the conditions for the conversation that unfolds in the *Republic.* The dialogue's setting belongs entirely to Piraeus, the harbor and marginal area associated with mobility, immigrant homes, trade, and empire. Piraeus operates for Athenian democracy much like the many metics that live there: it helps sustain and give meaning to an autochthonous order. On my reading, the underappreciated liminality that opens and envelops this work functions to air a concern with democratic difference and hierarchy that then runs through the rest of the dialogue. That the metic frames the *Republic* suggests, in my view, that the text does not simply comprehend the nativist political realities of its setting but assumes its importance to Athenian democracy, uses this relation to frame (its concerns with) the city, and attempts in the course of the conversation to consider, often indirectly, its workings and political effects. The fact that the characters in the dialogue never leave the home of the immigrants Cephalus and Polemarchus means that a metic home inflects the claims that are made throughout the dialogue, including the proposals for a new city called "callipolis" (527c2). I propose that they are impossible to disentangle from each other.

Chapter 4 advances a new reading of the noble lie in this spirit. I argue that once the *Republic*'s metic realities and rhetorical structure are taken into account, the much-studied passages are not endorsing political difference, as typically assumed, but laying bare the artifice by which regimes, like the Athens of its setting, produce membership status as a natural or essentialist category. And yet Socrates does more in these moments than show us how regulatory fictions work. He makes specific recourse to an autochthony myth that would have resonated strongly with his audience and with Plato's. The narrative structure of the scene that imagines the construction of political difference for the callipolis, in other words, invites an informed reader to reflect on the political divisions of the Athenian city in which it is staged. I read Socrates' discussion of the artifice of natural difference, then, as a charged intervention into his own symbolic and political order. Plato's *Republic* makes an open secret of the regulatory fiction that a person's *genos* expresses a pregiven status, a loaded and fitting insight to deliver in a metic's house. With this move, I argue, the *Republic* actually exposes the constituted nature and political effects of an essentialist politics that it is widely held instead to originate and prescribe against a supposedly unessentialist democratic order.

Chapter 5 sets its sights first on the *Republic*'s explicit remarks on democracy, this time revisiting the widely discussed depiction of the democratic regime in Book VIII as status blurring and chaotic. Socrates argues that in democracy, metics and citizens act like each other, as do women and men, free people and slaves, young and old (562e–563a). The passage is most often read as a Platonic complaint about the collapse of natural status distinctions in democracy. I suggest it is more fruitfully read as a denaturing argument. In Greek, the *Republic* figures this democratic instability in a language of mimesis, a critical idiom of imitation and performance that has gone almost entirely unanalyzed in this political and historical context. I restore the concept's political meanings to the text and use them to wager that the passage actually reveals the fragility of the naturalized distinctions democracy employs to order its residents. The democratic chaos Socrates describes thus concerns the presumed or incomplete hardening of a membership role and neither, as usually thought, the constitutive rebelliousness of a democratic regime nor the Platonist desire to reinstate "natural" order between people. The *Republic* begins from the premise that democracy does distinguish – just on dubious grounds and to ambiguous effects.

Approaching Book VIII with Athens in mind leads me to ask, at the end of Chapter 5, why mimesis of all ideas should appear as the culminating practice of democratic freedom. I consider the textual history and dramatic setting of the *Republic* and recast the passage as a clever but unsettling rejoinder to Pericles' Funeral Oration. In his fifth-century history, Thucydides depicts Pericles insinuating that a mimetic relationship between Athenians and non-Athenians is the foundation of the city's freedom and autarky. To serve as a paradigm for the rest of Hellas, Athens famously opens itself to all and suffers the risks that come from bringing foreigners into its city. The city's freedom and expansion would appear to depend on the emulation and affirmation of its ideals by noncitizens. Athenian exceptionalism rests implicitly on the hegemonic claim that emulation only brings about "mere" mimicry: no matter how fine a copy, the metic will always stand at a detectable distance from his autochthonous model. And so I read the *Republic* passage against the political conceits of the Funeral Oration to argue that Book VIII also amounts to a trenchant critique of Periclean mimicry because it reimagines that exceptionalist concept as mimesis, a much riskier and all-encompassing operation. For mimesis works in both directions. To read Plato's mimesis in this light is to suggest that the familiar Platonic concept bears new and specifically political implications in the democratic context of its staging. Not only are the juridical and symbolic borders of the Athenian demos (of any demos really) fundamentally unstable. The *Republic* depicts democracy making the ambiguity of its own distinctions apparent. In Plato's hands, Athens shows us that the myth underlying its democratic-expansionist order is a fragile but necessary noble lie.

Whether the question emerges in the Piraeus setting, in a metic's home, or in the wager that democratic power comes to reside in the sort of behind-the-scenes politicking of a foreign sophist, Plato invites us to ask whether the practices that define the metic's inclusion-exclusion (e.g., freedom, economic mobility, military service, sophistic teaching) do not so much preserve as imperil the autochthonous definition of citizenship as a natural and exclusive practice of civic participation. I use the word "imperil" here not because metics are portrayed as realizing their political capacity as active participants in the city's juridical institutions. No one, not even Athenians, comport themselves as active citizens in democracy, from the *Republic*'s perspective. In fact, citizens come to act a lot like metics in Plato's dialogue because they forego participation in many of the city's public institutions. The extent to which the metic threatens the stability of the city's political distinctions, then, is the degree to which the metic models for the citizen a contagious, because imitative, form of insinuating, mercantile membership.

Chapter 6 brings us face to face with the real-life dangers of this status instability by looking carefully at an actual Athenian trial about passing. In Demosthenes' *Against Euboulides*, a politically active Athenian citizen named Euxitheus appeals the sudden decision by his deme to disfranchise him. How could he actually be a metic, the speaker wonders, if no one has seen him act like one? The accusation that his citizenship is fraudulent, we learn, is based not simply on his lineage, which is polysemous, but also on the work his family does for a living. In Athens, however, socioeconomic status cannot serve as a reliable proxy for membership status either – democratic equality in blood, after all, bestows equality in law above and beyond matters of wealth and family background. Then what can account for the risk and desperation that infuses Euxitheus' speech?

Institutional and juridical explanations notwithstanding, I argue that the illegibility of Euxitheus' status is made possible by the specific symbolic conditions of a membership order that claims blindness to wealth at the same time that it delimits democratic citizenship by blood. In a regime in which metics live freely but permanently excluded from full membership, practices like work become particularly charged; for it is in and through work that the difference between citizens and metics will ultimately be sought on behalf of blood. Demosthenes' speech enables an examination of how the very membership rules that should protect a laboring family like Euxitheus' end up making the citizen poor newly and differently vulnerable. If the autochthonous citizenship rules that promise political equality to the earth-born make possible the "metic," then they also produce the permanent menace of the dangerously good and laboring citizen impersonator.

Before I turn to Euripides, let me offer a final word about my selection of texts. This book might have featured chapters on metic thinkers like Aristotle and Lysias. One of its aims, however, is to explore in depth the unexpected importance of *metoikia* to classical theorizations of democratic life that, especially in the *Republic*'s case, are so widely read and cited as to have shaped countless conversations in political theory and to avoid insinuating that the topic of the metic is of most or primary concern to thinkers who lived as metics in Athens. For these reasons, I do not offer an exhaustive exploration of the metic's figuration in Athenian thought. The texts I have elected to read are unique in their ability to bring out the metic's critical power, and my ability to show how they do this careful work would have been greatly curtailed by a survey-style approach to the metic. *Metoikia* provokes the dramatic action and political arguments of the *Ion* and the *Republic*. I read both texts as rewritings of the Athenian founding myth of autochthony that helped construct the fiction of the metic's permanent difference. Both, in other words, are mythopoetic attempts to recast the democratic origins story that enables the metic's exclusion and reveals the citizen's precariousness. If they invite us to see the workings of the Athenian democratic order anew, then Demosthenes shows the urgency and political stakes of their efforts in practice.

There is a sense in which Aristotle does speak in this book. He does so not as a passing Athenian or a canonized political theorist but as a metic would. He talks from the edges, setting the course for each discussion in epigraphs that frame the chapters and contribute aporetically to their meanings from a liminal spot, at once inside and outside the space of argumentation. One passage in particular, from the first book of the *Politics*, gives us a point of entry. Aristotle recalls the common view that the difference between the well-born and the base-born, the free and the enslaved lies in kinship, which he eventually calls nature (1255a–1255b). What undergirds this blood-based political calculus, however, is a false analogy, he says. We tend to assume that good people are born from good people, just as humans are born from humans, animals from animals. We imagine that power and privilege are like a species inherited. But nature is not so determinative as to guarantee this state of affairs.

CHAPTER 2

Immigrant Passing in Euripides' Ion, *the Tragedy of Blood-Based Membership*

> *Compare Homer's words "like some dishonored immigrant"; he who is excluded from the honors of the city is like a metic. But when this exclusion is concealed, then its object is to deceive fellow inhabitants.*[1]
>
> – Aristotle, *Politics* 1278a37–1278a40

Euripides' *Ion* is a relentless exploration of the tenets of Athenian exceptionalism. Unparalleled as a sustained engagement with the founding myth of autochthony, the tragedy has drawn curiously little attention from readers interested in analyzing the workings of a democratic order.[2] The critical tendency to overlook the *Ion* as a work of political thought may have something to do with the general impression that the text solves its own conflict and equivocates on its own tragic and critical force.[3] A recognition scene (*anagnōrisis*) between Ion and his estranged Athenian mother establishes peace where mistaken blood ties previously threatened familial violence. For some readers, the mother–son unification gives the tragedy a happy ending that restores Ion to his proper and formerly unknown identity as a fortunate native Athenian. Ion's new blood knowledge sends him safely back to Athens, the city he left as a baby, where he is supposed to ensure the pure reproduction of the demos and its empire – the two dimensions of the city's self-conception promoted by the autochthony myth that was popularized in the fifth century BCE.

On closer inspection, the political realities established by the *Ion*'s ending are not as sanguine as they first appear. The question of what, if any,

[1] I have altered Jowett's translation to highlight Aristotle's use of the Greek terms *metanastēs* (immigrant) and *metoikos* (metic).

[2] Cohen (2000: 85–87), for example, reads the *Ion* as a deeply critical and mocking exploration of Athenian (and democratic) identity.

[3] Sustained political theoretical interpretations of the play include Foucault 2010: 75–147; Lape 2010: ch. 3; Loraux 1993: ch. 5; Saxonhouse 1986: 257–260; Saxonhouse 1992: 76–89. I discuss these readings later on in the chapter.

political theoretical meaning we might find in this tragedy turns partly on whether we see the figure of the metic at work in this text. Although Euripides' singular use of marginal and liminal characters in this text is well noted – the tragedy is rife with illicit but apparently necessary mixtures – critics have generally failed to appreciate that much of the dramatic action revolves around analyzing, averting, and ultimately acquiescing to life as a metic. And in the *Ion*, I argue, figurations of the metic lead us to the text's tragic and political theoretical insights about democratic Athens. No resolution is ever reached, on my account, because the tragedy's central political conflict actually lies elsewhere, not over the characters' blood ties themselves but in the problems that the mobility of people creates for the blood-based calculus that is supposed to order this movement and mingling. Ion is actually made to reconceal the news of his Athenian blood as the condition of his return to Athens, its future as a democratic hegemony, and its colonization of Ionia. Thus Euripides' tragedy closes not with the triumphalist departure of a native son recovered, as typically thought, but with the imminent immigration of a foreigner whose nativity has been covered over. Once read from this angle, the recognition scene does not imply a happy restoration of a predetermined political status. For despite his autochthonous bloodright, Ion will go to Athens as a metic.

Taking this different lens to the tragedy, the following chapter reflects on the critical import of Euripides' new etiology for Athens' democratic-imperial regime. Ion's disquieting fate suggests that, contrary to what the autochthonous polis promises its natives, the possession of Athenian blood need not decide one's membership experience in Athens. But Ion's knowledge of his maternal Athenian lineage does accomplish something in this play: the news compels a young man to turn his kinship into a secret and, rather than repatriate, to immigrate, which is to say pass as a resident foreigner. That Ion refuses to go and live as a metic in Athens earlier on in the tragedy, when he mistakenly thinks that is his "real" blood-based assignment, makes the ending only more urgent to work through. Becoming Athenian in Euripides' tragedy amounts to taking on one's parentage as a secret. The closeting that reveals blood's failure to decide membership practice in advance is the very gesture that keeps this blood-based regime intact. In the strange logic of Euripides' tragedy, the concealment that makes an autochthonous son a metic, that reveals the city may not always deliver on its promise to the "well born," is the one and only act that can safeguard the city's future as an autochthonous (and colonizing) demos. Somehow the instability of these blood-based membership lines establishes the political utility of blood for future generations of the regime. The question worth considering is what this Euripidean innovation helps us see about the fifth-century polis into which the poet retrojects it. In what sense does the new myth serve the democratic city it founds?

I argued in the last chapter that Athens grounds *isonomia* (equality before the law) in *isogonia* (equality in birth) and in this way generates a political desire for blood knowledge in a context of migration and mingling. What interests me about the *Ion* is not only that it depicts a family grappling with the demands and uncertainties of this political order but how, when read as a work of critique and political theory, the tragedy can help us analyze – can articulate a rationale for – the polis's interests in this particular membership calculus and its less-than-salutary political effects.

Reading the *Ion* afresh as an immigration fable, I try and understand why the concealment that reveals that Athens does not deliver on its civic promise is precisely what Athens' perpetuity requires. I suggest that the function of the closing secret is to show us how a blood-based, hierarchical membership order emerges. The secret founds a future, fifth-century Athens as a political order for which citizenship means a stable, hegemonic, and expressive status: the logic of concealment-disclosure establishes political membership in Athens as a "natural" fact that may be hidden or disclosed, like the content of a secret, a status that may be known prior to and in spite of its performance. That it culminates in an act of passing, however, suggests Ion's closeting has an additional constituting effect on the Athenian order: Ion's boundary crossing provides a paradigm of Athenian membership. Ion's passing founds a democratic future in which it will be possible and may be politically urgent to read a person's membership practice as the "wrong" (or "right") performance; inserts this instability into the foundation of the polis; and reveals that (the accusation of) masquerade is an effect of a political decision to construe membership as an expressive, internal attribute that promises but fails to determine membership performance in advance. If the *Ion* makes imposture and status flux foundational and therefore permanent Athenian risks, it provides a sort of alibi for the democratic policing of "natural" autochthonous difference in the city (and beyond) that we will encounter most explicitly in my reading of Demosthenes' court speech in Chapter 6 – not in order to endorse practices of detection, in my view, but to explain and reveal their political utility. From this vantage point, Euripides depicts Athens *needing* a notion of aberrational performance like the one Ion undertakes at the end. And therein resides what I see as the *Ion*'s arresting gambit: the perpetuity of Athens as an autochthonous regime depends on a secret that does not simply establish political difference as an expressive attribute but also, and for this reason, lays the foundation for its continual and strategic undoing. If Athens needs Ion as such, that is because an imperializing democracy needs membership to stand as a pregiven and natural status about which it can also be mistaken.

Founding Athens

Initially, as Vincent Rosivach points out, the term *autochthōn* was used to describe Athenians as a people that had always lived in its land.[4] By Euripides' production around 412 BCE,[5] Athenian autochthony had likely taken on a strong genealogical dimension, symbolized by the incorporation of another long-standing origins story – the myth of Erichthonios, the early king and Athenian progenitor who was born from the earth itself.[6] By "attributing to themselves collectively the autochthony of Erichthonios," writes Nicole Loraux, citizens gained an exemplary status among Greeks as children of their land.[7] To claim all Athenians were born from the earth was to collapse successive generations into one. This tactic of belying biological reproduction in a context of interpolis mobility had in practice the opposite effect of entrenching its political value. Athens granted citizen status only to those who could persuasively claim an uninterrupted and uncorrupted blood tie to their native founder. Laws governing marriage, citizenship, and inheritance concretized the emphasis on descent: on the basis of blood, they disenfranchised metics and their offspring. As we saw earlier, only the children of two married freeborn natives were eligible for democratic citizenship.[8]

[4] Rosivach 1987: 294–306, 297.

[5] There is no consensus on the *Ion*'s production date, but commentators posit it sometime between 415 and 412. I accept Zacharia's argument that the play was produced in March 412 (2003: 1–3).

[6] Athenians are referred to as "the demos of Erechtheus" in Homer (*Il.* 2.19) but by Sophocles' time have become his descendants (*Aj.* 202). Rosivach sees this as a shift in Athenian self-conception: Erechtheus was eventually seen as Athenians' eponymous ancestor (Rosivach 1987: 295). But the story of the infant Erechtheus is actually one stage in the larger foundation myth of Athens. Erechtheus, the second earthborn king of Athens, is the figure most explicitly associated with autochthony. He is "probably the 'adult double' of the autochthonous infant Erichthonios," mentioned earlier. Here, however, Euripides makes Erechtheus the descendant of Erichthonios. See Zacharia 2003: 56, 60, 63.

[7] Loraux 2000: 10, 33–34.

[8] As mentioned in Chapter 1, Periclean laws of 451/450 (reenacted in 403/402) prescribed double endogamy. That is, qualification for citizen status hinged on birth from two citizens. The law may have relaxed during the Peloponnesian War, however. See Patterson 2005: 267–289.

The double meanings of autochthony as original, uninterrupted habitation in a land and intergenerational purity of birth together service the exceptionalist view that Athenian democracy is founded in landedness, not mobility, and inheritance, not choice.[9] When Athenians cast their descent from Erichthonios as a metonym for their own chthonic origins, they deterritorialize citizenship but resacralize the territory. So long as ancestry provided for citizenship, children born in colonial outposts to citizen parents were Athenian citizens regardless of their participation. This superior claim of blood over residence, socialization, and social mobility was played out vividly in the domestic context, in which Athenian-*born* children of metics inherited their deprivileged status despite a condition of assimilation and constrained participation in the Athenian community. Athenians born abroad thus came to mirror metics and metics Athenians. In the play, these two forms of social mobility are perfectly instantiated in the protagonist's duality: Ion is an autochthonous Athenian who will live as a metic in Athens before colonizing Ionia as an Athenian abroad.

The myth of autochthony emboldens a citizenship politics concerned with ancestry in a curious way. It eschews generational time to make each citizen appear as the unmediated offspring of the land. The figurative landedness – one is born *of*, not on, the land – implied that Athenians were ethnically and culturally antecedent and therefore superior to all other *poleis*, whose citizenries were, by contrast, the products of settlement, invasion, and migration, even as the city tracks this purity through consanguinity.[10] Such a conception of inherited immobility, however, encourages physical mobility in and out of Athens while attempting to address the blurring and contaminating effects of interpolis flows. Those persons born outside of Athens but in its colonies could acquire citizenship through ancestry, while those persons born in Athens or its colonial outposts without dual Athenian ancestry could not.

Against this background, in 412 BCE, Athenians found themselves humbled and weakened by a disastrous military campaign to Sicily waged as part of the Peloponnesian War. This was a dark period for Athens, writes Katerina Zacharia, with "civic morale shattered, faith in democracy . . . beginning to fail, and the dockyards and treasury . . .

[9] Here I invert a point Honig (2001: 75) makes about the myth of an immigrant America, an exceptionalist account that "recuperates foreignness" for a national project by "drawing on and shoring up the popular exceptionalist belief that America is a distinctively consent-based regime, based on choice, not inheritance."

[10] See Thucydides, Book 1; Lysias 17.2–4; Plato, *Menexenus* 245d.

empty."[11] The ideology espoused by autochthony had promoted an expansionist policy whose realities were now leaving the myth and its implications vulnerable to scrutiny and contestation. In the midst of Athenians' awakening to the political and psychic costs of their bloodright, Euripides produced a rewriting of the founding myth that, like any mythopoetic encounter, bore opportunities for assessment and renewal.[12]

Secrets and Lies

Set much earlier than the classical period, the *Ion* opens two generations after the original autochthonous birth of Erichthonios, with his daughter and grandson struggling to bear the burden of their lineage. Kreousa and her son Ion, the product of her rape by Apollo, are the first of generations of Athenians to face the problems that come with ensuring one's ancestral heritage stays tied to a privileged political status, a predicament classical audiences would have recognized. All the action in the *Ion* is dominated by attempts to conceal or disclose what are supposed to be permanent and unalterable relations of kin. The effect is that in the *Ion*, blood ties emerge as unstable disclosures that acquire the semblance of ontological truth while remaining open to interpretation and revision.

The action unfolds in Delphi around Apollo's temple. Hermes opens the drama, relaying that, years ago, Apollo raped Kreousa near the Acropolis. She gave birth to Ion as a result but left the newborn baby to die (8–18).[13] Unbeknownst to her, Apollo had Hermes rescue the child and bring him to Delphi, where he has been growing up since, ignorant of his biological parentage (28–40). Kreousa has kept the incident a secret even from her eventual husband, a non-Athenian war hero named Xouthos (20, 57–58). When the audience meets them, the childless couple has just arrived from Athens to ask the oracle if they will procreate and continue their royal bloodline. The trip to Delphi, Hermes explains, was

[11] There were also "fears of a general imperial secession," Zacharia argues, which fits with the "marked emphasis on Ionianism at the beginning and end of the play." Consider as well that in March 412 the Erechtheum, the shrine to Erechtheus, "stood half-finished," and all parts of the Acropolis building project that "concerned the inalienable mythical past of the city" were suspended for financial reasons (Zacharia 2003: 1–3). See also Thucydides 8.1.

[12] Like many Euripidean tragedies, the *Ion* is innovative because it engages in mythopoesis, a radical reworking of traditional myths. Such mythmaking is pedagogical insofar as its departure from the traditional myth invites comparison that animates reflection on the productivity of all myth. Because tragedy is characterized by ambivalence and paradox, its representations of mythological traditions serve to illuminate the myths' irreconcilable demands and multiple meanings in the polis.

[13] Citations to the play indicate the Greek lines, which are the same as those in the English of Euripides 1997 (the translation by K. H. Lee), cited throughout the chapter unless otherwise noted.

masterminded by Apollo to precipitate an encounter between Xouthos and Ion (64–68). Apollo's plan is for Xouthos to mistake Ion as his own son and invite Ion back to Athens to be his heir. Ion will join the Athenian ruling class and his descendants will go on to found Ionia, part of the fifth-century Athenian empire (69–75). Only once in Athens, or so Hermes thinks, should Kreousa recognize Ion as her biological son so that Apollo's affair may stay safely concealed (72–73). Kreousa and Xouthos will then have their own biological children together. But things don't exactly go according to Apollo's plan. Kreousa and Ion recognize each other while still in Delphi. The incident provokes Athena to insist that they keep their blood relation a secret from everyone, including Xouthos. For Athens to realize its democratic, hegemonic future, everyone (but the audience) must believe Ion is Xouthos' long-lost biological son.

Two scenes raise the question of Ion's homecoming and residence in Athens. In both scenes, the possibility of Ion's departure is raised in light of his newly discovered biological identity. In both, at least one character speaks from the assumption that there is a stable correspondence between this blood knowledge and political status. Yet on both occasions, shortly after a recognition scene, Ion's political standing fluctuates: he moves from a statusless temple servant to an Athenian metic to an autochthonous Athenian back to an Athenian metic. In each case, Ion's political membership is (re-)constituted by some act of concealing or disclosing of status – what the city suggests is mere uncontroversial facticity.

Xouthos takes to heart the oracle's insinuation that his first encounter out of the temple will be with his (long-lost) son (534, 536). This, conveniently, is Ion, who appears incredulous of Xouthos' disclosure and finds him foolish (526). But Xouthos perseveres and asks his newfound son to come back to Athens with him, precipitating an argument two foreigners might have about the costs and benefits of moving to Athens. Ion's long reply, to which I will return, imagines his life as a metic in Athens to be without privilege and full of danger, resentment, competition, and censure. In addition to the social discrimination he would face, his arrival in Athens would cause Kreousa, now his stepmother, embarrassment and pain (617–620). He begs Xouthos to let him stay in Delphi, where he is happy.

Xouthos dismisses Ion's hesitance. He tells him to stop talking and to think instead about the success he will enjoy there (650). (Given metics' exclusion from public political speech and their reputation for economic prowess, the advice is appropriate.) Xouthos acknowledges the problem of Kreousa's feelings, however, and to this at least responds,

> I'll take you, as a sight-seer, of course, and not as my son. For in fact I do not want to cause pain to my wife, childless as she is, while I am fortunate myself. But in time I shall grasp the right moment and induce my wife to allow you to inherit my rule over the country. (655–660)

The proposal calls for the reconcealment of what Xouthos has taken to be Ion's newly recovered biological identity. The implication is that Ion will *act as someone else*, a tourist this time, not an immigrant looking to infiltrate Kreousa's family/polis. The interaction ironically anticipates Athena's closing dictum that Ion will have to reconceal his "real" autochthonous identity. That secret will fulfill a similar purpose, but it will keep Xouthos, not Kreousa, unsuspecting.

This is the first of several instances in which Ion, an Athenian progenitor, acquires and then sheds a kinship position, and it contrasts sharply with the notion of permanence and transparency that the autochthonous twinning of ancestral and political identity purports to secure. The characters' efforts to discover their blood ties at all costs may appear to underscore their belief in blood's univocality, but the same characters – Xouthos in particular – also exhibit a perceptive grasp of how easy and necessary it will be to fake these relations from time to time. The plan to dupe Kreousa is the play's first signal of blood's inability to dictate membership in or as a practice. Ion may *be* Xouthos' son, but, as Xouthos says, he does not have to act like it. No one will know the difference.

Still, secrets and lies cannot seem to undo autochthony. They may even work in its service. In order to affirm Ion as his birth son, privately for a while and then publicly in time, Xouthos asks that he pretend *not* to be his son. (Ironically, playing Xouthos' son will turn out to be the role of Ion's lifetime.) The request to misrepresent the biological relation Xouthos thinks he has just restored may signal kinship's instability, but it also attests to (Xouthos' belief in) the forcefulness of blood to constitute and organize political society. That Ion should perform a role in spite of who he has learned he "is" indicates that Xouthos grasps the indecisive yet productive power of blood's importance in Athens. Xouthos' plan may express an awareness that one's blood-based status in Athens is irresolvably unstable because it is performed, but this does not neutralize the political utility or effects of blood's invocation. The plan to hide Ion's identity as his birth son actually helps Xouthos establish the necessary conditions for perpetuating his ancestry within the polis' kinship economy of membership. With Ion in Athens, Xouthos can hope to bequeath to his son the household he has married into. Like a good immigrant, Xouthos reproduces and exhibits his allegiance to the patriarchal order of inclusion of the host city that has done him well.

Unlike Pericles' Funeral Oration (2.39), which, in Thucydides' version, figures Athenian hospitality as a source of civic pride for the polis that is open to all, Ion's protestations present an exclusionary underside to this openness as equally (in)famous. The city may be welcoming to foreigners, but within the polis, hospitality has its limits. Athens incorporates autochthonous persons into the demos but keeps other long-standing and native residents disenfranchised. Foreigners like Xouthos willingly go to Athens to live despite these conditions and affirm the city's attractiveness above and beyond the costs – censure, powerlessness, and danger. Ion rejects Xouthos' invitation because he thinks these are costs from which no wealth can insulate an individual. There will always be discrimination against the nonautochthonous, he says: the law may establish some parity between an Athenian and a successful, assimilated metic like Xouthos, but metics experience exclusions that the law does not capture. For Ion, the myth of autochthony invests Athenians in a politics of belonging that extols proper parentage above participation in its institutions. In Athens, good blood displaces good character as the criterion for political inclusion.[14] There is no way to live in Athens without feeling the effects of this coupling of blood and membership, he says. If he lived in Athens as a metic and a child born out of wedlock, he would always be inferior if not invisible. Voiced from the safe distance of Delphi, Ion's reply to Xouthos offers a heartfelt account of a metic point of view:

> They say that renowned earth-born inhabitants of Athens are not a people brought in from outside. I shall land there suffering from two disadvantages: being the son of an outsider and being myself born out of wedlock. Burdened by this slur, if I stick to a position without influence, I shall be spoken of as a nobody. But if I aim for a place in the first ranks of the city and strive to become someone, I shall be detested by the powerless. Superiority causes offence. On the other hand. . . . I shall attract ridicule for being foolish, because I do not stay in the background in a city full of censure. Then again, if I manage to acquire a standing superior to +those again chroniclers+ having dealings with the city I shall be hemmed in by their votes [. . .] Those who control cities and enjoy privilege are full of hostility towards any rival contenders. (585–606)

[14] Although the play does not call Xouthos a naturalized citizen, the tragedy might have brought this possibility to mind. The classical approach to naturalization avoided granting membership to average foreigners who might actually use it and instead bestowed citizenship to benefactors as a way of facilitating diplomatic objectives. In the view of Ion, naturalization would not insulate an outsider from Athenian prejudice. The division between the autochthonous and the foreign-born persists and trumps social and legal equality. See M. J. Osborne 1981: 5–6.

No ways of living with virtue appear open to Ion in Athens. How could he consent to inhabit the margins of political society when doing so would mean leading no (political) life, not just a restricted one? If Ion does not make himself invisible in Athens, he will engender the scorn of insiders who will block his political ascent and effectively disenfranchise him. And then there is Kreousa, whom the speech invokes in its most explicit identification of a metic's way of living with death. "Moving into a strange house as an outsider to face a woman who is childless," he will "incur her hatred," just as he would the demos', and put himself and Xouthos at risk of murder (606–607, 611, 616–617).

For Xouthos, who adopts the conventional Periclean view in this interaction, all the difficulties of living in a foreign city can be overcome by wealth, which secures influence and safety in an adoptive city, as it would for Ion, who would acquire his newfound father's. The idea holds no sway for Ion, who argues that money in the hands of a nonnative brings the same sorts of pains as political visibility (630–631). Besides, it is not wealth that makes life worth living in a city. In Delphi, where Ion leads a moderate (*metrion*, 635) life, things are good, better than in Athens even (645). There is peace, leisure, and happiness – not just for the few but for everyone – because everyone in Delphi is transient (640). There is no myth of exceptionalism at work, no status to dole out.

Ion inhabits an outsider's perspective more than once in this scene. He puts forward criticisms of Athens through a projected meticness that displays a deep knowledge of an Athenian citizen's view of the insider-outsider. He criticizes wealth for being inadequate (for metics) to trump law and custom. When he praises life in Delphi by contrast, he does not do so because he enjoys the privileges of an insider there but rather because Delphi circumvents that distinction altogether.

The answer Xouthos gives Ion to all this is dismissive – "Enough of this talk! Learn to be happy!" (650) – and, in spite of the concerns his new son has voiced, shifts back to planning for Ion's arrival. Xouthos effectively talks past his son. That may be his new right as a father, but the incompatibility dramatized by their discussion about Ion's immigration begs a prior question about the argument Ion has just given. Might Ion have talked past Xouthos, too?

Recall that it was the need for an heir that first motivated Xouthos' invitation to Ion. Ion "will be seen" in Athens as *eugenēs* ("well born") on account of inheriting not Athenianness but "life's comforts." Ion's immigration is further justified for Xouthos by his desire for familial restoration. "For your part you have found what is most dear, though you did not know it earlier," he says when he first sees Ion (571). But Ion thinks about his immigration differently – in terms of what it will mean for his everyday life above and beyond the material comforts or power that a family tie to a foreign resident could secure. He talks past Xouthos not because he has not heard the blood reason Xouthos offers for his immigration but because he does not yet share his father's Athenian view that this counts as a sufficient reason to act as Xouthos would like.

As a foreigner, Xouthos may never be a complete insider in Athens, but he buys into the polis order and represents its wishful self-conception as hospitable, which may be true by comparison with some other *poleis* but not, as Ion has pointed out, by comparison with Delphi. When the news of their kinship relation opens lines of action and destiny as far as Xouthos is concerned, his request of Ion bespeaks his Athenian sympathies. In Athens, blood matters. For Ion the situation is less certain: blood does not dictate a course of action. Even if Ion's speech fails instrumentally (he does ultimately consent to going to Athens *twice*), it draws our attention to the Athenian interest in blood-based difference and stages a gap between the status bestowed by a fact of blood (Ion's supposed tie to Xouthos) and the activity that should follow from it (Ion's prospective *metoikia*).

This first broaching of Ion's immigration may look like an ironic foreshadowing of Ion's eventual and seemingly proper repatriation at the end. The audience knows Ion is not really Xouthos' son and that he should therefore not be worried about his place in Athens. Indeed, his encounter with Xouthos provokes a series of dangerous mishaps that ultimately push Ion and Kreousa toward their own recognition scene. As we shall see, despite or even because of the near misses and thwarted murder plots that threaten the future of Athens, many interpreters conclude that Ion's departure for Athens feels like a triumph. Ion does find out who his birth parents are after all. But the play has also suggested that genealogy is a truth that, though rife with political significance, may only be contingently detected in practice. Rather than reassure us, then, the near misses around family violence and misrecognitions have another effect. They make visible the unreliable and paradoxical character of the polis' blood criterion for membership. Origins are a thing about which the city, and we, may well be mistaken – but that does not neutralize their political utility.

Ion warily consents to Xouthos' plan in the end. He prays that his unknown mother will turn out to be an Athenian so that he can enjoy *parrēsia*, the privilege of speaking publicly and freely in the city (672). But the chorus of women has overheard their scheme. They cite his foreign ungratefulness (702–704) and, equating the plan with a foreign invasion, call for Ion's death in the name of Athenian self-defense (719–722). The women disclose the secret plan to Kreousa and the old tutor. He convinces Kreousa to murder Ion as a way of keeping him out of her household. The plot backfires once Ion realizes he is about to be poisoned (810–815, 845–846). And having identified the basket in Ion's hands as the one she abandoned him in as a baby, Kreousa finally recognizes her son (1355).

Ion rejoices at the news but, as Kreousa explains, it is not all good. Not only was Ion born to her out of wedlock, he is actually Apollo's son, not Xouthos', and born of a rape that she has concealed from everyone, including her own husband (1468–1487). The revelation of the secret only confuses Ion: why would Apollo want to give his own son away? "[Apollo] does you a favor in setting you up in a noble house," Kreousa unsatisfactorily explains. "If you were known as the son of the god you would never have got a house as your inheritance nor the name of a father" (1539–1553). Ion wishes to confront Apollo and hear it directly from him, but the god never appears in the play to give a reason for Ion's adoption by Xouthos. Athena arrives to affirm everything Kreousa has said and closes the tragedy with a forecast (1574). Ion will go to Athens. His descendants will "settle in the island cities of the Cyclades and the territory on the sea-coasts," giving "strength" to her land and settling parts of Asia and Europe (1584–1588). The Ionians "will win glory" for her and the Athenians, and Xouthos and Kreousa will go on to have their own biological children, the progenitors of the Dorian tribe (1589–1590).

For all this to occur, Athena warns Kreousa, "Keep it a secret that this boy is your son, so that Xouthos may happily retain his delusion and you too, lady, may go on your way enjoying your blessings" (1601–1603). Ion now accepts the importance of blood to which he earlier objected and, as Xouthos' son, prepares to move, with Athena as his escort. He accedes as well to the notion that he has a role to play in Athens' imperial destiny. Ion sets off for Athens not knowing how long he will have to live as a noncitizen before his descendants carry the banner of Athens to a new imperial outpost.[15]

In light of this closing reprisal of Ion's immigration, let us treat Ion's earlier speech to Xouthos, with its anxious elucidation of a metic life in

[15] Thucydides reports that the Ionians asked Athenians, their "mother-city," to be their leaders after the Persian Wars, and Athenian acceptance led directly to the formation of the Delian League or Athenian Empire (1.95).

Athens, not as a typical dramatic obstacle en route to a happy ending but as a mirror and prediction of this final scene. Does Ion's ultimate compliance neutralize the concerns he voiced about *metoikia* when he did not know that autochthonous Kreousa was his mother? It may, or that earlier speech may yet ring in our ears. Ion never reconsiders his speech to Xouthos. Life as a metic will be his and it will be what he feared unless he learns to take Xouthos' advice to love talk less and be happy. In other words, Ion will for the time being have to give up any hope of *parrēsia*, the speech of truth and justice that comes with political freedom in Athens. Ion's "true" blood and the insider status it is said to bestow will not determine his experience of living in Athens.

Romanced by Blood

From Ion's perspective, life as a metic could hardly be called happy. Yet most readings of the tragedy argue that the play ends on a surprisingly upbeat note, even going so far as to call it a "happy" ending.[16] Efforts to make sense of the *Ion*'s treatment of autochthony tend to foreground, even celebrate, the recognition scene between Ion and Kreousa.[17] This interpretive habit has tended to distract readers from considering the political problems created by the same kinship tie's immediate reconcealment.[18] To illuminate the stakes of this general approach, I elaborate on three issues that appear to ground this "romance" reading: the shape of the plot, readers' expectations for the tragic genre, and a lack of attention to *metoikia*.[19]

The anticipated and long-threatened reunion between Kreousa and Ion certainly drives the play's plot. If Ion finally leaves Delphi to take his place in Athens' line of rulers, it is because he has received information about the autochthonous heritage he inherits from his mother. But this is not just about Ion. The homecoming will also shore up Athenian hegemony.

[16] In addition to Loraux's reading, Zacharia 2003 is an exception to this conventional view. She writes, "We are not given a wholly neat and tidy (happy) ending; we are left with loose ends: Xouthos will remain deceived; Ion will remain illegitimate" (Zacharia 2003: 99). See Loraux 1993: 184–236. See also Walsh 1978: 301–315.

[17] Critics who think the play is ambiguous about and in some cases sympathetic to the nativist ways the polis creates divisions include Dougherty (1996: 249–270); Loraux (1993); Rehm (1992: 131–147); Saxonhouse (1986); and Zeitlin (1989).

[18] This is perhaps starkest in the case of Zacharia, who is alert to the range of conflicts in the play but maintains that "Athena's appearance" does not make a "serious claim to any directorial function" because "she only comes at the point when all the serious conflicts have already been resolved (e.g., the prevention of the killing of son by mother and mother by son)" (Zacharia 2003: 146).

[19] Lape (2010: 95) calls the *Ion* a "family romance of Athenian racialism."

On Athena's closing prediction, Ion will retroactively domesticate Ionia, a colony that was controversial at the time of the play's staging.[20] His return will also ensure the continuity of the kinship calculus democratic Athens uses to justify *isonomia*, the principle of political equality based on birth (from the Athenian earth). Insofar as the mother–child reunion leads to Ion's departure for his city of origin, autochthony's (and the polis') tenuous future does look secure. For many of *Ion*'s interpreters, then, by sending Ion safely on his way to Athens, the play celebrates the autochthonous logic the city uses to constitute legitimate families and authentic citizens.

This romance reading finds further support in the view that the *Ion* subverts the genre expectations of tragedy.[21] Under the assumption that tragedy is predominantly characterized by human destruction, much secondary commentary misidentifies the cessation of physical violence in the play with the resolution of the tragedy's tension. By the time Ion's reconcealment occurs, readers have already settled the play's conflict: Kreousa and Ion's plans to kill each other are set aside when they discover their autochthonous blood relation; the peace that "true" blood knowledge apparently brings – discounting the colonization of Ionia it precipitates – gives the play a sense of closure.[22] Ion "is successful at Delphi" in part because "he avoids killing his mother," writes Carol Dougherty.[23] Similarly, for Froma Zeitlin, "Ion's story is a success. What threatened to become a typical tragic scenario in which misrecognition between kin led, as in the *Bacchae*, to a mother's destruction of her child has been turned into a series of happy reversals" that "initiate those present into the happy forecast of the future." The play does not lead to a "destructive negation but to a joyful if complicated ending about parents and children, lost and safely found," Zeitlin says.[24]

Not only do those "lost and safely found," including their relatives, live complete and happy lives on these sanguine accounts of birth family

[20] For a discussion of the play in the context of Athenian imperialism, see Zacharia 2003.

[21] Donald J. Mastronarde, however, emphasizes that tragedy was an innovative and changing genre in the classical period; see Mastronarde 2010: 44, 47, 51.

[22] The costs to Ion's citizenship in Athens do signal autochthony's violent effects, however, which include the structural exclusions of imperialism and its costs to human life.

[23] Dougherty thus looks elsewhere to salvage the *Ion*'s tragic sensibility in spite of its "happy ending" and finds it in its use of Delphi, which "functions in Greek tragedy as a dramatic topos . . . where things work out . . . and contradictions can be reconciled" (Dougherty 1996: 263–264). For a view that opposes reading the play as a "Delphic tragedy," see Loraux 1993.

[24] Zeitlin 1989: 154. The discourse of happiness is also used by Saxonhouse, though she rightly senses the "disquieting tone to the successful and happy conclusion to the plot" (Saxonhouse 1986: 272, 257–260).

reunification. Recognition by one's birth parents provides one's political standing.[25] Ion's autochthonous family reunion should therefore restore his citizenship. And while birth-mother reunification does drive Ion's move from Apollo's sanctuary into Athenian political society, Athena's introduction of the secrecy requirement makes a full (political) restoration difficult to argue for. What is more, an avoidance of death is not the same as an avoidance of political conflict. Readers for whom tragedy's conflicts are legible only within an arc of murderous plotting are misled by the play's avoidance of violence and neglect to attend sufficiently to the criticality that the play mobilizes both before and after the recognition scene.[26] The failure to account for the secret keeping that occurs at the end of the play and the effects it will have on Ion's standing enlists the *Ion* in a wholesale positive valuation of restoring biological identity – the very belief that sustains Athenian hegemony. When readers displace the politics of *metoikia* from this rewriting of autochthony, they risk reproducing Athens' self-conception, an idealized vision in which the demos, like the play, is invulnerable to contamination by the metics that are otherwise everywhere.

To see precisely how and from what the metic's erasure diverts readers of the *Ion*, it is necessary to explicate the broad lines of Nicole Loraux's interpretation of the tragedy. Loraux offers a bridge between the romance reading, which sees the *Ion*'s central conflict as one of violence averted through the recovery of biological identity, and the one developed here, in which the play troubles the autochthonous claim that blood settles questions of membership and belonging at the same time that it seeks to incorporate that instability into the democracy's etiology.

Loraux's way out of the romance reading is to see the play's tragic dimension not in the plot, where critics often seek it to no avail, but in its autochthonous theme.[27] This promising shift in register allows her to argue both alongside and against the familiar view that the recognition

[25] Ion's repatriation signals his *compliance* with Athena's instruction and her invocation of Athenian destiny but little more as far as his own sentiments are concerned. Euripides gives us no reason to assume that Ion goes home happy or that he will live a happy life there.

[26] Such emphasis on violence leads Dougherty, for example, to argue that the recognition scene not only "avoids murder" but "restores all participants in timely fashion to their proper and productive identities" (Dougherty 1996: 264). The play, she and others suggest, is restitutive not destructive, and for this reason quite unlike a tragedy. Even Zacharia calls the end "superficially" happy but tempers her assessment by seeing it as a means to an end. For the play's logic "is not just there to lead to the happy ending"; it "has a thought-provoking function of its own" (Zacharia 2003: 148–149). We should note, however, that violence nevertheless haunts this play, from Kreousa's rape to Ion's impending colonial efforts.

[27] Loraux 1993: 184.

scene may resolve conflicts in the plot but that this in and of itself does not alleviate the play's tragic tension. In fact, the way Euripides "resolves" Ion's incorporation into Kreousa's family, says Loraux, exposes the paradoxical and therefore tragic nature of any autochthonous narrative.[28] What gives autochthony and, by extension, the *Ion* a tragic quality for Loraux is that it expresses a demand to repeat (over generations) what can only happen once (the original birth).[29] Loraux focuses on the play's treatment of gender, particularly its depiction of Kreousa, to illustrate this paradox. Kreousa captures the impossibility as well as the attractiveness of autochthonous birth because, as a woman, she is both unnecessary to the original autochthonous birth (from earth) and necessary to the biological reproduction whose monitoring will sustain the myth, and the Athenian people, in and over time. Thus, when Loraux concludes that "woman is restored to the shadows" by the end, with the "dilemma" of incorporating Ion into an Athenian household "only in extremis . . . resolved," she invites us to see that the final scene functions as an instructive elaboration of an autochthony paradox.[30]

Athena anchors the identity of Athenians as a mythically pure (and colonizing) people in a concealment of the very blood tie that the city claims to celebrate above all else. From Loraux's vantage point, Kreousa's restoration to the social realm expresses the ambivalent role woman plays in the myth of autochthony. The myth is premised on rejecting the women it nevertheless depends on to perpetuate itself on (not from) the ground. The paradox of Kreousa's "return to the shadows" is that it occurs in spite, if not because, of her importance to political life.

An open secret, however, is not the same as a resolution. Loraux does not consider the disorderly effects of a restoration that is *shown* to rely on a lie. Kreousa may be emblematic of the paradoxical role woman plays in the autochthony myth, but even that category's construction is shown to be dependent on a secret, which, as the chorus demonstrated, can always be revealed. Loraux's analysis seems to assume, despite the addition of Athena's secrecy requirement, that the play simply mirrors, rather than critically recasts, the meanings (of woman, metic, autochthonous, Athenian) that the myth of autochthony aims to secure.

My quarrel with Loraux, then, concerns this move away from an initial willingness to seek the politics of tragedy at the discursive level, where new meanings are produced and not simply represented by the play. Rather than treat the *Ion* as an autochthony story par excellence, I want to read it

[28] Loraux 1993: 230. [29] Loraux 1993: 195. [30] Loraux 1993: 204.

as an active participant in the construction of new meanings. This involves asking how the secret helps construct and does not simply reflect the city's ideology. Loraux provides the conceptual language to do this when she suggests that all tragedy is mythopoetic. Let us extend the claim and say that the *Ion*, like all mythopoesis, is engaged in reproducing an original (myth) anew: tragedy, whether as text or performance, always marks a difference between an original (autochthony) and its copy (the *Ion*).[31] The question is not how the *Ion* enacts the paradoxical maneuvers that are demanded by a myth of autochthony but how it rewrites the myth to shine a critical light on Athenian membership politics.

Closeting Ion

One reason Loraux's reading overlooks possibilities it otherwise licenses may be that it focuses on the category of woman to the exclusion of the metic. Insofar as the reconcealment restores Kreousa to the private realm, as Loraux thinks it does, the ending of the *Ion* fulfills (her) Athenian expectations by bringing full circle the inclusion-exclusion that makes Kreousa a woman and the *Ion* a tragedy. But this is only half the story. What Athena demands of Kreousa she also demands of Ion. And in Ion's case, the reconcealment makes a metic out of an Athenian man who should be a citizen. The decline of an autochthonous son into *metoikia* is hardly reassuring. Ion's metic predicament presses us to look again at what it means that secrecy constitutes the political order for a regime like Athens. That Ion admires Athens is made clear in the play. The question is why, in this rewriting of the myth, Athens needs Ion as such. Why should autochthonous blood need to be hidden to secure its subsistence as the city's membership criterion?

Consider again that the function of the autochthony myth is not simply to ground civic equality in a notion of shared and superior birth but also to guard against the kind of mingling and confusion of identities that blurs discrete lines of demarcation in the social order. To prevent this chaos, Athenians promote a civic ideology according to which social and political difference, and the categories that signify it, have meanings that preexist their production and figuration by the myth. Autochthony establishes difference in claims of nature – specifically in earth and blood – to give these categories an antecedent status. The natural difference autochthony insists on between a metic and a citizen, then, is one version of the city's

[31] This makes tragedy an especially interesting mode for exploring the theme of originality.

secret. Woman is not the only category that reveals the irreconcilable tensions that generate the polis' ideas of belonging, exclusion, and political membership. The metic also resecures and reperforms the value of autochthony as being at the expense of those outsiders who are at once and always the product of, but also the condition for, democracy's regeneration.

But the metic perspective sheds light on something the play's politics of gender imply and are implied in but cannot obviously illuminate: if a native Athenian can pass as a metic, a metic can pass as an Athenian, for the so-called facts of blood do not speak for themselves – and, as Ion told Xouthos, they do not determine a course of action either. This is a worrying thought from an Athenian hegemon's perspective. And yet it is precisely what the marriage of imperialism and autochthony spawns while trying to suppress.[32] When a polis colonizes but restricts full membership to natives on the basis of blood, it cannot but produce the metic, a figure whose inclusion-exclusion – whose ability to pass – bears the promise and the risk of that form of citizenship. In asking Ion and Kreousa to keep his autochthonous identity a secret, Athena indicates that the polis' seemingly inviolate identifications are really vulnerable performances of naturalized identifications. From this perspective, the *Ion* does not merely equivocate on or reproduce the claims of the traditional autochthony story, as other readers have suggested. Nor does it simply expose a tension between political membership as blood-right (status) and political membership as a lived experience (practice). Euripides' tragedy lays bare the Athenian practices that function to ascribe a pregiven quality to the city's categories of standing. As the subsequent section will suggest, Ion's fate makes manifest the violability of these categories and suggests it is this violability that is foundational to and servicing of Athenian citizenship politics. This is the groundwork for passing, and it is what the *Republic*'s myth of the metals will try to preclude.

So far my efforts to recover the political implications of the *Ion*'s treatment of autochthony have focused on the ways the tragedy draws on figurations of *metoikia* to destabilize settled views of hereditary attachments and publicize their known instability. I have argued that if the play is a reworking of a traditional myth (*mythopoesis*), it does more than criticize an existing myth. To make sense of how the *Ion* reconceives of the democracy's civic ideology by way of the concealment, we need to think more carefully about the secret's symbolic effects. The secret does more than unsettle the traditional myth after all. It sits at the core of a new one.

[32] For a discussion of the play's twinning of imperialism and autochthony, see Dougherty 1996.

The marriage and inheritance practices of the fifth-century context in which the play was produced shed some light on the reasons for the secret, but they ultimately cannot explain its constitutive effects on the founding myth. All the attractions of Erechtheus' house (name, power, wealth) belong to Kreousa's side. Because she has no brothers, Kreousa is *epiklēros*, heir to her father's *oikos*. Loraux suggests that Athenian law was probably particularly strict on issues of inheritance at the time of the tragedy's production. In order for name and power to stay inside the family, standard practice would have ensured that a female heir marry her close relative. Kreousa's marriage to a foreigner makes her situation abnormal from the perspective of family law and practice. For Loraux, this may be the play's way of exploring some of the tensions in Athenian exceptionalism, particularly around gender: the fact that Kreousa "alone transmits to her son the name and power of the Erectheidai" highlights the polis' commitment to kinship, its self-image as a clan or family.[33] At the same time, however, the city builds alliances with foreigners. When an Athenian royal like Kreousa marries outside the clan for political reasons, she does something Athenians in the audience would recognize. She forges a political alliance as a reward to Xouthos for aiding Athens in war.

But Kreousa cannot perpetuate the autochthonous line by way of her marriage to Xouthos, which is (so far) fruitless. The marriage suggests that from time to time, Athens must go outside of its autochthonous line to renew itself. Each time Kreousa and Xouthos' union resorts to adoptive, extrabiological measures to procure an heir, as it does again with Athena's forecast, the couple plays out the idea that the polis cannot sustain itself through a marriage of imperial power. This is not just to reproduce biologically but for the city to secure its capacity to maintain itself. It is a problem Xouthos acknowledges early in the play when he hopes for Kreousa's eventual and painful acquiescence to Ion's incorporation into the family. Athena invokes it, too, when she intimates that Kreousa will remain childless unless she endures Ion's inclusion as an apparent foreigner in the house of Erechtheus. Only then will she and Xouthos go on to have a *koinon genos*, a "common race" (1589), which the tragedy outs as really a mixed race.

If Kreousa represents Athens here, as Loraux's reading claims, what might the closing secret say about the city? Kreousa was raped by a god, bore an illegitimate child, and married a foreigner whom she needs to secure and define her future. This feminized Athens should be

[33] Loraux 1993: 203.

autonomous. Kreousa, after all, has an *oikos* of her own. But a female-headed household is not adequate under Athenian law. This patriarchal polis depends on violence, foreigners, trickery, and coercion to reproduce itself. There is no future for Athens without cultural mixing.

One reason for this condition is that the Athenian political order is inevitably self-limiting. As Jacqueline Stevens notes, "The appeal to intergenerationality is always paradoxical" because it rests "on the naturalized rules of kinship that are produced by political societies," the very same political societies that turn to kinship as their natural ground.[34] The secret at the center of the polis, then, is that the blood ties the city relies on are actually its own production.[35] From a fifth-century perspective, a woman in Kreousa's situation could bequeath her family's inheritance only to a son of a legitimate union, which Ion is not. Only if Ion is thought to be the adopted son of Kreousa and the nonautochthonous, natural, but illegitimate son of Xouthos can he inherit and play a role in Athenian destiny. Through the secret that transforms him into Xouthos' metic son, he inherits wealth (and military power) from Xouthos, though not full citizenship, and gains some status in the polis as well as its legacy.[36]

Here, however, Loraux issues the useful caution that the play's historical contexts cannot do the work of rendering the secret a necessary or understandable solution to the tragedy. The tensions created by the polis's laws for membership are never actually solved, she reminds us: "Xouthos is and remains an intruder who cannot therefore really be the legitimate father." Echoing Ion's worries, she surmises that "in the eyes of the Athenians, given the standing of Xouthos, Ion could at most be regarded as an adopted son, unable to inherit the oikos of his adoptive father."[37] Loraux may be right about this. But the absence of a neat solution to the play makes the theoretical significance of the secret all the more necessary to pursue.[38]

[34] Stevens 1998: xiii.

[35] For this reason, Zeitlin's use of the phrase "mysteries of identity" (also the title of her chapter on the *Ion*) to argue that the play represents the self as performed does well to point to the fragility and uncertainty surrounding subjectivity, but it does not recognize the further political implication that Athens maintains and profits from the uncertainty and the appearance of verifiability (rather than verifiability itself).

[36] Similarly, K. H. Lee has argued that the secret is necessary "because there is little likelihood that Xouthos would allow an adopted child [Ion] to exclude from his inheritance any son which may be born to him later." See Lee's commentary on lines 71–73 of the tragedy in Euripides 1997: 166–167.

[37] Loraux 1993: 204n85.

[38] It is surprising that Loraux does not see this and relegates her discussion of the secret instead to a provocative footnote: "Thus, read in the light of the present, Xouthos' illusion (1602)—which prevents the disclosure that Ion is Kreousa's son—is unfortunate, since the city as an entire community will be involved, and Ion will continue to be considered an intruder." Loraux 1993: 200n69. See also Loraux 2000: 20.

In the context of the *Ion*'s production, inheritance laws serve as just one instance of the range of institutional practices driving the insistence on and attachment to familial identity and its knowability. The desire Xouthos feels for his son's return might also be an effect of the polis's insistence on the importance of kinship.

Zacharia brings us closer to the secret's meaning when she suggests, "the outsider must be allowed in if what lies within is to be rescued."[39] She rightly shifts attention back to the necessary role the foreigner plays in securing autochthony's perpetuity, but her language betrays the autochthonous view that there is a stable inside to begin with. From Zacharia's perspective, the *Ion*'s criticism of autochthony on this issue amounts to little more than its empirical debunking. In other words, one effect of the *Ion*'s retelling is that it posits retroactively an Athenian founding in which foreigners were just absorbed into the polis (maybe even the demos) and a native was left out. Zacharia is not wrong, but her case and its dyadic structure are driven by their exclusive focus on Xouthos' foreignness. The future of autochthonous Athens certainly needs Xouthos' inclusion, but what of the performative, shifting, in-between foreignness Ion expresses? In the play, Xouthos and Kreousa's procreation hinges only in part on Xouthos' deceptive inclusion. It also requires Kreousa's and Ion's silence about Ion's nativity and Ion's living in Athens as Xouthos' metic son.

In Foucault's reading of the *Ion*, the future of Athens also depends on an exclusion – of what he calls oracular pronouncements of truth – that makes space for Athena to found the city instead in a political order of *parrēsia*, the practice of political freedom.[40] Foucault's account depends, like other happy-ending readings, on understanding Ion's return as a homecoming not a *metoikia*. Indeed, Foucault sees "the truth of Ion's birth and his right to exercise power now in Athens" in Athena's closing pronouncement.[41] If Foucault cogently perceives the power of Athena's dictum, it is in decidedly rosier hues than Ion, who knows his life will lack *parrēsia* in Athens. Foucault is right to fasten to the generative power of Athena's "truth under the reign of a share of illusion," but his sanguine view of Ion's standing implies that the political order he takes it to generate may be similarly idealized. Once seen in terms of Ion, the exclusion at the play's end founds the field of citizen truth telling, as Foucault insists, but only insofar as it establishes an autochthonous order in which *parrēsia* will be claimed as the special privilege of natives.

[39] Zacharia 2003: 101. [40] Foucault 2010: 145. [41] Foucault 2010: 144.

At this point, a couple of recurring questions remain. Why should Ion's secret keeping serve as the act that secures the city's political order? The concealment that establishes in perpetuity the pregiven difference between the autochthonous and the unnobly born is the same one that demonstrates its instability. How might this apparent contradiction enable, rather than simply undercut, the claims of the regime?

To take stock of how the concealment is not merely privative but also helps to refashion the myth and the notion of Athenian membership that belongs to this political order, consider it an act of closeting, the sort of discursive act Eve Kosofsky Sedgwick analyzes for its generative effects. Addressing the discourse of sexuality in the nineteenth century, Sedgwick maintains that sexuality comes to mean a "function of stable definitions of identity (so that one's personality structure might mark one as a homosexual, even, perhaps, in the absence of any activity at all)."[42] What enables the shift to conceive of sexuality in terms of conscious identity rather than a spectrum of behavior, she explains, is the act of closeting, which moves sexuality out of an economy of activity and into an economy of knowledge. "'Closetedness' itself," Sedgwick argues, "is a performance initiated as such by the speech act of a silence."[43] So long as same-sex desire has the status of a fact that can be disclosed or hidden, it remains a matter of being, not behavior. To bring this idea to bear on the Athenian case is to see how Ion's secret keeping establishes blood as the natural and univocal ground of political status, a pregiven difference that can be concealed or revealed. From here on out, political status stands as an object of potential suspicion. Ion's act of closeting turns him into a (temporary) metic in order to found Athenian membership in static, oppositional terms (citizen/metic). And yet this effort at stabilization is precisely what Ion's anticipated metic masquerade exposes as the city's necessary and generative maneuver. Closeting Ion's nativity works in the service of Athens' autochthonous project even as it appears to betray it.

By reconcealing his Athenianness, Ion secures the metic/citizen binary that is both the condition and product of the hegemony espoused by autochthony. The secret tries to keep up the appearance that all forms of membership, even if deprivileged, are inviolate identities. Naturalized status in the *Ion* is not merely a fact to be covered, recovered, discovered, or disclosed. It is a reminder of the city's efforts to make statuses seem like facts. The *Ion*'s rewriting of autochthony thus exposes the Athenian prioritization of a status-oriented citizenship and suggests it is the

[42] Sedgwick 2008: 83. [43] Sedgwick 2008: 3.

inevitable outcome of privileging circumstances of blood. Euripides' tragedy shows Athena founding a democracy and a conception of citizenship in which all, even citizens, are vulnerable to threats of exposure.

The *Ion* unsettles the forceful presumption that the right blood establishes citizenship, but it does so in an unconventional way. The tragedy does not focus on a person with the wrong blood who nevertheless infiltrates Athenian society undetected by virtue of active participation in the polis' institutions. But there were cases of this, as Chapter 6 will attest, as well as a politics of suspicion around such infiltration. In the *Ion*, practices of disclosure and concealment are exposed as the daily work that enables the city to give its self-serving and exclusionary guarantee that status, bestowed by blood, grounds a practice of citizenship. Euripides suggests that there are practices, like secret keeping, that make political status look prior to and generative of political practice, and so the tragedy founds the possibility of passing, that is, of a deceptive membership performance. The resolution of the play, however, implies that Ion's passing tragically resecures the citizen/metic binary it also unsettles.

PART II

A Metic Republic *in Three Acts*

CHAPTER 3

The Republic *as a Metic Space*

> *... There is quite as much trouble in the reformation of an old constitution as in the establishment of a new one, just as to unlearn is as hard as to learn.*
>
> – Aristotle, *Politics* 1289a3–1289a4

Nowhere do we find figurations of metics with the prominence or historical specificity that we do in the *Republic*. Plato's dialogue unfolds in Piraeus, the Athenian harbor synonymous with empire, merchants, travel, importation, and immigrant residence.[1] A metic entreats Socrates to stay and talk. His home furnishes the space for the examination, eschewal, and rethinking of the city's membership lines. The site of the famous imaginary expedition to found a just city belongs to a family with no autochthonous claim to rule.

In the grand scheme of the *Republic*'s argumentation, this setting is only marginally visible. Yet as a dramatic conceit, it bears a crucial theoretical insight. If in Athens the autochthonous citizen is constituted by the metic's exclusion, Plato's dialogue enacts this logic of democratic difference. For the *Republic* presents the Athenian definition of the citizen against the metic by literally staging a conversation about membership in the house of one. It would seem that, without this figure, we could not grasp Athens in its entirety or be moved to think it otherwise.

The Aristotelian epigraph that introduces this chapter establishes an equivalency between the trouble of altering an existing polity and the difficulty of establishing a new one: both activities involve a critical

[1] Based on epigraphic evidence, Whitehead (1986: 83) observes that Piraeus had the second highest number of metic residents in Attica. While metics tended not to live in rural demes but were scattered across many "urban and suburban" ones, Whitehead estimates that almost 19 percent of all metics lived in Piraeus. Among Piraeus' additional associations is democratic power in the form of the fleet. Aristotle remarks on its strong democratic connotations in *Pol.* 1303b7. See also Lysias 12 and Plutarch's *Life of Themistocles* (19.2–4). For a historical account of the Piraeus and its Athenian significance, see Von Reden 1995: 26; Von Reden 1998; and Garland 2001.

distance that is hard to acquire. I invoke the passage here to suggest, as subsequent chapters elaborate, that the *Republic* attempts both enterprises simultaneously. Plato defamiliarizes Athenian democracy by presenting it in a metic frame in which the established lines of Athenian membership will come unmoored: they will reemerge as a question, not a given, for political life and pave the way for imagining a new polity in the form of the callipolis.

The liminality that opens and subtends this narrative, however, is rarely named and less often analyzed.[2] Readers have been curiously reluctant to consider that Plato's allusions to *metoikia* might be contributing specific political theoretical meaning to this text. When the metic does register in studies of the dialogue, it appears less as the generative analogue to the foreigner or woman of Greek tragedy – the established linchpin of unsettling meditations on the naturalness of Athenian membership lines – than as a set of codified historical references working to reinforce the hegemonic status quo that Athenian drama, by contrast, is taken to trouble. One reason for this interpretive conclusion is that scholars assume the rhetorical function of the metic begins and ends in the first book, where the immigrants Cephalus and Polemarchus speak, and that it consists merely in confirming the poor quality of the early definitions of justice. The noncitizen status of Socrates' wealthy hosts appears to evince the superior acumen of the citizen characters who quickly supplant the metics as the main interlocutors. If these liminal figures seem to mark, by contradistinction, a proper orientation to reason and politics, then Plato's text affirms the citizen's permanent distance from the noncitizen's despite (if not because of) the way it places persons of varying statuses together – attending the same spectacles, praying to the same goddess, gathering privately to talk about politics. What Plato codes "metic," then, is thought to underscore, rather than call into question, the Athenian order of inclusion. Just as the *metoikos* helps bring into view a certain democratic ideal of the deserving (because well-born) citizen, so its deployment in Plato's text is assumed to indicate, by way of some dramatized inadequacy, the right way to think and speak. It is as though the real philosophical work of the dialogue could not commence without his putting metics back in their natural place.

[2] Honig, for instance, wonders in passing why "the house of a foreign merchant" is the setting for the dialogue but does not pursue the issue. Her answer to whether Plato means to "imply that justice, or perhaps philosophical dialogue itself, is occasioned by engagement with foreignness" is yes, but she understands the function of the "foreign" as supplying for Socrates a figurative foreignness that enables an outsider perspective on the city he is criticizing (Honig 2001: 3 and 124n8).

The desire to reinforce Athenian political distinctions is a strange one to attribute, however inadvertently, to Plato, a thinker otherwise persistently read as deploring democratic practices.[3] Not only does the *Republic* resist positioning deprivileged figures at or outside the boundaries of intelligibility.[4] Plato's characterization does not systematically tie variations in philosophical aptitude or interest to Athenian political or social status. There are, for instance, several citizens in the metic's home that night who say nothing at all.[5] And while the scenic space of the discussion seems to fall away as the speakers limn the abstract space of the callipolis with greater specificity, the home of Cephalus and Polemarchus never disappears. Though most visible in the opening scenes, this house envelops the whole conversation.

The straightforward premise of this chapter is that the *Republic* is a metic space and that a good deal more could be said about how this feature (if it can be reduced to that) works to provoke and inflect the political theoretical concerns of this text. By "metic space," I mean not only that metic figures enable and provide the conditions for the imaginary founding that ensues. The topography of the text also belongs entirely to Piraeus, an area characterized by intermixture, mobility, and liminality. In what follows, I argue that Piraeus functions symbolically for Athenian democracy, much like the metics that had homes there, to give definition to the city's autochthonous order. That the metic frames this dialogue suggests that the *Republic* does not simply register the nativist political realities of its setting. The dialogue assumes the importance of metic to Athenian democracy, uses this relation to peer into the city, and attempts over the course of the evening to consider its workings and political effects.

This chapter takes it for granted, then, that setting is one of many resources Plato uses to signify meaning in the *Republic*, and it attempts to

[3] Plato's chauvinism and anti-democratic sentiment are taken for granted and (uneasily) brought together in Fracisco L. Lisi and Gabriele Cornelli's assessment: "His writings show a clear rejection of the Athenian democratic regime as it existed in the fifth century BC, but his own attitude is one of an unequivocal Athenian patriotism, and he even considers democracy to be the system that corresponds to the Athenian nature (cf. *Menexenus* 238c5–239a4)" (Cornelli and Lisi 2010: 6).

[4] Pace Irigaray 1985.

[5] Seldom noted is the presence of three quiet citizens. They are Cleitophon, a supporter of Thrasymachus who speaks once and early on (340b); Charmantides, a wealthy, politically active contemporary of Plato's; and Nikeratus, son of the wealthy and prominent democratic leader Nikias (327c, 328b). Like the metics in the house, they watch from the sidelines. Besides the slave, whose speech provokes the encounter on Munychia, all those Socrates reports to be in attendance are free, including Lysias, the metic speechwriter who is also Polemarchus' brother. The disparity of the group at once underscores the differences in formal standing and resists this level of analysis altogether. For a historical account of the figures in the dialogue, see Nails 2002. Blondell (2002) discusses the *Republic*'s characters in depth.

take stock of the actualities of democratic power he links to this home and to the *politeia* discussed therein. The discussion that imagines a colonial expedition to found a just regime unfolds in a place encoded with Athenian meanings far more specific and politically charged than typically acknowledged. We rarely appreciate that Plato might have chosen a different place to dramatize the Athenian world that provokes this city in speech. Thus the pages that follow ask what it means that "the metic," as a place, as an inherited status, as a way of living – I use the term in all these senses – makes up the background of this discussion. The argument I advance has an unusual objective as a result. I aim to reconstruct an atmosphere of autochthony and draw out what the *Republic* lightly activates. Part of the argument's function is to set the stage for subsequent chapters in which I recast some of the dialogue's explorations of "natural" political difference and democracy in the context of the dialogue's immediate interest in the nativism that runs through Athenian membership politics.

In Chapter 1, I wagered that the metic's difference is constitutive of citizenship in democratic Athens: if the metic is free but barred from citizen status intergenerationally on the basis of blood, Athenian citizenship is not fully accounted for as a practice of freedom. Citizen status is assigned first and foremost as a privilege of kinship, which means that freedom is a necessary but insufficient condition of full membership and, perhaps most relevant here, that it also characterizes a metic's way of living in Athens. To argue that Plato stages this metic–citizen dynamic through the dialogue's setting is therefore to claim that the dialogue adopts the dynamic as a device for re-presenting the Athenian *politeia*; it uses this unjust relation as the dramatic and structural catalyst for the city's transformation into the callipolis. Yet in drawing on Piraeus, Plato is making use of a place that already operated in Athenian discourse as a *topos* for theorizing and organizing hierarchical relations. He sets the *Republic* in Piraeus, in other words, so as to present and reorder a hierarchy that this particular space was already and variously called on in Athens to arrange.

Neither Piraeus nor the specific home in which the dialogue unfolds is therefore sufficiently understood as one of many tropes used by Plato to generate a desire to flee the chaotic openness of democracy for the ordered, just, and immobilized world of the callipolis. Plato depicts a world of mingling not chaos to signify a fifth-century Athenian reality.[6] The first

[6] As Cohen (2000: 21) remarks, the *Republic* does not confirm a "sundered dichotomy of *politai* and foreigners" but portrays "the metic hosts as 'friends and virtually kinsmen' of their citizen guests, an absence of social differentiation recurrent throughout Plato's dialogues." In stressing the

fifteen lines of the dialogue are peculiarly thick with references to Athenian relations of power: Piraeus, Syracusan metics, Thracian residents, a slave. The question of hierarchy, in other words, does not emerge with the callipolis. It is already in Athens, in Plato's situating first line, "I went down to the Piraeus yesterday" (327a).[7]

Once we read the first lines in this light, Book I's interest in the relation between what is politically marginal and symbolically central is hard to miss. The opening maps their interplay repeatedly. The narrator focuses immediately on the distance traversed between town and harbor and in the sometimes-uneasy gathering of citizens and metics. One gets the sense when reading the first book that Plato is concerned less with securing this difference than with depicting its negotiation. The opening evokes or enacts a series of Athenian practices that spans a contiguous but differentiated area. The festival that brings Socrates to Piraeus will involve two segregated parades celebrating the same foreign goddess. One belongs to natives, the other to metics. He will find their conduct equally good and, with this observation, shift the reader's thoughts, momentarily at least, to the reason for their division. If not a difference in capacity, then a difference in kinship must account for the rule that separates them. But here, in the *Republic*'s portrayal, that descent-based rule betrays itself as a regulatory fiction. The internal attribute that is assumed to dictate a person's place in the social order fails to materialize as such in practice during the very civic spectacle that is segregated so as to evince it: Socrates sees no difference in their performance. And so begins the *Republic*'s slow, at times oblique, examination of this unjust and precarious arrangement. The lines of Athenian membership will not be taken for granted in this text. Plato starts the *Republic* by putting the lie to the myth of autochthony.

The importance Athens places on metic–citizen distance and proximity finds further expression in the first book by a series of locating comments. Socrates would prefer to make his way back to town. Cephalus would like him to visit more often (328d). We can surmise from all this that Athenians do not simply cross a hierarchized space. They order a space

intermingling in this scene, however, we should not assume that difference in juridical or political status ceases to matter in the dialogue. Consider as well that Cohen's reference is to ***philous te kai panu oikeious*** (328d6), a line I read at the close of the chapter to suggest Plato is making a claim about the link between citizenship and kinship. How the lines between friends and enemies and insiders and outsiders are drawn constitutes a central matter of contestation in the *Republic.*

7 References to the Greek of the *Republic* are from Plato 2013. Translations of the *Republic* are by Tom Griffith (Plato 2000) unless otherwise noted. I have also consulted Rowe's translation (Plato 2012b).

they must cross. I say "must" partly because what helps sustain life materially in the city of the dialogue's setting is empire, immigrant labor, and trade. The importance of mobility, of peoples and goods, to the Athenian economy is evident in the *Republic* whenever Socrates worries about containing the influence of money on politics but also specifically when he asks Cephalus about the comforts wealth might bring him (329e), as if to stress a conventional association between metics and mercantilism. With money, however, the *Republic* will turn out to be saying something less about metics *per se* than about the democratic membership order of which the metic is both a product and a signifier. I argue toward the end of the chapter that Plato figures democratic membership as a way of life characterized by participation less in celebrated political practices like *parrēsia* than in unaccountable and social acts of flattery, trade, and private discussion, not unlike the one staged in Polemarchus' house. If the agora was "the heart of Athenian commercial and social life," this "blending of the civic was uncomfortable for some contemporaries," notes Alex Gottesman.[8] Aristotle (*Pol.* 1331a19–1331b13) would recommend separating the functions spatially, reserving one area for rule and citizens and another for trade and, presumably, noncitizens. A metic may signify a mercantile way of participating in the city's political life. (Cephalus, for example, leads a free but disenfranchised life.) But in Plato's hands, this way of living acquires the status of a collective democratic habit.[9]

There is a further reason for thinking mobility and mingling constitute some of the central concerns of Book I. The *Republic* foregrounds a series of spaces and practices, the function of which is to stratify and integrate the noncitizens on whom the demos depends for its autochthonous self-conception yet maintains are wholly superfluous to it. The distance depicted in the opening scene may be bridged, but it is always marked. Distance works, like the opening procession, to allegorize a certain precarious interdependence between citizen and metic, center and periphery, polis and harbor. And so the metic functions in Plato's text, as I will argue Piraeus also does, to draw attention to the specific terms of this democracy's self-definition. For this reason, Piraeus, like the metic, poses a specific threat to Athens. The city depends on the harbor for its

[8] Gottesman 2014: 28. On the integration of metics in the agora and the space of Athens more generally, see also Mansouri (2011: ch. 3).

[9] Plato's dialogue dramatizes this blending when it depicts citizens, metics, and slaves sharing spaces. As I mention in Chapter 6, citizens, metics, and slaves also worked side by side as craftsmen, as was the case in the building of the Erechtheion (R. Osborne 2010: 89).

autarkeia.[10] What Aristotle (*Pol.* 1328b6–1328b15) would later understand as the needs a polis must meet to achieve self-sufficiency – the provision of food, the practice of arts and crafts, the bearing of arms, the provision of material wealth, the establishment of religious worship, and the means to determine what is appropriate and just in people's dealings with each other – are all fulfilled in, or with the help of, Piraeus.[11] Under these conditions, how could a city ensure that a permanent distance separates citizen from metic? Plato's *Republic* does not seek to resecure this regulatory fiction in my view but to present it for our immediate and critical examination.

The reading I bring forward seeks in these ways to demonstrate that Book I is not a second-rate component of the dialogue, as some readers assume. And the beginning of the dialogue generates critical insights into democratic politics that do more than simply describe, in order to critique, the democratic-imperialist vision of orderly cultural mixing and hospitality famously celebrated in Pericles' Funeral Oration.[12] The democracy portrayed in the *Republic*'s setting depends instead on an openness that may be more accurately and less euphemistically described as mobility – to compensate for infertile land, to found colonies where soil is arable, to collect tributes.[13] These materialist and symbolic rationales may be displaced from Pericles' Funeral Oration, but they are not absent from the *Republic*.[14] Like the place they live, the wealthy, shield-making, colony-settling, immigrant family of Cephalus symbolizes migration, trade, colonization, war, the democratic *ordering* of persons and spaces, and the instability of these status assignments. For like mythical Ion in the last chapter, the real Cephalus became a metic in Athens before becoming a settler of a colony (Thurii) on Athens' behalf. At each point, the flux in his status was the effect of a physical movement, but it was also apparently a consequence of a Periclean invitation – of a call to serve Athens.

This chapter unfolds in four sections that focus attention around two persistently underanalyzed features of the *Republic*'s opening: the

[10] Von Reden argues that the Piraeus "seems to have been used in what has been called the 'rhetoric of otherness'—that is, the emphasis of the cultural limits of citizenship, which were essential for the self-consciousness of the Athenian polis" (Von Reden 1995: 32–33).

[11] This is Manville's gloss on the needs and political functions of the polis as articulated by Aristotle (1990: 41).

[12] I explore these readings of the dialogue in the next section.

[13] On the barrenness of Attic soil, see Thuc. 1.2.5–6. Bresson explores the agrarian dimension of Athenian colonization and notes the city's "external dependency" on fertile territories was the effect of colonization: "The desire to take over external territories that produced grain, or to have access to grain trade routes, was certainly a powerful motive for Athens' foreign adventures in the second half of the sixth century" (Bresson 2016: 410).

[14] I discuss the Funeral Oration in Chapter 5.

figuration of metics and the dialogue's setting in Piraeus. In the first two, I diagnose the interpretive assumptions that have made it difficult to appreciate that the metic functions as a site of discursive and political theoretical meaning in the *Republic.* I then suggest we read Cephalus as the embodiment of a troubling kind of democratic power (autochthonous, mercantile, stealth) that is not exclusively possessed by metics but, when read with Book VI in mind, illuminating of Athenian membership more generally. Section III returns us to Piraeus to provide a close reading of the Bendis festival, arguing that the processions signify the city's autochthonous order of rule. What Socrates sees in Piraeus, I conclude in the final section, calls into question the citizen's natural difference from the metic and clears the way for a new membership order called the "callipolis" (527c2), which I consider in Chapter 4's reading of the noble lie.

If the *Republic*'s allusions to *metoikia* have seemed too marginal to take stock of until now, that may be because they are "casual and stressed," to borrow Edward Said's evocative language, "both incidental, referred to only in passing, and absolutely crucial to the action."[15] Rather than assume that the dialogue begins with an autochthonous reordering that marginalizes metics and sets Book I's struggling arguments on the right track, let us look again at how this text begins and where it remains, in a space overdetermined by hierarchy of a most uncertain kind.

A Hermeneutics of Assimilation

The opening of Plato's *Republic* is often understood as a nexus of failures – of argumentative acumen, Socratic method, and philosophical consistency – redeemed by the commitments and cohesiveness of the dialogue's subsequent books. This common reading of "thwarted ascents" finds its basis in the apparent instruction of the dialogue, which in Book I displays a series of starts and stops that begins with Socrates' frustrated attempt to leave Piraeus and culminates in his

[15] The expression is used to describe the imperial activities Jane Austen refers to in *Mansfield Park.* What makes Austen's uses of empire casual and stressed, according to Said, is that life in Mansfield Park is enabled by this "overseas sustenance" (1993: 89). The approach Said takes in *Culture and Imperialism* is instructive for a reading of the *Republic,* in which Plato's allusions to *metoikia,* mobility, and trade establish the dramatic world of the text without explicitly referring to these Athenian dynamics. For the point is not only that "allusions to the facts of empire" have an outsized, if quiet, presence in the nineteenth- and twentieth-century British novel but that to overlook these figurations would be to further marginalize the already-circumscribed representation of "inferior classes and races" in these texts and the constitutive relation they call attention to between the so-called center and periphery (1993: 80).

supposed quashing of Thrasymachus' efforts to dominate the discussion by way of a successful, albeit figurative, escape to the callipolis.[16]

Otherwise unable to reconcile what they perceive as inconsistencies in style and argument, commentators used to argue with frequency that the first thirty lines were remnants of a lost Platonic text added to the *Republic* at a later date.[17] The "hypothesis of its early composition," wrote Gregory Vlastos, "may be favored in the strength and preponderance of the stylistic evidence."[18] In recent years, readers have been less inclined to see the book's fit as a question of composition continuity. Yet the tendency to cast its theoretical importance in terms of inadequacy persists. Thus, in C. D. C. Reeve's estimation, the *Republic*'s opening misfires but in a way that is purposeful, performed, and pedagogical. Readers may feel frustration and disappointment at Socrates' inability to offer sufficient arguments early on, but this experience is illuminating: it instructs readers in the philosophical importance of argumentative style. And so in Book II when Glaucon suggests Socrates may not be achieving his aim if it is really to convince them, Plato provides a "new beginning" that suggests the failure of Book I is part of a narrative arc. What makes the opening a critical component of the *Republic* on these views is that Book I adumbrates several important themes unsatisfactorily that are treated more substantively in later books.[19]

Such efforts to understand the significance of Book I's function within the *Republic* take as paramount the text's thematic coherence. Even so, these attempts to understand the critical purchase of Book I prioritize a doctrinal reading of dialogue. They judge the theoretical importance of Book I largely by the validity of the claims that proceed from and correct

[16] Seth Benardete (1989: 9) refers to the beginning of the *Republic* (327a1–328c4) as a "thwarted ascent," but I pluralize it here to capture the multiplicity of failure readings I find in the scholarship on Book I.

[17] In 1839, K. F. Hermann proposed that Book I did not belong to the *Republic* but was instead part of a different dialogue by Plato on justice that had yet to be found. On the issue of the opening's complete disavowal, see Charles Kahn (1992: 131), who recounts and argues against the long tradition of reading the opening as a separate enterprise; see also Reeve 1988: 3–4. Nevertheless, a long gap seems to have separated the composition of Book I from the composition of Books II–X. Plato had already written the first book by the time he opened the Academy around 383 BCE (though this date is debated). "Between the school's opening and his second visit to Syracuse in 367," writes Danielle Allen, Plato probably composed the rest of the dialogue. See Allen 2013: 166n13. Reasons for dating the Academy to 383 (not 387) are explored in Nails 2002: 248. This is also the date adopted by Allen 2013.

[18] Vlastos 1991: 250–251.

[19] The point is made with regard to Cephalus, who, despite departing midway through Book I, is said to help the argument along by introducing themes like piety, which plays a crucial role in Socrates' delineation of justice later on (331a4). See Benardete 1989: 15.

for the shortcomings of the opening, their (in)ability to provoke consensus and the argumentative success of later speakers. As responses to the dialogue's stark shifts in characterization, tone, and conversational style, the accounts bring a certain set of expectations to the *Republic*'s opening. They treat the first book as a stylistic and philosophical outlier and unwittingly inhibit a reading in which other features of the *Republic*, such as its staging and characterization, might generate their own meaning and pose political questions by rhetorical means.

To assume the marginality of the opening is therefore also to underappreciate the specifically metic resources Plato utilizes in these scenes. Under the presumption that the first book is lacking, critics tend to treat the metic status of the hosts and liminal spaces and practices of the text's milieu as largely irrelevant to the *Republic*'s central political and theoretical concerns. That these metics appear to drop out of the discussion after Book I only underscores that sense. In an essay titled "Who Is Cephalus," for example, Peter Steinberger sets out to correct for this "marginal" character's underappreciation,[20] but as Sara Monoson notes, "neglects" even "to discuss the family's status as metics."[21]

The *metoikia* that is rendered theoretically unimportant by way of an erasure may be just as disavowed by the rare reading that attempts to take its full measure. The relatively few critics who address the metic in the *Republic* – Ruby Blondell and David Whitehead among them – tend to read the metic figure not as a site of political theoretical meaning but as a literal and historical referent to a legal order of inclusion with little symbolic importance for the dialogue's arguments. Their accounts, while brief, are crucial to work through because they glimpse but then curiously retreat from the metic's peculiar theoretical power: its resistance to neat classification within the citizen/foreigner dyad that governs studies of classical democratic citizenship.

I argued in Chapter 1 that the category "metic" classes free, economically diverse men and women, and their children born in Athens. The metic's figuration in the *Republic*, then, need not function to secure the binaries (citizen/slave, native/foreigner, mass/elite, male/female) that scholars traditionally use to articulate Athenian membership politics. For the metic troubles each one. When readers fail to grant this disquieting in-betweenness to the metic, they assimilate its figuration to one of two dominant categories: foreigner/anticitizen or quasi-citizen/citizen. Critics

[20] Steinberger 1996 names Cephalus as a metic in the first line of his essay but never explores the issue.
[21] Monoson 2000: 215n21.

oscillate between positioning the metic at the outer limits of the political (like the foreigner, a symbol of pure externality) or assume, as they do with Cephalus, that the metic is so much *like* a citizen that his figuration in the *Republic* cannot signify deprivileged membership. This interpretive habit culminates in an elision of the metic's particularity and amounts to reading past the metic altogether.

To spell out this argument and explore its political theoretical stakes, the remainder of this section looks carefully at what I call a hermeneutics of assimilation. Without appreciating the sense in which the metic constitutes the outside that is permanently within the polis, readers inadvertently enlist this figure in support of an autochthonous ideal: the notion that there is a stable inside and outside to begin with. Once his *metoikia* is restored to the *Republic*, Cephalus emerges instead as a powerful example of a precarious liminality: he is citizen-like only because he is first and foremost a metic and thus illuminating not of what democratic citizenship means juridically but of what it is always in danger of becoming (in practice).

Ruby Blondell's chief concern in her engaging and wide-ranging study of Plato's dialogues is to make a case for the philosophical importance of their literary features. Her reading of the *Republic* raises a number of crucial details about the real Cephalus and his family but ultimately turns away from addressing how these matters of historical context bear on the political or theoretical meaning of the metics in the *Republic*. She writes,

> The historical Kephalos was not an Athenian citizen but a wealthy Syracusan who had settled in Attica with his sons as a resident alien or metic. This particular metic family was unusually well known as such, thanks to its victimization by the Thirty Tyrants. In socio-political terms, this status is an ambiguous one. Metics were not, of course, enfranchised members of the polis, and were sometimes viewed as a kind of "anticitizen." As such they were associated with crafts, *banausia* (manual work) and money-making. The setting of *Republic* at Peiraeus recalls the fact that metics could not own property within the city walls of Athens without special dispensation ... Many, like Kephalos, were not only wealthy but well-connected. Plato never mentions that Kephalos and his family are foreigners, and in real life they seem to have moved in the highest Athenian democratic circles.[22]

Elsewhere in the discussion, Blondell stresses the deprivileged standing of this family – the "setting" in Piraeus, she adds, "emphasizes rather their

[22] Blondell 2002: 166.

status as outsiders" – but she nonetheless concludes that the family that provokes the *Republic* is especially difficult to categorize because of their money and their influence.[23] What makes Cephalus' classification indeterminate for Blondell is not the messiness of metic status. (Recall that in her view, metics are anticitizens.) The difficulty concerns the family's exceptional biographical details, which Blondell takes to mean that Cephalus transcended his *metoikia*. Despite the eventual execution of his son Polemarchus by the Thirty in 404 BCE, Cephalus' family is assumed to have mitigated the unsalutary effects of their precarious status by socioeconomic means.[24]

This view that the hosts of the *Republic* are exceptional metics aligns with the conclusion reached by David Whitehead, who argues that Cephalus' prominence is less an effect of his *metoikia* than an escape from it. Whitehead turns to Plato's depiction of Cephalus to support a mounting historical argument about the ways metics' wealth, education, and social ties could compensate for the inequalities their juridical status afforded. The *Republic*'s figuration of *metoikia* provides evidence of this social reality, he thinks: "It might be ironic, but I doubt it: Cephalus has simply reached the stage – economically, socially, intellectually – where Plato is oblivious of any connection between him and the *metoikoi* and *xenoi* who, in a democratic *polis*, tend (deplorably) to become assimilated to *astoi* (563A)."[25] It is worth keeping in mind that Cephalus is a metic figure of rare density in Athenian political thought, and he recurs in Whitehead's study of the metic to underscore the important historical claim that juridical standing was only one "criterion of differentiation" in Athenian society.[26] High levels of social or economic status, Whitehead argues, are not captured – indeed they may even be mischaracterized – by the title *metoikos*, a point he supports with reference to the "reluctance" Athenians felt about calling the immigrants who made "enormous" contributions to the city "metics," even though "that is what they were."[27] Whitehead's argument attributes an explanatory power to this conventional practice of (not) naming, which he then attributes to the *Republic*:[28]

[23] Blondell adds, "[The name] Polemarchus may also be read as a reminder of his metic status, since *polemarchus* was the title of the Athenian official responsible for metic affairs" (Blondell 2002: 166n4).

[24] Compare to Nails (2002: 84), who argues that, despite Cephalus' wealth, he was a metic and "should not be confused with the aristocratic citizens with their inherited wealth or 'old money.'"

[25] Whitehead 1977: 19.

[26] Whitehead 1977: 19.

[27] Whitehead 1977: 18. On the importance of metics' economic contributions to Athens, see Adak 2003.

[28] Wijma (2014) shares this view.

the wealth and education of a man like Cephalus could "confound" metic status in Athens; that Plato never *refers* to the well-known family as *metoikoi* attests to their high status but also, paradoxically, to the sense in which they were not really metics after all. If this sounds like Xouthos, who in the previous chapter attempted to convince Ion that social and economic mobility could nullify a metic's status, that is because both views imply that a rich immigrant's legal status does not capture his lived experience in Athens, which is, at least in practice, equivalent to a citizen's. The *Republic,* on Whitehead's reading, does not figure the metic way of life I have been tracking so far in this study, because in Plato's eyes, Cephalus was no different from a citizen.

There is, however, nothing in the text of the *Republic* to discount the possibility that the dialogue is interested in the very *metoikia* Whitehead seems to downplay or conflate with citizenship. Plato's dialogues do not typically announce the juridical status of their historical characters. A contemporaneous audience is likely to have known this particular family of immigrants by name (Cephalus was one of the wealthiest men in Athens) and, as Blondell indicated, to have known the special risk they incurred during the reign of the Thirty. Although we need not perform the sort of assimilating move on Cephalus that Whitehead suggests (perhaps too sanguinely) that Athens did, there is nonetheless a crucial insight in his reading of this character that, while he does not extend it to Plato's text, may be worth pursuing for the possibilities it opens up in the *Republic.*

The sense that Cephalus is like a citizen in Plato's text leads Whitehead to conclude that under certain conditions, juridical status ceases to matter in democracy. Such metic–citizen similitude, he suggests, functions as a way of eliding the metic's difference from the citizen and so it conveys, supposedly on Plato's behalf, the conventional Athenian view that wealth trumps blood. Once again this is a version of Xouthos' claim: blood-based status does not decide Athenian membership practice, not because blood is indeterminate and uncertain of action but because in this autochthonous regime, the wealth that a metic is free to secure can compensate for a lack of juridical (and inherited) privilege. But there is another possibility. Money and high social status bestow influence that rivals or, worse, starts to define what it means to share in a *politeia* for citizens as well. This claim is not the empirical observation Whitehead would like it to be. It is a theoretical point, and it is afforded not by blindness to Cephalus' *metoikia* but rather by an acknowledgment of its peculiar contours. To consider what it means to say that Cephalus is like a citizen in the *Republic* means first seeing him as a metic. It involves addressing how a metic's freedom and exclusion from rule are conditions that, when taken together, represent a uniquely qualified form of membership that may be emblematic of what Athenian citizenship comes to mean in Plato's postfiguration of a Periclean moment.

The *Republic* raises the possibility of a similitude between metics and citizens in Book VIII, where Socrates provides an explicit articulation of this sort of blurring. He asserts there that in democracy, citizens are made equal to each other and vice versa (563a). This passage, which I read closely in Chapter 5, constitutes the only reference to the metic *qua* metic in the *Republic*. Curiously, it is the one Whitehead emphatically disarticulates from the figuration of Cephalus in Book I.[29] Whitehead's argument keeps Plato's figuration of metic characters separate from the characters' statements about metics despite the fact that their connection would actually serve his view that Cephalus is *like* a citizen for the *Republic*. It is important to figure out how Whitehead's argument can hold the similitude between metics and citizens to be theoretically insignificant at the level of characterization while nevertheless attributing theoretical significance to its invocation in Book VIII.

Consider again the conclusion that Cephalus is like a citizen for Plato because this metic is wealthy and socially prominent. On this line, Book VIII's anxieties about proximity and blurring would have to concern poorer metics like *banausoi* (craftsmen) exclusively. For Whitehead, then, wealth neutralizes Cephalus' political difference in Athens and therefore should for Plato, too. And though he concedes that "even men like Cephalus, high 'scorers' on some counts, were ultimately fettered by the limits of political immobility,"[30] he stops short of asking how this limit might also factor into the *Republic*'s interest in Cephalus. Neither he nor Blondell considers the possibility that the almost-but-not-quite-ness of Cephalus – the exclusion and the wealth that characterize his way of living – is the very metic-ness at stake in Book I. If in Athens, the citizen is constituted against the metic's (uneven) exclusion, then the peculiarities of the metic's inclusion might lead us to understand the citizen differently as well.

Right off the bat, the *Republic* associates Cephalus with economic mobility and religious worship. These details are typically read as signs of the metic's Athenian conventionality, of a piety and materialism unhampered by metic status, even though they are the only areas of civic life into which the metic was officially permitted. "Unlike the slave," as Mary G. Dietz observes, the metic "is granted access to the agora yet unlike the

29 See Whitehead 1977: 129. See also Chapter 5. 30 Whitehead 1977: 19.

citizen he is denied political capacity in the assembly."[31] Any influence a wealthy metic acquires is thus partly a consequence of this particular kind of freedom. Freedom might enable wealth and influence, but as my reading of Demosthenes will suggest, wealthy metics are not the only ones who can pass as citizens. The possibility not only of being "like" but also of (deceptively) masquerading as a citizen is open to and suspected among the working (immigrant) poor precisely because they too are included in the demos.

To the extent that Cephalus is a "model metic," then, he is a figure of "conditioned inactivity" who avoids the law courts and, like his sons, keeps to his own affairs, tending to his fortune, his religious rites, and the military needs of his adopted city.[32] As Lysias recollects in a moving speech, his father did not just take from Athens. Cephalus gave back, arming Athenian soldiers, presumably in the Peloponnesian War, with shields he produced in his factory. His trade protected Athenians even, we can assume, in their expeditions to fight against his native Syracuse. He served Athens and Athens served him. The seasoned colonist who leaves the evening's conversation before it turns to the question of founding a colony is a reminder not or not only of the limited privileges afforded the metic but also of the metic's economic and symbolic importance to Athenian politics.

We are now in a position to question the common view that Cephalus, like Polemarchus, his son, has no real hand in establishing the callipolis that takes shape after Book I because he is either too staid or too traditional to partake in the rewriting of the order by which he has done well. For the act of piety that draws the old man away from the conversation before it has found its footing is a religious sacrifice, the very purification rite Greek colonists performed before laying down their foundations in a new place. The much-noted departure of Socrates' host might be less a sign of his exclusion from the discussion than a mark of his crucial participation. Cephalus' role in the founding of the Athenian colony at Thurii suggests this metic is familiar with what the ventures entail. What if his sacrifice in the *Republic* is the move that enables the founding of the callipolis to proceed?[33]

But I am getting ahead of myself. What Cephalus represents in his so-called success, then, is not full participation in the institutions of the polis –

[31] Dietz 2012: 279.

[32] I borrow this language from Whitehead's reading of Lysias, who portrays his father in his speech *Against Eratosthenes* (Whitehead 1977: 58).

[33] On Greek colonization and its rituals, see Dougherty 1993 and Tsetskhladze 2008. For a discussion of Cephalus and the founding of Thurii, see Monoson 2012: 165–167; Nails 2002.

it is not citizenship – but the insinuating and necessary membership enabled by a political condition of liminality. This is a way of living freely and vulnerably, of "merely" abiding, of possessing a political capacity and the disallowed potential to exercise it.[34] These dimensions of *metoikia* fall to the wayside when readers assimilate metics like Cephalus to the citizen or the foreigner. And when the metic's precariousness drops out of the picture, so does its power for signifying democratic politics and membership. To see this more clearly, let us turn to Book VI.

Metic Citizens

I have been suggesting so far that the *Republic*'s interest in the metic's liminal status and political power in Athens – what *metoikia* means as a democratic category and way of life – bears on and opens up the dialogue's political theoretical arguments. The specific historical meanings of the metic inform its symbolic role in the *Republic* and shape its power as a figuration that generates critical insights about democratic membership and Athenian hierarchy even when the metic *qua* metic is far from view. This new angle onto the text permits us to use what we know about metics in Athens and what the dialogue figures about them, in its characterization, setting, and callipolis proposals, as a lens for reading other passages about Athenian democracy – moments in the text that seem, at first glance, to bear only an incidental relation to the metic. This is the case with Book VI.

Though far from a systematic or comprehensive account, the sections I consider in what follows sketch a picture of insinuating, liminal membership as the specter of a corrupt democratic power that crosses citizenship boundaries. The figure of the unaccountable yet omnipresent sophist-orator, whose work behind the scenes of the assembly and the courts trains citizen speakers and in some cases even produces their speech, emerges as the real source of political influence in democracy and constitutes the main problem to which Plato's writing is so often some response. The primary targets of Socrates' critique of democratic membership here are political speech and voting, celebrated hallmarks of citizen life that nonetheless appear wholly ineffectual in this account. That the dialogue stages the frankest speech inside a home, not in a political setting, is perhaps an early signal to this charge. Soon we will see Socrates invert the Periclean adage to suggest that Athenians actually direct their public lives to private matters.[35]

34 Dietz 2012: 286.

35 This is an inversion of what Manville says about Pericles' Funeral Oration (Manville 1997: 16).

The metic, as the figuration of a certain unaccountable and vulnerable political power, is the key to drawing out the critical democratic import of this state of affairs.

We read that a politically active and ambitious citizen can have no future unless he joins secret clubs where he can forge allegiances of influence and garner support to use later in the assembly.[36] He will pay teachers of persuasion, like the foreigners Gorgias and Thrasymachus, in order to learn the methods of argumentation and force that make up the "wisdom of the assembly and the lawcourts" (365d). The private, furtive dimension of politicking – the only one open to metics – may be formally unaccounted for, but it is as good as institutionalized in Socrates' remarks. Participation in the deliberative institutions of democratic politics (i.e., the assembly and the courts) does not by itself constitute or illuminate membership in his account. Socrates places them within a range of formal and informal gatherings that, in their role of sustaining democracy, paradoxically end up undermining the privileges exclusively afforded citizens.

The *Republic* pares democratic politics down to the actions not of citizens but of the teachers and sophists who educate in private – who can "turn [*paideuein*] young and old, men and women into anything they want" (492b) – and thus reach a political community that, like the noncitizen rhetor himself, exceeds the boundaries of the demos and belongs to the polis as a whole. These students and their private educators breed a culture of conformity, fear, cynicism, and hopelessness that makes disagreement, whether in "assemblies," "courts," "theaters," or "military camps" – any of the public sites at which "the multitude" (*plēthos*) gathers – unpopular if not impossible (492b).[37] "How can he avoid agreeing with the crowd about good and bad, following the same way of life as the crowd, and being like the crowd?" (492c). It would be folly to try and stand up to them, for there is not, never has been, and never will be a different type of *ēthos* trained in *aretē* "in defiance of the education these sophists provide" (492e). The *Republic*'s account of the widespread indoctrination of citizens by sophistic types, not just self-proclaimed sophists, recasts the democratic relation in terms of domination not equality, but it is a relation nevertheless secured by a practice of emulation, akin to a collective act of conformity.

In Athens, teachers of sophistry, like Gorgias, were often foreign. But in the dialogue, it is worth stressing, foreign origins do not render this formative dimension of democracy, this sophistic way, alien or unnatural

[36] Ferrari (2007: 46n.17) notes that these clubs became "notorious hives of oligarchic conspiracy."

[37] This is my translation.

to the city. Socrates' further point is that each of these paid teachers is in fact teaching nothing but the *dogmata* expressed by "the general public" in its gatherings and which they call wisdom (493a).[38] The troubling elements of democracy's political culture, in other words, are not imported. They are part of a self-affirming democratic operation that relies not only on intimidation but also on an underclass of free resident aliens whose political influence, because restricted, lies in pandering to and mirroring what citizens already think and desire.[39] The conduct that sophists model for their students to emulate, then, is the sort of behavior one would expect from someone keeping a "large, powerful creature," someone who gets to know "its likes and dislikes, how to approach it, how to handle it, when and why it is most awkward and most amenable, the various sounds it is in the habit of making in different situations" (493a–493b).[40] Political success or survival means being with the animal over a long period of time and devising a way of teaching its habits, or this sensitivity to habit, as though it were itself a kind of (political) knowledge. "The message," Malcolm Schofield concludes, "is that the Beast controls" the animal keeper, "not the other way around."[41] But the animal-keeper is the one educating the Beast in the values and styles of subservience, flattery, and indirect approach. Socrates' remarks would seem to anticipate Book VIII's bidirectional mimetic blurring, which Chapter 5 will explore in detail.

What passes as political speech in Athens, whether we cast it as teaching, public address, or the art of rhetoric, is in the *Republic*'s account likened to a cautious process of assimilation. An outsider gains fluency in democratic speech by learning the vulnerabilities and desires of the wider culture the outsider must infiltrate without unsettling.[42] It is a job most obviously done and figured by a metic, whose meaning for the city shifts precariously between the extraneous and the necessary, but it emerges unequivocally in this dialogue as a democratic ethos. No one, whether foreign or native, citizen or alien can disagree with the demos without risking one's life (493d). By convincing the public of what it already thinks is true, the teacher of

[38] The idea overlaps with Honig's argument that "the foreigner" is often figured "as a device that allows regimes to import from outside (and then, often, to export back to outside) some specific and much-needed but also potentially dangerous virtue, talent, perspective, gift, or quality that they cannot provide for themselves (or that they cannot admit they have)" (Honig 2001: 3).

[39] Insofar as this is a description of the kind of mimesis that occurs between metics and citizens, we might ask whether citizens desire to mirror metics.

[40] In the *Gorgias* (521a–522a), Socrates describes the dynamic in Athenian courts along similar lines: like a pastry chef before a group of children, the prosecutor who feeds his jurors pleasantries succeeds at persuading them.

[41] Schofield 2006: 65.

[42] We could consider silence a version of this, too.

persuasion finds a safe place from which to reflect the demos back to itself and thus models emulation as a political art. We will hear echoes of the sophist-orator-citizen of Book VI in Chapter 5, when we encounter the imagined metic listener of Pericles' Funeral Oration and consider Socrates' metic impersonation in the *Menexenus*. Pericles' metic listener will serve to reinvigorate and reaffirm the city's political culture and transform himself in the process from a potentially divisive force into a vessel of democratic virtue.[43] The *Republic*'s presentation of democratic virtue could not be further from the one celebrated in Pericles' speech, which describes excellence in terms of heroic public acts. In the Funeral Oration, political activity will involve an obsequious practice of (metic) flattery, the most pleasing form of which is imitation itself. In the *Republic* and the *Menexenus,* however, the citizen is just as implicated in the act of imitating as the metic.

The simplest point to take from all this is that the metic's way of living in democracy is not unique to the noncitizen. Forbidden from making any real changes to the city's way of life, people learn that only the "person who takes the city as it is, who is the people's most beguiling servant and flatterer, who creeps into their good graces, who anticipates their wishes and is adept at satisfying them – this person they will declare a fine man, a man profoundly wise" (426c). The democratic city honors the submissive and stealthy person Socrates so famously reviles in Thrasymachus' character. The *Republic* figures public speaking as a kind of sophistic operation that charges clients to recirculate old and flattering ideas. Such speech is not the exclusive, salutary, or deliberative practice through which the citizen and only the citizen actualizes his membership. Here speaking in front of the assembly, an activity from which metics were formally barred, is impossible even for citizens. The assembly's exclusive goings-on are really dominated by private, mercenary educators, and so they are like any public gathering at which attendance is hardly policed (558a).

Book VI provides us with one (but not the only) sense in which "the metic is made equal to the citizen, and the citizen to the metic" (563a).[44] Citizens are insiders who become formally disenfranchised, while noncitizens gain the same, if not more, access to the informal practices that are as much produced by as they are generative of democratic rule. To see how the institutions which bestow citizenship and enable the well born to

43 Among the many uses of foreignness Honig finds operating in democratic theory is the foreigner who reinvigorates the country's institutions and values by choosing to become naturalized. See Honig 2001: 3–8, esp. 4.

44 This is my translation.

practice it are corrupt in this sense is also to see how easily citizens may be effectively disenfranchised, how easily they may become "like" metics. Socrates' interest in the range of spaces in which politics takes place, the scope and intensity of the encounters Plato depicts between metics and citizens, and the text's focus on democracy's blood-based lines of division have already begun to suggest that how a city is shared and how its residents are arranged deeply shapes expectations for, perhaps even constitutes, the meaning of membership in a polity. This possibility will find clearer expression in my reading of the setting and opening scenes. With this in mind, let us go back to Book I.

What Happens in Piraeus

It may seem like a truism to say that Socrates spends his evening trying to escape Piraeus, first literally then figuratively. The narrator remembers that he intended to walk back to Athens but was unexpectedly detained. In the course of reading, we realize he spent the whole evening there concocting an alternative regime from the one in which he lives. It is partly this uncontroversial portrait of the dialogue's frame and its relation to the text's arc that leads Jacques Rancière to conclude that the "whole political project of Platonism can be conceived as an anti-maritime polemic." For Plato, he adds, the "sea smells of sailors. It smells of democracy," which means "the task of philosophy is to found a different politics, a politics of conversion which turns its back on the sea."[45]

We could read the *Republic*'s setting as an elaboration of the harbor's general associations with demotic power, the sorts of connections that in antiquity made this place "a sacrilege . . . to the traditional, antidemocratic elite."[46] This picture, however, is incomplete if not misleading. The political and symbolic meanings of Piraeus are not univocal, and they are certainly not as unhierarchical as the earlier assessment would lead us to believe. To the extent that our view of Plato's "politics" depends on how we think about the relation between the callipolis and the place in which this "city in speech" is taken up, it is worth having another look at

[45] Rancière bases this understanding of Plato's view of the sea primarily on a passage from the *Laws*, however, in which the Athenian character elaborates on the specific political conditions of – and risks borne by – a city on the sea (705a–705b). He extends the character's views to the *Republic*. See Rancière 2007: 1, 2. Von Reden also uses the *Laws* to claim that Plato "saw a fundamental contradiction between land and sea" and believed the sea "had negative effects on the polis" (Von Reden 1995: 24). The sea carries further associations with the democratic resistance and the oligarchs' decision to turn the Pnyx away from the sea.

[46] Von Reden 1995: 28.

the signifying powers of Piraeus and the activities that go on there. Let us consider more carefully not just what kind of democratic power is figured there but how it is figured. Let us ask, in other words, to what Athenian state of affairs the callipolis is responding. For while hardly novel, the critical view that the callipolis is born of an act of turning *away* from democracy depends on a series of interpretive assumptions about this democracy (not to mention the "sea" by which it is figured) that are difficult to square with the political realities of democratic Athens, the meanings of Piraeus, and perhaps most crucially the rhetorical strategies Plato uses to bring them all together in this text.

Athenians left from Piraeus to settle colonies on behalf of their city. But the characters that make up this dialogue never go anywhere. In fact, the project of imagining the callipolis is enabled by, embedded in, and inseparable from the seaside where it is taken up. What is more, the conversation takes a decidedly Athenian form when Plato portrays it as a colonial expedition. As much as the callipolis might eschew the order of its Athenian setting, its founders do not. Socrates makes use of his city's practices and idioms to imagine this alternative place. The imperial dimension of Athenian maritime power and the mobility and hierarchical membership with which it is bound up is nevertheless occluded by readings that tether the sea exclusively to the demotic power of the fleet, as if that demos were not itself directly constituted by the same autochthonous difference that justified imperial expansion. "There can be no doubt that Piraeus was both a condition for, and a symbol of, democracy," as Sitta Von Reden notes. But since "both democracy and the maritime empire were the result of the orientation of the Athenian polis towards the sea," the dialogue's staging of "the relationship between the harbor and the city of Athens" is also an evocation of democratic mobility, imperial expansion, and the city's autochthonous order.[47] The *Republic* thus permits a reading in which these historically variegated meanings inflect its figuration of Piraeus as a real inhabited place and provoke reflection into the workings of democracy as such. If the sea smells of democracy, it also smells of empire, immigrants, and trade.

The *Republic*'s topography has not been entirely lost on commentators. To the extent that critics take the opening's geospatial allusions to conjure egalitarianism, they assume that their function is to anticipate the descent and ascent evoked later by the allegory of the cave. These allusions, in other words, are assumed to lay the groundwork for Socrates' figurative flight

[47] Von Reden 1995: 29.

from the liminal place of Piraeus. The stakes of casting the rhetorical function of the *Republic*'s setting this way are significant. So long as Piraeus is understood to elicit a desire to escape democracy for a kind of utopia (an abstract, antidemocratic, rationalizing space), the *Republic*'s landscape signifies little more than a kind of privation. If Piraeus is in this dialogue in order to be transcended, Plato figures the place for the same reason he is assumed to represent the metic: both are deficient and serve to make the retreat to the callipolis seem desirable and urgent.

Together, these two interpretive assumptions – Piraeus signifies a form of unsavory egalitarian power; the text instructs us to leave this place behind as it gives shape to the callipolis – work to impede a reading in which Plato's interest in democracy extends to the blood-based membership practices that helped sustain it, not simply to lament them but to present them critically. The setting of this text need not function just to demarcate two spheres, pure and impure, philosophical and political, high and low, abstract and embodied. For one thing, the two textual spaces of the *Republic* are not so easily separated. Plato makes one the condition for the other's discursive construction. One zone emerges inside the other.

The problem is therefore not with the interpretive tendency to contrast Athens with the callipolis (I do so myself in the next chapter). My quarrel has to do with the habit of thought that presumes their neat separation is necessary, which is to say, somehow dictated by the text's narrative structure, or even the most illuminating way to take stock of the layered structure of this dialogue. Such prying apart not only risks obfuscating the extent to which one space serves as the ground for the other. It also distracts us from reflecting on the historical specificity of the conversation's location and the theoretical possibilities this specificity enables.[48]

The more Plato deploys direct dialogue to construct the callipolis, the less we hear from the narrator, whose voice so famously locating in the opening lines – "I went down to Piraeus yesterday" (327a) – recedes after Book I and irrupts into the action of the text only occasionally thereafter. The Piraeus starts in the foreground. That it shifts to the background, however, does not mean that it ceases to bear on the action the narrator presents in the foreground or that it should not factor into our interpretation of the text. The difficulty is how to make interpretive and theoretical sense of a place that seems to fall away but never actually disappears.

[48] As Worman (2014: 202) explains, landscapes in ancient Greek texts "are not abstract spaces in any true sense" but deeply rooted in the ground of civic practices, organized and assigned value in relation to recognizable transactions in familiar places.

To see this issue more clearly, consider how a tragic performance uses scenic space to generate "meta-theatricality." For Rush Rehm, a meta-theatrical space emerges when a "playwright momentarily foregrounds the fact of dramatic performance by alluding to theatrical representation . . . by parodying dramatic and other performance genres . . . by manipulating various 'plots within plots.'"[49] The point here is not only that Plato's text thematizes the means of its own construction when it has Socrates mime Plato in the act of constructing a mimetic world. It is that this kind of imaginary play always bears a relation to the fictive (i.e., scenic) setting in which it is taken up.[50] Theater, as Rehm stresses, is not an empty space, which means that the meta-mimetic aspect of Plato's text, the construction of a fictional world within a historically locatable but mimetic place, produces a doubled textual space that invites a reading of one against the other.[51] Plato takes pains to hold together two spaces, then, the liminal yet politically significant home of Cephalus and Polemarchus and the mimetic space of the callipolis that emerges within it. He does this, I have been suggesting, to provoke reflection on what we might call a third, Athenian democracy.[52] Piraeus is the literal and figurative space of democracy and empire's interrelations, which means the opening confronts us with the contiguity democracy posits between blood and inclusion, foreignness and exclusion, citizenship and power. The implications of this framing for the political theoretical reception of the *Republic* will become clearer in the next two chapters, in which I advance close readings of the noble lie and Socrates' portrait of democracy in and because of the interpretive field I construct here. For now, let us focus on what it means for the opening scenes.

I noted earlier that the relation between Piraeus and Athens was a familiar *topos* for imagining and contesting various conceptions of Athens and its autarchy. The sense that "the Piraeus became the true centre of the polis" was "a chimera . . . in anti-democratic texts" but one that nevertheless reflected a real shift in everyday activities from the polis to the harbor throughout the period of the *Republic*'s

[49] Rehm 2002: 23.
[50] On Plato as a prose dramatist concerned with both the performance of the dialogues and the question of performability, see Charalabopoulos 2012. See also Blondell 2002.
[51] This movement is often described as a *theoria*, a journey or religious pilgrimage (Nightingale 1995).
[52] For Ferrari, the "background" described by a narrator – what the Piraeus amounts to in the *Republic* – has a different effect on a reader than a background conveyed by a character's direct speech (about it). The latter, he thinks, draws greater attention from the reader. In the *Phaedrus*, he adds, "the background will not stay where it belongs. It becomes . . . a direct cause of the conversational action rather than, as one would expect, at most an indirect influence on its course" (Ferrari 1987: 3–4).

setting.[53] Elite critics of democracy were not the only ones who sought to contain the harbor's political influence, however.[54] Concerns that the port might come to overtake the privileged position of the town it was working to sustain materially and symbolically found expression in specific democratic measures aimed at limiting the harbor's political autonomy. Despite the fact that Piraeus was one of Athens' demes, it occupied a kind of second-class status not dissimilar from that of the metic. Residents of Piraeus, for instance, did not select their own demarch. He was selected in "town" (Arist., *Ath. Pol.* 54.8). While it may have emerged as a rival urban center, in other words, Piraeus did so "under close control of the assembly."[55] Even in its street design, Piraeus "was constructed conceptually as a colony at the periphery of the polis."[56]

The Athenian need to manage its precarious relation to Piraeus figures greatly in the *Republic*'s opening scenes. In crafting the *Republic* against this metic backdrop, Plato invites the reader to consider the democratic polis as both the bounded Athenian community its laws were drafted to police and the political community that sustains and exceeds it. Cephalus may complain that Socrates does not make the trip often to his house, but the point is that he does come (328c). That the harbor's residents, while remote, make up the political community and culture Socrates services and learns from is reflected by his decision to return to their house that evening, as he does at least occasionally.[57] But it is the festival spectatorship Plato uses to open this dialogue that poses the most trenchant challenge to the democratic membership order. The activity that provokes the trip to the home that will serve as the site and incitement of the creation of the callipolis demands our careful analysis. The question to keep in mind is how this opening activity bears a relationship to the imaginary political founding to which it gives way.

[53] By the time Plato wrote in the fourth century, Von Reden (1995: 26) notes, the harbor was "no longer primarily associated with naval power" (and empire) "but with commerce." Notwithstanding this "shift," both empire and trade concern themselves with the outsider; whether or not we mean the wholly external or the foreign that is permanently within, the outsider functions to signify a specific kind of Athenian dependence.

[54] Von Reden 1995: 29. [55] Von Reden 1995: 27. [56] Von Reden 1995: 27.

[57] Schofield (2006: 25) notes that in the *Apology*, Plato "construes his philosophizing as a public service" and that in the *Crito*, "conversely, it is he who is portrayed as the beneficiary of the city." From both senses, we arrive at a reciprocal notion of citizenship, in which Socrates gives to and takes from the city. Applying this to the *Republic*, we find that Socrates stretches the bounds of citizenship (or public service) to include not just the activity of philosophizing but a more expansive notion of membership. He engages metics in conversation, and the expectation is that he (and the city) will have something to gain from this even if only because they share the polis.

Foreign cults were not uncommon in classical Athens, but the story of the cult of Bendis, whose inaugural celebration Socrates ventures to the harbor to watch, is especially illuminating of metics' integration in the city. Thracians had apparently brought Bendis to Athens several years before the festival. And it is the "influence and presence" of these metics, Sara M. Wijma explains, that accounts for Bendis' eventual acceptance "as an official polis cult."[58] Upon its inauguration in 413/12, the polis festival for the goddess included two separate processions and a torch-race on horseback, the two spectacles around which Plato organizes Socrates' physical movements in the *Republic*.

Worshippers who performed sacred rites (*orgia*) for gods or heroes were usually organized into groups around a particular deity. These groups were composed of members of Athenian phratries, kinship groups that over time acted as the principle networks through which access to citizenship was controlled. Sometime between the late fifth and early fourth centuries BCE, however, metics were allowed to become *orgeōnes* without being allowed into phratries.[59] The city permitted Thracian worshippers of Bendis living in Athens to organize and worship the goddess at Munychia along with citizen worshippers.[60] Although the polis-wide festival was controlled by the Athenian demos, both *epichōrioi* (local natives) and Thracian metics shared in the celebration as part of the "same Athenian worshipping community."[61] The "religious behavior" of these metics was "hardly distinguishable" from that of their citizen counterparts, and yet they worshipped Bendis in "their own way."[62]

According to Corinne Pache, the case of two distinct "ethnic groups" that "worship the same goddess, participate in the same sacrifices and festival, organize themselves in different associations bearing the same name, yet never mix or fuse into one single group" suggests Athenians saw Thracians as something more than "barbarian." She reads the historical case of Bendis in Athens to mean that the city's dealings with foreigners and foreignness were characterized by a degree of ambivalence. And yet, she adds, the decision to Hellenize the foreign elements of Bendis' worship

[58] Wijma 2014: 130–131.

[59] The inclusion of metics in the tending of the *hiera* is the focus of Wijma (2014). Her study makes a strong historical argument for seeing metic religious participation as indicating (qualified) membership in the polis. She considers the possibilities, long dismissed by scholars, that phratries might have accepted Thracian *orgeōnes* on account of their management of Bendis' cult and shrine in Piraeus.

[60] See Pache 2001: 8. Wijma (2014) argues that, despite the separate parades, there was only one group of *orgeōnes,* unlike Pache, who suggests the groups never fused.

[61] Wijma 2014: 142. [62] Wijma 2014: 155, 142.

and maintain two separate rituals is evidence that the polarity that existed "at the ideological level" between the two groups was also upheld in practice.[63] Similarly, for Von Reden, the Bendideia bespeaks less of "a general toleration of foreign cults" than of the "powerful strategies" Athenians had "for maintaining cultural boundaries."[64]

In his notes on the *Republic*, James Adam points out that the dialogue is referring to Thracian metics not mercenaries or envoys when it depicts Socrates at the first of these festivals, and he stresses on this point their residency and influence. Metics lived "for commercial purposes in the Piraeus," he says, "which at all times contained a large admixture of foreign population. It was part of Athenian policy," he continues, "to encourage commercial settlers by allowing them to exercise their own cults."[65] This casts the Bendideia in a slightly different light. It invites us to read the figuration of the festival not as a sign of polarity or inclusion but as an Athenian concession to a material and symbolic dependence.

Alert to this possibility, I want to look again at how Plato starts the *Republic*:

> I went down to the Piraeus yesterday with Glaucon the son of Ariston, to offer a prayer to the goddess. Also I wanted to watch the festival, to see how they would conduct it, since this was the first time it was being celebrated. The parade of Athenians struck me as excellent, and the show put on by the Thracians was every bit as impressive, I thought. (327a)

The *Republic* commences with a festival that, like the polis overall, is divided by blood. "Ritual differentiation" may have been "instrumental in the carrying out, displaying, and (re)affirming of the constituent parts of the polis and the (re)creation of identities and hierarchies,"[66] but the dialogue does not take these intentions for granted. The narrator immediately adds that one parade appeared (*ephaineto*) just as good as the other. The remarks provoke reflection on the criterion for their division and its salience. The dual parades are supposed simply to convey the expressive difference that separates the two kinship groups.

We will see later that Pericles encourages the foreign listeners of his funeral oration to emulate Athenians. He intimates, however, that they can only ever approximate the citizens they copy. Whether reassuring or

[63] Pache's interest lies in assessing the stability of the barbarian marker, but she concludes, surprisingly, that the "notional boundary between Greek and barbarian" escapes slippage (Pache 2001: 9).
[64] Von Reden 1995: 32.
[65] See Adam's commentary on the first lines of the *Republic* in Plato 1963: 2n5.
[66] Wijma 2014: 10.

menacing, the speech implies that an autochthonous difference is apparent during the carrying out of Athenian deeds; the acts work to confirm the exception that is said to precede them. They correspond to a difference that in such cases as the Bendideia is open for all to see. In Plato's rendition, however, the sort of spectacle and spectatorship needed to affirm this Athenian exception leads to a much less salutary, we might even say contrary, judgment. The problem is not just that the parades rest on a fictional autochthonous difference – the noble lie will suggest this is true of all founding myths – but that this noble lie is *apparently* fictitious, which is to say, it regulates the production of citizens poorly, because it ends not in the confirming clarity of a pregiven difference but in a demonstration of its ambiguous effects.

Recall that the definition of the demos and the rationale for empire rest on the same autochthonous logic or what Derrida calls an "aristo-democracy of brothers."[67] In the previous chapter, I read Euripides' *Ion* to suggest that when a polis colonizes but restricts citizenship to the "well born," it generates the metic, a figure whose inclusion-exclusion enables both the promise and risk of this form of membership not only because it makes it possible or inevitable to "pass" but because it calls into question the very pregivenness of the metic's exclusion. Only a scene as carefully and uniquely crafted as the opening of the *Republic* could deliver a similar insight. Plato studiously avoids depicting a disordered polity in these first lines. He stages a polis-sanctioned event, whose very design as a segregated spectacle represents the city's autochthonous ideal (in the form of a spatial division) and thus requires the spectatorship that threatens to undo it.[68] These necessary practices of segregation, worshipping, parading, and spectatorship follow a prior act of cultural mixing: this polis is apparently used to absorbing foreigners like Bendis. Athenians are (again) acting like metics.

In the *Republic*, Thracian metics are observed performing the tending of sacred rites, a citizen deed, just as well as Athenians. The metics possess a political capacity, in other words, that the city disavows at the same time that it helps them actualize it. Such a revelation is, if not the clearest

67 Derrida 1997: 94.

68 An interesting parallel exists in the making of funerary monuments, a practice that "ascribed status and value, and established expectations" (R. Osborne 2010: 263) and yet, in the case of metics, did not emphasize their deprivileged status. In his discussion of monuments figuring metic women, Osborne notes that "the pressures on the metic community to conform to local practice, and indeed the expectations of sculptural workshops, will have ensured that metic monuments were shaped in the image of citizen monuments" (R. Osborne 2010: 263n51).

indication that the membership lines of Athenian democracy are constructed and unstable, then a precursor of things to come. What gives the *Republic*'s insight critical power is that Socrates' judgment of the parades comes about as a consequence of the city's own arrangement, a point we might just as easily apply to the representation of passing we found in Euripides and will soon see figured in Demosthenes.

What if the rest of the *Republic* were a response to this state of affairs? The dialogue opens by showing us the wrong way to keep an autochthonous order looking fixed and pregiven. Then it shows us the right way. Book I's staging of democratic flux clears a space not for any autochthonous regime but specifically for the callipolis. This "just" polis will not only assign status on the basis of performance (not blood); it will also arrange its members, practices, and institutions so as to ensure that the artifice of its "natural" order will remain hidden from its members at all costs.

Razing Ground

The callipolis takes shape after the first book, and so it lacks, with some exceptions, the contributions of metic characters. Eventually, as if to thematize this absence, the Athenian speakers move to ban foreign residents from their imaginary city. This may be the reason Whitehead thinks the metic "holds a very minor place in Plato's *oeuvre* until *Laws*." Plato, he continues, "had no time for metics in his best *conceivable* city as delineated in *Republic* (witness the acid comment at 563A)."[69] However we interpret the passage on metic–citizen blurring Whitehead invokes parenthetically (I return to Book VIII in Chapter 5), it is worth pausing to consider the theoretical implications of such a sweeping assessment. Whether we think Book VIII is the only place metics appear in the *Republic* depends on what we think counts as a site of meaning in this text. Whitehead discusses Cephalus and Polemarchus, of course, but as we saw, he does not treat characterization or setting as zones of argumentation. The *Republic* is ultimately indifferent to metics on his account because – and this is crucial – there can be no metics in the callipolis. All residents of the callipolis are citizens, though they are not all rulers. And no foreigners are allowed to reside there permanently. I have been taking it for granted that the text of the *Republic* is not reducible to the proposals the characters offer for the callipolis; these moments of dialogue cannot be extracted from the textual conditions under which they are said. The *Republic* "is a narrated dialogue," as Arlene Saxonhouse reminds,

[69] Whitehead 1977: 129.

which means that it invites an interpretation of the membership rules in the context in which Socrates recalls them to have been relayed.[70] What is striking, then, is that the policy of restricting foreigners from settling in the callipolis is proposed under conditions that are enabled and marked by *metoikia*. The suggestions to equate residence with citizenship and restrict the movements of persons in and out of the callipolis arise in public. They are spoken during, and even inspired by, a trip to a metic's home. What can we make of this loaded configuration?

Silence is not unique to the noncitizen characters present that night, but the fact that it comes to characterize the metic host after Book I is intriguing, and it suggests Polemarchus' withdrawal is a sign not of inadequacy but of nervousness, the sort of reticence we might expect from a host who suddenly finds himself held captive by a visitor, alerted to his precarious status, reminded that, even in his own home, he is, as in Athens, always a guest.[71] We saw in the *Ion* that silence is not the same as lack or absence. In the *Republic*, Polemarchus' silence hangs over the discussion like a pall, weighty, dense, noticeable.

The question this raises in closing is not whether the *Republic* is uninterested in metics but in what sense it is interested in them; why they might constitute the consummate provocation of this text; what sorts of democratic problems they help figure; and how in conclusion we can begin to take stock of the text's efforts to imagine a polity in which the metic would be an unthinkable category – a possibility, it bears repeating, that is aired in metic company. We could conclude that the *Republic* is offering an *apologia* for nativism here, that it recommends the exclusion of foreigners because Plato is a Laconizer and, as any admirer of Spartan *xenēlasia* might, he seeks a less ambivalent chauvinism than the sort Athenian autochthony enables. Such an assessment would surely fit with Plato's reputation as a theorist of isolationism, essentialist difference, and general conservatism, but it cannot account for – and may even occlude – the text's interest in examining blood-based membership critically, in presenting what we will subsequently see is productively read as an exposé rather than as an endorsement. Instead of reading the exclusion of immigrants as a lack of interest in metics or a commitment to nativism, I take it as Plato's attempt to draw the reader's (knowing) attention to the Athenian politics of this scene.

70 Saxonhouse 2009: 730.

71 Derrida (2000: 123–125) describes inverted guest–host relations at work between Oedipus and Theseus in *Oedipus at Colonus*.

There are to be no metics in the callipolis not because the foreigner lacks an ability to act politically, quite the opposite in fact. The question of the foreigner's inclusion in callipolis is not presented as a question of blood or natural difference (or even territory). Whether one actualizes one's political *capacity* is a question of power: one who is granted metic status is not vested with the privileges to live in Athens as an active and unqualified member of the polis. The *Republic*'s mode of presentation (the layered spaces, its dialogical form) makes it possible for us to see that it is the characters who decide whether to exclude metics from the callipolis. Their imaginary founding act anticipates what we will soon understand more clearly: the metic's inclusion-exclusion in Athens is similarly artificial. The disenfranchisement of the metic has political not natural origins. Socrates shows this to his quiet metic host just as Plato shows it to his Athenian audience.

Let us consider once more that the figuration of one political reality (life in Piraeus) is the condition for the characters' undertaking a similar act, the construction of "an example of a good city in speech" (472d–472e) that rearranges the political order of Athens.[72] "The inquiry concerning the 'paradigm of a good polis' (427e)," as Eric Voegelin observes, "is organized as a play within the play."[73] One mimetic act begets the other. And while this second "play" is most often called a founding, it is worth elaborating finally on what I have been suggesting all along – the rarely explored matter that "Plato casts Socrates in the role of *oikistēs*" (a settler, colonizer, 378–379a).[74] The callipolis is imagined as the settlement of an already inhabited area; its founding will require the displacement of some people (541a). The reason for this displacement will turn out to be the same reason for the ban on immigrants.

By now it might come as little surprise that Piraeus of all places inspires Socrates to fashion himself a colonist. Plato's writing, says Nicole Loraux, exhibits an unusually pronounced concern with settlement. "Foundation and colonization are one and the same," she adds, "and the philologist intervenes opportunely with the statement that of all classical prose-writers, Plato boasts the greatest number of *katoikizō* [and *oikizō*] . . . He who envisions the polis in its essence would be an *oikistēs*, then, before being deemed legislator or statesman."[75] What is opened up by this shift in emphasis from founding a polity in an empty place to founding a polity in a place already inhabited – for Piraeus, for Athens, for the making of

72 This is my translation of *paradeigma epoioumen logoi agathēs poleōs*.

73 Voegelin 2000: 88.

74 While Voegelin translates the Greek as "founder" here, he is among the few readers to make the immediate connection to colonization. See Voegelin 2000: 89.

75 Loraux 2000: 122.

a polis – is not immediately clear. The move sounds in any event like the act Plato himself undertakes: the idea for the callipolis emerges not in an empty space but in a home, in a city already populated.

As a way of tying these various threads together, let me introduce one more. Plato's text fundamentally links the act of founding to the act of speaking. It is obvious that the *Republic* figures settlement as a matter of discourse, but the sense in which it does this and the political theoretical effects that are produced by such a framing are less so. "We are not poets at present," Socrates declares abruptly in Book II, following a discussion of stories, "but settlers of a city" (*oikistai poleōs*).[76] Founders set the patterns (*tupous*) according to which poets compose their stories (379a). They fix the framework within which all speech and imagination will occur henceforth. No wonder Socrates introduces the noble lie shortly after this scene. As the invention of that regulatory fiction will also attest, the founding of a polity involves more than the occupation of a physical place; it entails an initial act of imagination that forms the basis of all subsequent thought, what the callipolis residents will think is real, the conditions of possibility, the relations that hold between kinds, "the movement of each opposition," and, most urgently for my purposes, the difference between insiders and outsiders.[77]

The reason Socrates calls for the displacement of some inhabitants from the callipolis, then, has nothing to do with a pregiven and determinative difference. The reason concerns the very distinction established earlier between founders and poets. Persons over the age of ten must leave the callipolis at its founding and reside permanently in the countryside because their inculcation in the new order is impossible (541a). The patterns the founders establish for the settlement would never take hold; they would become "mere" stories, and like autochthony myths, they would inform and regulate conduct but never fully or well enough to hide their own status as fictions. The only people impressionable enough to believe they are really born from the earth are children, children who never meet adults with other ideas about how membership lines are drawn. Immigrants from other polities, like the displaced inhabitants of the callipolis, not only lack the ability to internalize the noble lie. They can demonstrate its artifice and permanently alter the city's culture. All the city's residents help set

[76] This is my translation.

[77] Although Derrida is referring to *phusis* here, he means it in the regulatory sense that I discuss the noble lie in the next chapter. The comment comes from a larger discussion of the *Republic* and the *Menexenus* in *The Politics of Friendship*; see Derrida 1997: 90.

expectations for membership, in other words, regardless of where they fall in the order of rule, just as the animal keeper of Book VI suggested.

"Banishing elements of a population from a city to the surrounding countryside was not without historic parallel," G. R. F. Ferrari notes, "and in the Greek world in general populations were relocated with what to us would seem alarming frequency."[78] The practice was used in Sparta, Ferrari adds, which had a "core of citizens surrounded by non-citizen subordinates in the villages and countryside."[79] Rather than divide its population physically, Ferrari argues, Athens encouraged citizens of "all social ranks" to "engage in a full range of commercial, agricultural and other activities likely to produce wealth."[80] And yet cohabitation and collaboration do not, on their own, render stratification inefficacious. They might instead give rise to an insinuating kind of membership and to an increased fear of disorder – the justification for more policing of boundaries not less.

It is worth revisiting in this light the infrequency of Socrates' visits to Piraeus, the theme of Book I usually taken to confirm the distance of Piraeus, its difference and unsavoriness. According to Cephalus, Socrates stays away because he does not feel at home there. That will not do now that Cephalus is too old to visit Athens, so he tells his guest to "come and be" (*sunisthi*) with the young men in his company from here on out, to make them his companions by arriving and departing so regularly that, as Adam translates *phoitaō*, he will make the metic home in Piraeus his "resort." Cephalus requests that his Athenian guest regard them as (*hōs*) very good friends (*para philous*) and kin (*oikeious*). Socrates complies (328d).[81]

We are told later in the *Republic* that the greatest evil for any city is what tears it apart and turns it into many cities instead of one (462b). To avoid this stasis, Socrates suggests that every time the guardians of the callipolis meet someone, they should assume they are encountering a family member (463d). "It would be ridiculous for them merely to use the names of relationships, as a verbal convention, without the corresponding behavior," for what one "speaks" about these relations is also what one "thinks" (463e–464a).[82] Cephalus' invitation that Socrates treat the metic's home

78 Ferrari 2000: 251n24. 79 Ferrari 2000: v. 80 Ferrari 2000: xv.

81 Blondell 2002: 167–168.

82 The "Phoenician" noble lie uses a kinship idea to describe citizen relations, but it does not say that the citizens *are* "born of the earth" as "brothers." It issues rather that they regard each other as such (414c–414e). The *Republic*'s myth models a proscription for conduct, not a criterion for or description of membership.

as his own and regard the metic family as if they were kin anticipates the noble lie not only because it invokes an idiom of kinship but also because it invokes kinship as an idiom. Who better to introduce the artifice and political utility of blood than a metic, and a successful one at that? The passage calls attention to the act of speech that makes some kin, which is to say, it focuses once again on the Athenian decision that renders some residents autochthonous and others not. It would seem that, for Cephalus, being "like" a citizen is not enough.

Democracies make a prior distinction about who counts as kin. In Athens, those equal before the law are brothers because equality in birth (*isogonia*) is said to bestow their civic equality (*isonomia*). Socrates' trip to Piraeus muddies this distinction and sets into motion the citizen/metic hierarchy it undergirds. Cephalus suggests the appellation of kin ought to reflect practice, not the other way around. Socrates would be his kin because they would do more of what they do already: they would live together.

CHAPTER 4

Plato's Open Secret

For the law has no power to command obedience except that of habit, which can only be given by time, so that a readiness to change from old to new laws enfeebles the power of the law.

– Aristotle, *Politics* 1269a20–1269a24[1]

Generations of readers have interpreted the noble lie (*Rep.* 414b–415) as a straightforward endorsement of "natural" hierarchical difference starkly opposed to the democratic politics of its Athenian setting.[2] What makes this habit curious is that the *Republic*'s narrative frame actually presents the idea that one's political "kind" (*genos* [501e]) expresses a pregiven, stable nature as a regulatory fiction. In these scenes, Socrates contrives the noble lie as an "artifice" (*mēchanē* [414b]) by which regimes, including the Athens of the dialogue's setting, found and reproduce membership status as a naturalized category. The awareness that Plato's framing affords the reader, not to mention the characters listening inside the house, implores us to consider these scenes as revealing, not concealing, that the "natural" distinctions of an exclusionary citizenship politics are the effects of willful political power. I argue in this chapter that Socrates' disclosure carries unexplored critical meaning in the Athenian and specifically metic setting in which he offers it and from which criticism has persistently displaced it. This recontextualizing, and the sensitivity to narrative structure that it entails, does more than counter the critical tendency to see the noble lie as a template for essentialist politics or an act of political

1 Plato's *Republic* is similarly alert to the difficulty of ensuring the obedience of residents who are not wholly indoctrinated in the city's ways of life: the need to ground the city in a founding myth (i.e., the noble lie) is the dialogue's concession to the instability inherent in all customary arrangements and therefore to the political utility of naturalizing these arrangements.

2 Chapter 5 examines the argument of Rancière (2006) that Plato's rejection of democracy concerns *its* rejection of a natural title to rule. See also Reinhard 2012: vii, on how "modern philosophy and critical theory have generally agreed in denouncing [Platonism] as idealism, essentialism, logocentrism, or even proto-fascism."

deception.[3] Foregrounding the narrative and political conditions under which Socrates imparts his regulatory fiction, I maintain, also expands our understanding of the *Republic*'s criticisms of democracy.

Plato's presentation of Socrates' machination ostensibly serves a discussion about the callipolis, but it doubles as an open secret about Athens, which had its own noble lie. The story enables "insiders," by which I mean the slave, metic, and citizen characters of the dialogue as well as a historically alert audience, to see that the "natural" lines of democratic membership are also the effect of artifice, an idea so consequential in the metic context of this text that it can only be confronted obliquely. When Glaucon knowingly responds, "No wonder you were so embarrassed about telling us your lie" (414e), he is not noting the outlandishness of the tale, as traditionally assumed, but winking at its discomfiting familiarity. Any shame in this scene accrues from encroaching on a taboo. This chapter reads the noble lie, then, as an "open secret" so as to invoke an ambivalent mode of communication. For whatever knowledge open secrets signal to the already knowing need not be "claimed and acted on"; the structure of an open secret preserves the countervailing possibilities of denial and acknowledgment.[4] It is in this sense that Plato's open secret permits listeners not to pursue the implications of its narration for Athens or to admit them outright, as I attempt here.

The pages that follow restore the noble lie to the hitherto neglected dimensions of its dramatic and historical contexts to argue that the text addresses questions of democratic exclusion usually considered outside its purview. To carry out this reading, I construct a new interpretive context along two axes. First, I contend that the *Republic* makes discursive use of the practices of law and mythmaking Athenians relied on to produce citizenship as a "natural" status. Chapter 1 argued that, throughout the fifth and fourth centuries BCE, Athenian democracy functioned as an ancestral order that stratified its residents into three legal statuses of descending privilege.[5] Only those who demonstrated pure Athenian descent acquired the title of citizen, meaning that, similar to the callipolis, *rule* over the city was the inherited or "natural" privilege of one group even if

[3] As I argued in the last chapter, the dialogue's setting in a metic's home in Piraeus calls attention to the dialogue's concern with Athenian membership. Piraeus was "the gate to foreign trade" and empire, and it had a high "concentration" of foreigners "active in trade, commerce, and the fleet" who were politically influential yet disfranchised. See Von Reden 1995: 25.

[4] I use Anne-Lise François's working definition to characterize conventional theorizations of the open secret, which are decidedly not the ones she herself adopts or develops. See François 2008: 1.

[5] Ogden 1996; Blok 2009b; Lape 2010; Kamen 2013.

within the demos there was diversity of economic standing. The other two status groups in the city, metics and slaves, were excluded from ruling on the basis of ancestry, generation after generation. Yet readers have generally failed to consider that Plato's depiction of the symbolic production of political difference engages with themes of pressing democratic significance – that his opprobrium of democracy is concerned both with Athens' unprecedented egalitarianism and with the nativist practices that enabled it. The last chapter argued that the *Republic* is not simply attuned to this autochthonous dynamic but preoccupied with foregrounding, depicting, and critically examining it.

Once the metic dimension of the dialogue's context is brought into view, I argue, instructive parallels between Athens and the callipolis emerge by way of the noble lie. Though they are not identical, both hierarchized polities rely on founding myths of autochthony and invoke ideas of a "well-bred" (*gennaion*) citizenry to establish the fixity of political status. Following John Seery, I am alert to the "dramatic cues" that "invite us to think beyond the apparent logic of the text itself," and I treat the text's dramatic setting and its figuration of Athenian politics as part of a textual strategy that "splits the reader's attention" and encourages critical comparison between two perspectives.[6] The narrative's refracting strategies invite us to ruminate on the seeming givenness of Athenian divisions as we engage with the "positive" proposals of the callipolis.

The second axis along which I read the noble lie is rhetorical. As in the last chapter, I take it for granted that the *Republic*'s rhetorical aspects are central to any exploration of its political theoretical arguments. If there are figurative dimensions to political theory texts that cannot be accounted for simply in terms of "their legitimacy or validity or their grammatical correctness,"[7] then readers ought to adopt a critical approach for assessing how the noble lie's narration (not just its premises) contributes to the production of meaning. In this vein, I suggest that while the truth status of the noble lie has been the subject of numerous debates, much less attention has been paid to what happens dramaturgically in these scenes. Socrates does not tell a lie. He talks *about* telling a lie. Plato shows him recommending, out loud, by way of Athenian imagery, that the political use of a divisive rhetorical device should be kept hidden. Rather than focus on

[6] Seery 1988: 230, 244. Tarnopolsky thinks critical distance is achieved through Socrates' "pointed assertions" of the noble lie's outrageousness, a claim that depends on missing the Athenian resonance of the lie. We are shown "what it means to give birth to speech-acts" and taught to "question foundational myths" *in general*. See Tarnopolsky 2009: 30.

[7] Shklar 1985: 226.

Socrates' intentions to deceive, as many politically attuned readings have, I emphasize instead that the text's structure makes sure no one is duped by this imagined deception – not the audience, not even the characters.[8] Thus, my reading does not begin from a place that has Socrates working to conceal the constructed character of the callipolis order. It asks how the implications of the noble lie shift when we catch this Athenian character in the narrative act of disclosing the artifice of natural hierarchy as a secret to keep.

Several new critical-historical insights issue from this different interpretive orientation. Plato's *Republic* is usually read as creating in these founding moments what Leo Straus, Nicole Loraux, and Edward Andrew have variously described as a confusion between nature and artifice but that in my view is actually a demonstration of their mutual imbrication.[9] I contend that Plato's text is showing us the mechanism through which the very distinction between nature and something like convention is generated and maintained as a tactically useful opposition for fixing a polity's membership order.[10] Once restored to their Athenian context, the specific proposals for how the philosopher rulers will carry out the just city's architecture over time suggests the *Republic* does more than expose the artifice by which any polity draws "natural" boundaries of inclusion. It specifically challenges the Athenian reliance on claims of a "natural" attribute (i.e., blood) to fix membership lines in advance even as it seeks, paradoxically, to found a political hierarchy in an idea of pregiven difference (i.e., metal). The callipolis will assign and when necessary reassign people to their membership class on the basis of their performance in

[8] Even when readers emphasize the noble lie's transparency, they do so in order to claim that discernible natural inequalities between persons are a "falsity" for Socrates. As important as this argument may be for unsettling Plato's reputation as a "doctrinaire inegalitarian" (Andrew 1989: 580), a focus on the truth claims of Socrates' premises cannot address, indeed even discounts, the dramaturgical register on which the passages are engaged in an exposé (that can be picked up or not). See Andrew 1989.

[9] Loraux (1993: 127n76) uses the terms "confusion," "*physis*," and "*technē*." Strauss (1978: 102) says Socrates "blurs" the distinction between "nature and art" and later "nature and convention," by which I assume he means the Greek *nomos*. Andrew (1989) uses similar language. I refrain from supplying an oppositional term against which to contrast *phusis* so as not to misleadingly bifurcate and reify the uniquely plastic character of the Greek concept, which includes an idea of origins as well as the acculturative process that shapes it.

[10] This does not mean there is no operative distinction between *phusis* and *nomos* in the *Republic* but, rather, that this distinction is multiple, unstable, and itself an object of the text's theorization. The exposure and exploitation of this distinction's authoritative force and political usefulness is *part* of Plato's exploration of the relation between *phusis* and *nomos*. My use of the term "imbrication" suggests the *Republic* offers a deconstruction, not a blurring or erasure, of nature and artifice. To borrow Samuel Chambers's formulation, the dialogue "shows *how* the construction works" and "reveals *that* there is a construction going on in the first place." See Chambers 2009: 5.

a series of educational activities and tests. Member status is constituted by (and as) performance in two senses, then, as the effect of an acculturative, generative participation in a specific training and as an evaluation of that molding's success. A performative notion of citizenship thus need not exclusively serve a democratic regime. Nor is a democratic regime necessarily conducive to a performative citizenship, as we will see in Chapter 5.

Now it is true that Socrates suggests genealogy may serve as an expedient proxy for virtuous activity. "Most of the time," he imagines telling the rulers, "you will father children of the same type as yourselves" (415b1). But Plato's narrative advances this proposition that metals (and their corresponding behaviors) are more or less inheritable as part of the myth. Analyzed from the perspective afforded the reader (and the listeners) rather than the callipolis residents, genealogy takes on the semblance of determinacy because of politics (i.e., practices of mythmaking and assignment). This is precisely why "the first and most important instruction" (415b4) to the rulers is to watch out for people who seem to be in the "wrong" class: since they are most likely to expose kinship's determinacy as artifice, they must be immediately reassigned. The callipolis's risky and unstable practice of classification will have to be concealed from the residents – a political necessity for maintaining the appearance that coherent distinctions precede their performance and decide virtuous political activity. In this way, Socrates' membership rules appear to preserve a regime of "natural" difference. Plato's prose, however, lets the audience in on the regulatory production of political identity. The text reveals the political utility of claiming a blood criterion's determinacy. It does not assert that determinacy. Against what Athens would have its citizens believe, the *Republic* suggests that it is because genealogy is only *claimed* to have determinative powers that it cannot *guarantee* performance. We are reminded, on this score, of the equally impressive performance yielded by the "naturally" divided groups at the Bendideia.

I read the emphasis Socrates places on the need for reassignment, then, as a response to the Athenian political conditions that made it possible to be accused of passing as a citizen, that is, of acting counter to what one really "is." The *Republic*, by contrast, imagines a polity in which political mobility between membership categories is actually possible. The young person who, though born to bronze parents, acts like gold achieves gold status (415c). Passing, in other words, becomes inconceivable in the new regime. Accordingly, the issue for the dialogue is not to reject a "prior" political criterion for membership – one of its insights is that a political hierarchy requires one – but to attach it to achievement. While this has led some readers to conclude that the myth of the metals establishes a meritocratic regime,[11] the rhetorical reading I advance suggests a more critical possibility: both regimes (Athens and the callipolis) insist political standing is an internal attribute, but Socrates' narrative permits the insight that people's belief in a substratum that guides activity is itself maintained by a series of acts, not least of which are the telling of a regulatory ideal and the quotidian work of judging people and assigning them to the categories of standing first laid down by that fiction.

The proximity I establish between Athens and the callipolis may strike some readers as unlikely. While I think that their parallels would have been evident to an Athenian reader, this argument is not an exercise in recovering Plato's intentionality or historical plausibility. Rather, I build on the work of the previous chapter in showing that attention to the *Republic*'s political realities opens up the dialogue's interpretive possibilities and exposes some of the habits of thought that have made democratic difference seem irrelevant to Plato's text and therefore to the so-called origins of democratic theory. Just as modern regimes have claimed freedom and expansive citizenship as ideals despite, if not because of, their systematic exclusion of some persons along "natural" lines, Athenian commitments to equality and participation were, in the fifth century of the *Republic*'s dramatic setting, bound up with and sustained by a politics of empire and nativism. Plato's text does not fail to register this constitutive dynamic, and neither should we.

The rest of the chapter proceeds in two sections. The first part reconstructs the symbolic politics of Athenian citizenship to reveal parallels between the Athenian and callipolis membership orders and diagnoses the critical energies that have gone into displacing the democratic resonance of the *Republic*'s founding myth.[12] The second part uses this interpretive context to provide a close reading of the passages as an exposé of how natural difference is made. I then draw out the text's additional figurations of Athenian practices and demonstrate that the noble lie provokes new insights into the workings of democratic difference.

Democracy's Noble Lie

Scholarly interest in the historical, poetic, and intertextual contexts for the noble lie and its elaboration in the myth of the metals has focused on

[11] See Andrew 1989.

[12] Rosenstock (1994) reads the noble lie as a rewriting of the Athenian myth but focuses on (Plato's effacing of) gender.

recovering their aristocratic, foreign, and cosmogenic allusions while generally leaving its democratic connections underexplored.[13] At first glance, the *Republic* may seem to invite as much.[14] Although we "would expect" the lie (*pseudos*) "to be Athenian first and foremost as far as the Athenian Plato is concerned," writes Nicole Loraux, the text never explicitly mentions Athens as a precedent. In fact, the dialogue draws on so many other traditions, at least overtly, that it effectively displaces the noble lie from Athens (the very setting of its utterance) "so that it can take its Theban form."[15] This does not mean that Athens goes missing from the passage, she notes, but that Plato has opened up a space to (re)found the city "in alterity."[16] We have left Athens, Loraux says, only to see it more clearly.

The conspicuous absence of Athens from these otherwise Athenian scenes is thus an invitation to assess and refound the city. The following section begins that work by recovering the specifically democratic politics the *Republic* is figuring when it adopts an earth-born myth to found the callipolis. I show how a similar myth worked to entrench a legal policy of exclusionary and naturalized political difference in Athens and, along the way, identify two interpretive tendencies that appear to have stood in the way of this comparative reading until now. First, I suggest that commentators on Plato tend to treat the Athenian founding myth of autochthony as "mere" "fable,"[17] discounting it as a productive political discourse and turning away from the divisive work it performed in Athens. When readers acknowledge the callipolis's autochthony parallel with Athens, they usually note its sanguine political aspirations – civic unity across socioeconomic lines and natural equality – and downplay the extent to which autochthony was also an expansionist ideology that included, in the service of Athenian democracy's romantic ideals, the permanent and inviolable difference of some residents and colonial subjects. Attending to the full range of meanings carried by autochthony enables me to read the earth-born myth in the *Republic* as a particularized response to the politics that were working to fix democratic citizenship as a natural status constituted in advance.

[13] Aristocratic texts appropriated metal imagery from Hesiod's myths of the races, which leads Monoson (2000: 15) to present the myth of the metals as an instance of aristocratic (not democratic) discourse. In Herodotus, metals imagery is also tied to Persians, Lydians, and tyranny (Kurke 1995).

[14] Tarnopolsky (2009) foregrounds the text's connections with democratic Athens but by arguing that dramatic poetry and Athenian assembly debates over the relationship between war and democratic deception would be informing the noble lie. See also Hesk 2000.

[15] The noble lie is assumed to be Theban because Socrates announces the fiction has a "Phoenician" flavor, a reference perhaps to Cadmus, the Phoenician colonizer of Thebes who in Herodotus (3.414) sows his earth-born warriors out of the teeth of dragons. See also Hesk 2000: 160.

[16] Loraux 2000: 120. [17] Loraux 1993: 4.

As I mentioned in Chapter 1, autochthony discourse "forged strong ideological support for the democracy"[18] because it established the demos' common origins and naturalized the political equality that existed between native Athenian men.[19] But the logic that unified the demos was also an index of political difference. If only an inherited nativity provided for citizen standing, the criterion was a way of keeping the category of citizen safe from contamination by those non-Athenians born in the polis and the peripheries whose exclusion was more or less inevitable and pregiven. Residents found to be of mixed or non-Athenian descent were most obviously excluded by this nativism: immigrants, manumitted slaves, and their Athenian-born children were assigned *metoikia*. While metics' exclusion from citizen status was inheritable, they enjoyed a proximity to citizens that made passing and illegal enfranchisement possible if not frequent and therefore a source of anxiety.[20] In this way, imperial expansion and mobility made public trials for adjudicating questions of ethnic identity or genealogy particularly charged.

In the period of the *Republic*'s fifth-century setting and again in the decades leading up to its composition in the fourth, democratic citizenship was legally tethered to what Jonathan Hall calls ethnicity or what we might describe as Athenianness – a seemingly internal attribute that could not be earned except in honorary cases but could be proven through witness testimonies about kinship.[21] If citizenship depended on pure Athenian ancestry, the myth of autochthony helped found democratic citizenship in a notion of immobility, ensuring that movement into citizenship status was formally impossible except by special decree. An Athens-born metic thus inherited his or her noncitizen status despite a lived experience of assimilation and participation in Athenian civic life.

The callipolis's membership rules will revolve around a similar preoccupation with whether citizenship is an earned privilege or an inherited and fixed status. But the *Republic* will assume the necessity for mobility between naturalized political classes when the city's rulers warrant it, precisely because the class of a child's biological parents cannot determine the child's conduct, even if it may be some indicator of aptitude. To be

[18] Blok 2009: 154, 169. [19] J. Hall 2002: 204–205. [20] Davies 1977–1978.

[21] J. Hall (2002: 204, 219) makes the important point that if Pericles' Citizenship Law turned the demos into a closed descent group, Athenians "conspired to remove the ethnic criterion from definitions of Hellenicity only to redeploy it in patrolling the boundaries of their own civic identity." The Athenocentric notion of Hellenicity, according to which a Hellenic identity could be taught and learned, was "defined according to the cultural criteria decided by Athens." In this sense, it enables the mimetic relation between citizen and metic that I explore in the next chapter.

"well-born," as Carl Page puts it, "is to have impeccable origins, but it does not guarantee fulfillment of the very highest ends."[22] Indeed, the *Republic*'s admission of blood's indeterminacy focuses attention on a citizenship of performance, which was subordinated in Athens to good birth, an idea Plato evokes when he refers to the callipolis's founding myth as a *gennaion* (well-born) *pseudos*.

These citizenship parallels notwithstanding, political theoretical interest in the noble lie has tended to focus on evaluating the deception's legitimacy and validity. While some interpreters have asked how the dialogue can appropriate discourses it does not allow in philosophical discussion, others have sought to discern the precise epistemic status of the *gennaion pseudos* as a way of resolving what appears to be a moral problem or internal incoherence in the dialogue.[23] So long as the *pseudos* resembles the truth about how to arrange a just city, it is – at least in the *Republic*'s terms – a morally admirable fiction that leads one to sound convictions and virtue (382c–382d).[24] Socrates' act of deception "provides citizens a justification of their social differentiation."[25]

Such efforts to justify the *pseudos* from within the dialogue's supposedly closed philosophical system were, in Karl Popper's estimation, hypocritical, utilitarian, totalitarian, and tautological. Actions that "serve" the just city are "moral" in the *Republic*, he wrote, and "actions that endanger it, immoral."[26] Popper was troubled by what he took to be Socrates' illiberal and antidemocratic proposal that citizens be unable to engage in "*rational* considerations that have the power to motivate acceptance of a political authority by those who are to be subject to it."[27] According to Malcolm Schofield, Athenians would have been similarly outraged by Socrates' attempt to justify speaking falsehoods to the demos.[28] "Plato," he speculates, "must have known he was breaching the norms of the democratic political ideology of his own time and place."[29] Yet notions of "deceiving the people" were by no means foreign to classical democracy, as Jon Hesk

[22] Page (1991: 21) is inspired by the fact that the *pseudos* is not *kalon*, the word typically translated as "noble," but *gennaion*, which invokes birth origins.

[23] Hesk (2000: 152), for instance, writes that Plato "believes certain situations make lying a moral necessity" and thus obfuscates the lie's political power and effects. This move may be symptomatic of what Page (1991: 2) astutely casts as a tendency to extract the lie from its wider context *in* and relations to the rest of the dialogue.

[24] See Schofield 2007: 143.

[25] Wallach 2001: 254; Monoson 2000: 128.

[26] Popper 1971: 107. Page (1991: 2) finds that interpreters converge in objecting to Socrates' "paternalism" and his endorsement of "willful domination."

[27] Schofield 2007: 139. But liberal states also deploy metaphors of family to produce particular affective attachments, structure power relations in a polity, and regulate kinship (see Stevens 1999).

[28] Schofield (2007: 141) cites Demosthenes 19.184 to support this point.

[29] Schofield 2007: 140.

has pointed out.[30] In fact, Athenian oratory regularly drew on and debated the "powers and perils of deceptive communication on the part of elite speakers" and did not present deceptive rhetoric in oppositional terms of truth and falsity.[31] Athens even had a distinct discourse for policing and theorizing its own risky dependence on such speech.

It is curious that criticism's attempts to show how Athenian texts and practices unsettle "an (almost Popperian) Athenian ideological distinction between the open and closed society" do not ultimately pursue, as an instance of this democratic dependency, the foundational work that myths like autochthony performed in Athens.[32] Discussions of Plato consistently acknowledge the Athenian overtones of the noble lie but fail to consider that, contrary to Schofield, an Athenian audience might actually have found a noble lie familiar, as an illustration of how constitutive lies operate.[33] In underappreciating the generative power of founding lies for *democracy*, such arguments risk rehearsing the very precondition for Popper's view that (only) totalitarian regimes like the callipolis are founded on a big lie.

With the exception of Hall who asks whether Plato's "own myth of autochthony" might be objecting to, rather than endorsing, "the legitimation of primordial equality" in the Athenian version, *Republic* readers tend to defamiliarize the foundational lying they see in the *Republic*.[34] The impulse to estrange Athens from this poetic and political practice when confronted with its dramatization in Plato services and may be serviced by what Loraux sees as a general reluctance among readers to "give myth the place it deserves in the field of the historian of ancient Greece."[35] Despite the fact that the "celebration of Athenian autochthony (i.e. 'racial purity') is a frequently attested *topos* in the later fifth century and early fourth century"[36] or that myths of autochthonous descent were actually uncommon in ancient Greece overall,[37] critics tend to see no specific political resonance in the *Republic*'s figuration of an earth-born myth. "Socrates' mythmaking challenges the authority of traditional (and hegemonic) discourses in Athens," according to Elizabeth Markovits,

30 Hesk 2000: 2. 31 Hesk 2000: 4. 32 Hesk 2000: 4–5.

33 See Hesk 2000: 161. Although Hesk acknowledges that an "*Athenian* would know" a myth of autochthony was the kind of lie that was "good for a polis," he ends up stressing the shocking and unfamiliar quality of the *Republic*'s "state propaganda" (Hesk 2000: 159). Hesk may be drawing a distinction between the lie (as unfamiliar) and the myth of the metals (as familiar), obscuring the extent to which, in the dialogue, they are part of one regulatory ideal.

34 J. Hall (2002: 217) raises the question in a discussion of the *Menexenus* but does not pursue it beyond that.

35 Loraux 1993: 4. 36 Ogden 1996: 66. 37 Roy 2014.

simply by presenting them as objects for judgment and interpretation. If there is no particularized intervention to this challenge, it is because readers emphasize the myth's romantic aspirations of unity. The myth of the metals "would not have sounded completely foreign to Athenians," Markovits explains, because it aims to "solidify the bonds of friendship and loyalty" through "social control."[38] Here, even the stratifying work of the myth of the metals is made to serve an ultimate goal of solidarity, just as it is said (incompletely) to do in Athens.

Within such an idealized picture of Athenian democracy, autochthony's assumptions of "natural" forms of political difference appear peculiar to the *Republic*'s version of autochthony rather than (also) a democratic feature on which the text is drawing. Both myths may underwrite a political ideal of unity, but only the *Republic*'s is said to rely on an explicit politics of difference to do so. In bypassing the role that genealogy historically played in questions of democratic citizenship, readers are able to credit Plato with bringing back an older, inegalitarian, and "tribal" notion of "natural privileges for the natural leaders" (Popper, 1971, 95).[39] Once displaced to the *Republic*, democracy's own penchant for natural difference may safely ground aspects of Plato's antidemocratic legacy and inoculate readers against moments in the text that may animate or even undercut it.

It is for these reasons that Debra Nails's reading stands out in its attention to the exclusionary politics of the dialogue's historical context and its autochthonous ideology – until her account seeks a historical political referent for the callipolis. Nails inverts the aforementioned readings by arguing that the myth of the metals actually "directly opposes the founders' myth touted by the Athenians of the day" because it imagines an *inclusive* polity of unconditional membership.[40] She rightly reasons that, whatever their class, residents will share in the city, though she neglects to stress that they will not share in rule. When Nails looks for an Athenian precedent for the *Republic*'s three-part stratification, however, she curiously overlooks the citizen, metic, and slave categories of Athens. Though these are exactly the sorts of political divisions earth-born myths

[38] Markovits 2009: 124, 142–143, 140.

[39] That Rancière (2006) holds a similar view to Popper's suggests that a "Platonist" Plato frequently sustains not only (a certain kind of) liberalism but also its critique. In "Plato's Pharmacy," Derrida (1981) uses the term "Platonism" to characterize a persistent habit of reading that stabilizes the play of meaning in Plato's texts so as to locate in the text a series of hierarchically ordered oppositions, among which, we should stress, are political and ontological oppositions. For discussions of Platonism, see Leonard 2005, ch. 3.

[40] Nails 2012: 14.

figure, her reading fastens instead to Solon's much earlier efforts to arrange members of the Athenian demos – not the polis as a whole – on a descending scale of political privilege determined by wealth.[41] Nails concludes that the myth of the metals is actually replacing Solon's classes with "occupational groups based on the natural abilities individuals exhibit, their talents."[42] It is true that the callipolis stratification is occupational and that Socrates rearranges all residents of the city, but one of the aims of this stratification is that rule remain the purview of a specific and supposedly predetermined class, just as it was in Athens. If Nails misses this parallel, it is perhaps because she makes too much of the inclusive membership of the callipolis and not enough of its exclusive ruling class.

My concern is not to discount that there may be multiple historical contexts for interpreting the *Republic*'s division of members but rather to inquire into the habits of thought that might lead readers to select one over another.[43] Interpretive presuppositions about what "counts" as political discourse underlie the critical impulse to overlook Athenian autochthony politics as an illuminating context for the *Republic*'s founding story, despite the fact that mythmaking frequently serves in Greek texts as a metonymy for Athenian political practices (like citizenship rules) that distinguished citizens from noncitizens.[44] To some extent, the dearth of critical interest in autochthony's function as a historical and productive political discourse reflects myth's continued associations with nontruth.[45] But if we follow Luc Brisson in recognizing that Plato's text does not present *pseudos* or *mythos* as a form of verifiable discourse, we can shift attention away from the question of its truth status to the noble lie's rhetorical effects, which is to say, to the question of how the *Republic* narrates the noble lie.[46] The theoretical work performed by these well-known scenes, in other words, depends on the discursive conditions under which autochthony is disclosed as a secret for the callipolis. What makes the noble lie subversive, then, is not that it invokes deception *per se* but rather that foundational

[41] Curiously, Nails cites demographic estimates of the *whole* city (not just the demos), broken down into three tiers, as evidence for her reading; see Nails 2012: 6.

[42] Nails 2012: 14–15.

[43] For instance, insofar as the callipolis is drawing on (in order to critique) a Spartan model, one could also read the stratification as a reworking of the Spartan order, which also had a military class of guardians; see Menn 2006.

[44] As Pelling (2009: 474) says, "tropes of autochthony-thinking were so familiar that historians could allude to them subtly, without using the word 'autochthony' or making the relevance explicit."

[45] On this point, see Naddaf 1998: x.

[46] Brisson 1998: 90. Hesk (2000: 162) sees the productivity of myth in the *Republic*'s case, but whether he does so in the case of Athens is less clear.

lying is invoked to an audience (of characters and readers) whose attention is split. Socrates airs the notion of a noble lie in an Athenian setting in which the lie's presentation as artifice enables troubling insights about the democratic regime's own symbolic practices.

Outing Plato's Open Secret

Who should run the just city? The answer to this question depends in the *Republic* not on a preexisting criterion but on a series of activities. It is their performance by prospective rulers and the assessments of these activities by the current ones, Socrates suggests, that create the semblance of a prior and natural political criterion from which acts of citizenship and rule will appear to proceed. Socrates dramatizes the point when he instructs his fellow founders to "look for those who are the best defenders of their conviction"; "watch them from their earliest childhood"; "set them the kind of tasks which can make them lose sight of this aim"; and "then choose the ones who ... are not easily led astray" (412c–412d). The one who emerges from this sensitive process of interpretation unscathed is "pure" (*akēraton*) and "should be appointed" ruler and guardian of the city (413e7–414a2).

Allusions to birth, mixture, and purity populate these passages. They foreground the role that kinship, specifically "well-born" ancestry, plays in constituting citizens and force the question of why interpreters persistently turn away from the exclusionary politics of Athenian autochthony when they read Plato's *Republic*.[47] The appearance of *akēraton* ("undefiled," "unmixed," "pure gold") anticipates the myth of the metals, which will figure the rulers in terms of gold, but it also recalls the democratic *politēs*, whose uncorrupted Athenian lineage entitles him to citizenship and rule (cf. Plato, *Men.* 245c–245d). The *Republic*'s description of the testing and performance that produce a person's "natural" place recalls the Athenian institution of *dokimasia*, according to which, at eighteen, "each Athenian was accepted into his deme" following a scrutiny "to test his age and birth qualifications."[48] The scrutiny involved a deme in hearing accounts, from candidates and witnesses, that testified to a person's uncorrupted, dual Athenian parentage. When years later a man named Euxitheus is accused of

[47] Carmola (2003: 51) thinks *gennaion* turns up in a "sarcastic or defensive tone" as a way of registering a problem with parentage, which she understands as an issue of generational conflict. The noble lie is "falsifying the actual, familiar origins of the citizens" rather than, as I maintain, revealing the political and artificial character of all origins.

[48] Carey 1997: 212; see also Aristotle, *Ath. Pol.* 45.3.

passing, the subject of Chapter 6, Demosthenes (57) suggests on his behalf that juridical institutions like the *dokimasia* actually produce the natural and contestable "knowledge" of parentage and citizenship they purport merely to convey. Similarly, Socrates reveals the democracy's logic as a powerful if politically useful form of retrodiction when he suggests that in the callipolis, pure status follows from acts of observation – observation of activities that are subsequently rendered pure. To see here that practices of observation, interpretation, and decision making are working to ground the station one is suited to by "nature" is to see how they do so in Athens too. Well before autochthony is invoked, then, Plato's text invites the reader to compare regimes and, eventually, the multiple and contradictory definitions of citizenship that the language of *akēraton* can be used to figure.

We have seen already how democratic myth and law insists (autochthonous) descent qualified Athenians for a practice of citizenship. Membership on this score is the outcome of a preexisting purity. The *Republic*, by contrast, presents *akēraton* as an achieved status. And so purity is not a determinative attribute, as Athens maintains, but a performative status that follows from a series of acts that produce the identity it is said to reveal. What follows from the claim that one's place in the order of rule is earned not predetermined? Rulers and members are made not born. The *Republic* shows us that distinguishing between being (a citizen) and doing (citizenship) is a tactically useful practice for a regime.

Yet Socrates moves immediately to conceal this revelation from the city's imagined members, including those who would eventually take the reins. Citizens are more likely to accept their positions in the city's hierarchical arrangement, he suggests, if they believe them to be predetermined and for this reason fixed. The ignorance Socrates demands of his future citizens, however, he does not ask of his listeners. We now know that the just and stable arrangement of the callipolis depends on how well it maintains the appearance that political difference is fixed. In his imaginary role as colonist (*oikistēs*), Socrates may obscure the point, but this subterfuge, apparent to us, gives the scene a different meaning. It functions also to impart that the city needs to hide the traces of its efforts to make artifice look like nature.

We read further that the *gennaion pseudos* teaches citizens to believe that all the activities involved in their carefully monitored upbringing – performance, testing, education, and assignment – were a dream. In "truth" (*alētheia*), citizens are molded before undertaking the acts that, we were previously told, shape character and recommend class assignment (414d).

If they believe they were completely reared beneath and by the earth (*upo gēs entos*), citizens will not only treat the land as their mother and the other people as their brothers (414d–414e). They will think and act as if their political standing could be no other way precisely because it seems to express a naturally predetermined identity. Though a myth for the callipolis, the *gennaion pseudos* mirrors the democracy's citizenship ideals. Turning a series of activities into a natural fact requires a series of regulatory fictions, themselves acts of making (*poiēsis*).

This may be one reason Loraux thinks the dialogue's urgent task of founding is not a matter of legislating but of mythmaking, which renders political activity an expression of political status.[49] This shift from myth to mythmaking directs attention from the truth status of the pseudos, which the words "lie," "falsehood," and "deception" all stress, to the capacity of the *pseudos* to generate meaning. The noble lie does more than establish a permanent basis for political difference after all. It suggests this mythmaking is a foundational and continuous political activity. The pressing question is no longer whether an act of lying is legitimate or reconcilable with democracy (or the dialogue's own ethics). As we saw in the last chapter, the question is how all polities construct "truths" about membership and use them to establish expectations and opportunities for it.

If the first half of Socrates' *mythos* established the common roots of its citizens in the earth, the second proceeds by dividing them. Here, birth from the earth will not justify equal standing between the earth-born, as it does for the demos in Athens, but their differentiation, as it does for the population of Athens as a *whole*:

> You are all brothers, our story will tell them [*mythologountes*], all of you in the city. But when god made you, he used a mixture of gold in the creation of those of you who were fit to be rulers, which is why they are the most valuable. He used silver for those who were to be auxiliaries, and iron and bronze for the farmers and the rest of the skilled workers. Most of the time you will father children of the same type as yourselves, but because you are all related, occasionally a silver child may be born from a golden parent, or a golden child from a silver parent, and likewise any type from any other type. The first and most important instruction god gives the rulers is that the thing they should be the best guardians of, the thing they should keep the most careful eye on, is the compound of these metals in the souls of the children. If their own child is born with a mixture of bronze or iron in him, they must feel no kind of pity for him, but give him the position in society his nature deserves, driving him out to join the skilled workers or farmers.

[49] Loraux 2000: 28.

> On the other hand, any children from those groups born with a mixture of gold or silver should be given recognition and promoted either to the position of guardian or to that of auxiliary. (*Rep.* 415a–415c)

The choice of an earth-born myth is a provocation to read the passage in light of the political realities of its setting and production. The proposals for the just city's stewardship contribute to this sense. Ensconced in the noble lie's table of values, rulers perpetuate the fiction that an internal trait is not only determinative of conduct but also detectable *as such* in practice. The same can be said for Athens, where blood ties are held to possess the status of natural facts and used to decide political standing. As if to underscore his unsettling observations at the Bendis procession, where the citizen/metic difference failed to materialize in practice, Socrates takes up the logic and language of Athenian membership politics in ways that reveal the indeterminacy of a "natural" criterion and the naturalizing (and strategic) effects of its political use. The passage voices an explicit concern with the ambiguous effects of a blood criterion: genealogy's inability to guarantee performance is one reason the "first and most important instruction god gives the rulers" is to watch over the makeup of the children's souls and ensure each one is appropriately assigned or reassigned to a metal class.

The injunction to "assign the status (*timē*) fitting to one's nature (*phusis*)" thus works on at least two levels. Just as Athenians grant political status on the basis of supposedly stable facts of blood, the callipolis places citizens in their self-evident natural class. But the meaning of the passage is not delimited by the myth's *proposed* function in the imagined city. We already know that it is the guardians' "selection" that "determines nature" here, not the other way around.[50] The philosopher-rulers tasked with discerning the activities of young residents make "truths" about citizenship look like incontrovertible political criteria. The claim that there *are* decidable membership kinds generates the need for practices of discernment, and these practices in turn reassure the city that its political stratification reflects nature, now understood as a substratum.

In different ways, Strauss, Loraux, and Andrew have all noted that the *Republic* confounds the distinction between nature and convention here.[51] To observe that the text obscures what Andrew calls "the distinction between natural inequality and artificial or conventional inequality" is also to see that "there is no way to discern natural differences which qualify humans

[50] Rancière 2003: 18.

[51] See Loraux 1993: 127n76; Loraux 2000: 64, 117; Strauss 1978: 102; and Andrew 1989.

for different class positions or to differentiate the quality of the metal in the souls of the youth *prior to education*."[52] This means that the question of how Plato variously figures *phusis* throughout the *Republic* is not the same as how it is figured *for* the callipolis. In the myth of the metals, Socrates invokes a language of nature (and divinity) to imbue political distinctions with necessity and fixedness. The political order he imagines appeals to the authoritative force of nature to ground political meanings that we nevertheless learn are the functions of the order's own operations. In so doing, Plato's *Republic* sees nature as a question for political life as well as an ideological resource.[53] Mythmaking founds the prepolitical and necessary conditions of politics, and a series of political practices keep the divisions that nature purports to secure looking pregiven and inviolable. The determinative idea of nature – let us call it kinship – that indoctrinates people in the callipolis bears similarities to the Athenian use of blood, but it does not capture, and is in fact in tension with, the wide range of meanings of *phusis* in the text overall.

The meanings of *phusis* in classical thought generally militate against a consistent, unitary, or prediscursive notion of *phusis* even within a single thinker or text.[54] Plato's dialogue presents us with a sense of the multiple and conflicting articulations the "natural" can take, not simply between two polities but within one. Even when the dialogue appears to employ *phusis* to refer to a person's origin or character, it does so in a way that emphasizes the plastic quality of nature – its mutability and its vulnerability to the creative power of *mimesis*. "Imitations carried on for too long," Socrates says, "become a person's habits, even his nature (*phusis*), whether physically and in the way he sounds, or in the way he thinks" (395d).[55] Just as "[m]asculinity was still thought to be grounded in 'nature'" and yet "remained fluid and incomplete until firmly anchored by the discipline of an acculturative process," so is political status in the *Republic*.[56] The text frequently codes behaviors or ideas *para physin* (against

52 Andrew 1989: 585, 589 (my emphasis); Wallach 2001: 254.

53 Jill Frank (2004: 92) makes a similar point about nature's operation in Aristotle's *Politics*.

54 See Winkler 1990; Jill Frank 2004; and Holmes 2012; for Holmes, *phusis* designates "how a natural entity comes to be and develops, its stable attributes and its power to act on and be acted upon by other things, all topics that were open to investigation through the analysis of phenomenal evidence" (Holmes 2012: 29). Just before Plato, *phusis* was the term used variously "for the quality of action or 'manners,' the 'ways' of a people or a person, for the 'appearance' of an object—that is, for the qualities that one sees … for the human nature … and later for the man's moral and intellectual qualities" (Beardslee 1987: 3).

55 This is Christopher Rowe's translation in Plato 2012b.

56 Gleason 1990: 412. As Jill Frank (2013) notes, a philosophical nature is the product rather than the ground of an activity: the loving of truth and wisdom that is the condition for a philosophical soul.

nature) or *kata physin* (in accordance with nature) as a way of articulating what should or should not be off limits (456a) rather than to claim what is necessary and could not be otherwise.[57] It is the latter usage that appears in the myth-of-the-metals passage, where it serves as a necessary political tool.

In the callipolis, classifying members according to their *phusis* involves philosopher-rulers in an imprecise and risky activity of looking for supposedly discernible differences of aptitude and character that do not follow strictly hereditary lines. In this sense, the institution resembles another ancient practice, the "informal" science of physiognomy, by which people's "natures," especially those whose "gender deviance" needed decoding, were read according to their physical characteristics and style as "achieved states," independent of anatomical sex.[58] What drives the need for this kind of regulatory practice in the callipolis, Nails suggests, is its claim that "all citizens are amalgams, no one is pure, and all are related." If "like cannot be guaranteed to produce like," the ontological fact of their *mixture* creates "the need to monitor children's abilities"[59] not unlike the possibility of mixed gender signs – or, we might add, passing metics – which in Maud Gleason's expression "demands a science of decipherment."[60] A practice of sign reading thus makes the idea of a substratum and its distinct categories possible. In Plato's text, the decision that definitive distinctions have to be made generates the need for their subsequent monitoring. Likewise, democracy's hierarchical and imperial membership rules generate not only the need for institutions to decipher pure citizens but also the possibility of a figure like the metic – the excluded insider who is hard to classify but for this reason must be.[61]

The description of residents as amalgams deepens our understanding of how genealogy fails to *decide* aptitude and performance – those things that reify and become a person's nature in the *Republic*. If Socrates posits mixture,

[57] "The characteristic use of 'nature' was 'to indicate a fundamental cultural rule, of which one should not need reminding" (Winkler 1990: 199).

[58] Gleason 1990: 390–391; see also Winkler 1990: 199–200. [59] Nails 2012: 20.

[60] Gleason 1990: 391. To see how this practice of assignment works, consider it in light of what Fausto-Sterling (2000: 45) calls "the contemporary practice of 'fixing' intersex babies immediately after birth." Bodies that "exhibit sexual ambiguity" undergo techniques (surgery) that make them "male" or "female." A practice assigns them to one of two "normal" sexes and thus maintains the regulatory fiction that there are only two to begin with. If frequently the modern intersexual child "must leave the hospital 'as a sex,'" then we might say the child in the callipolis must be placed in the "right" political kind precisely because she can exhibit her own kind of ambiguity.

[61] The vulnerability of being (exposed as) a metic is demonstrated by an episode of "outing" (Davies 1977–1978: 111), in which the city disenfranchised as many as 4,760 people considered, during a shortage of corn, to be "illegitimately enrolled" and thus wrongly entitled to receive this sustenance.

not purity, as an ontological fact, then difference lies on a sliding scale, where citizens inhabit a continuum: in this context, a tripartite schema is a regulatory fiction. Unlike Athens or the callipolis, then, Plato's text is fully prepared to affirm that reproduction does not make distinct kinds because it has shown us that politics does. When statuses seem unambiguous, that is because the semblance of their discreteness is kept up in practice, through the careful differentiation of people's labor and duties and their constant observation. It is only when persons of different statuses start to act similarly that it becomes impossible to maintain their unambiguous and decisive difference. This is why in the callipolis, any behavior that diverges from the rulers' expectations for that class will immediately necessitate a different "nature" classification. The inevitable discontinuities between performance and membership class would manifest the city's social mobility and betray its secret.

If Athenian citizenship is premised on a notion of permanent political difference, it assumes immobility but creates autochthony trouble – the idea that people can act like what they are not – because, as Plato shows, blood does not determine action. In the *Republic*, we find a different solution to the problem Athenian autochthony creates: rather than seeking to prove who someone "is" in spite of what a person does, the ruling class yields to its judgments of practice. The new myth matches up with the just city's needs. Rather than creating the culture of exposure and vulnerability we saw in previous chapters, the callipolis reassigns people on the basis of performance and endeavors to make the idea of passing impossible. When Socrates introduces the possibility of social mobility, he does not simply reveal genealogy as an unreliable criterion for citizenship practice. He suggests that where one lies in the social order is observable, an interpretation of performance not origins.

The *Republic*'s *gennaion pseudos* naturalizes the polis's boundaries of exclusion and inclusion with a critical difference from the Athenian myth of autochthony. It shows us that the hierarchy *phusis* is called on to secure is the political work of the ruling class. A member's standing in the callipolis may appear to be the guide of membership performance when it is really the effect. Even if a degree of aptitude readies one for a certain type of conduct in the *Republic*'s view, the myth's purpose is to naturalize, not reflect, place – to make standing look pregiven. The disclosure of an imagined concealment is an incitement to ask what secret underlies any given polity. Restored to the political realities of its Athenian setting, Plato's text insinuates that an autochthonous designation is not so much the natural or stable effect of a biological fact as a fictional ideal that unevenly regulates the production of citizens.

CHAPTER 5

Of Mimesis and Metic

A Reading of Democracy in Book VIII

Imitators imitate ones acting.

– Aristotle, *Poetics* 1448a1[1]

The lines between metics and citizens blur in democracy. So announces Socrates in Book VIII. Fathers and sons end up acting like each other as do women and men (562e–563a). In Malcolm Schofield's observation, the problem is that citizens fail to respect what the law understands as difference. Their feeling that distinctions cramp and oppress, explains Arlene Saxonhouse, has the ironic effect of challenging their equality and ability to rule. In a reading of the same passage, Jacques Rancière contends that a general disregard for anything but pleasure leads the democratic character (the "egotistical man") to disregard "collective order." Democracy, he notes, "overturns all the relations that structure human society" – much to Plato's apparent distaste.[2]

The democratic city of Plato's *Republic* appears, on these accounts, to foster a love of freedom that eradicates the conditions of its own regeneration. Maintaining distinctions between people seems, on the one hand, necessary to and, on the other, undermining of democratic politics. Whether political theorists make this spirit of insubordination an object of admiration in their writing, they nevertheless converge in casting Book VIII as a critical moment in the history of democratic thought, a foundational site for equating democracy with a formless multitude signified by absolute disorder. Critics settle the meaning of Plato's status-blurring scene, in other words, so as to lend a Platonic force to a familiar late-modern paradox. For, as Alan Keenan observes, contemporary political theorists typically understand democracy as an arrangement "at odds

[1] I have revised this translation of the *Poetics* by Seth Benardete and Michael Davis (Aristotle 2002).
[2] Schofield 2006: 110; Saxonhouse 1998; Rancière 2006: 36.

with itself, torn between the closure necessary for the people's identity and rule, and the openness of contestation and revisability."[3]

To the extent that Plato anticipates this contemporary vision of democratic rebelliousness, however, he is said to do so unhappily. There is a strong sense in the political theoretical reception of the passage with which I began this chapter that Plato is haunted above all by democracy's rejection of a foundation in nature and its unwillingness to discern "real" differences among people. The common view that, after Plato, imagines democracy between the poles of stability and rupture also gives way to a romantic picture of what Patchen Markell has described as "the people insurgent, rising up in opposition to a regime or order, and so displaying the irreducibility of popular power to a fixed form."[4] It is in spite of Plato, in other words, that the *Republic* is made to stand as the (uneasy) theoretical origins of a redemptive democratic politics, according to which democracy is constituted by a tenacious and salutary drive to dissolve its own membership differences. The opportunity to theorize democracy's fundamentally emancipatory character emerges through and against the *Republic*'s unhappy vision of democracy in Book VIII.

This chapter offers a different interpretation of Plato's depiction of status panic. I question the iconic image of democratic unruliness that envisions the *Republic* reflecting desires to contain democratic disorder and expressing fears about the destabilizing of essentialist ideas of difference. What Book VIII provides, in my view, is a previously unnoted account of the performative character and fragility of all "natural" distinctions, democratic or otherwise, that directly challenges the tendency by political theorists to read the passage as the figuration of a certain kind of felicitous democratic insubordination. The chapter attends to the abundant yet persistently neglected invocations of mimesis that make up the passage in Greek and finds that the instability Socrates depicts has less to do with the constitutive rebelliousness of a democratic constitution than it does with the presumed or incomplete reification of a role. As earlier chapters have argued, Plato's *Republic* does not begin, as many of his readers do, from the unhistorical or idealizing premise that a democracy refuses to distinguish but from the assumption that it does, strategically and to ambiguous effects – neither totalizing nor negligible. The Book VIII passage invokes a wide range of statuses of age, sex, and kinship. Any sense of convergence

[3] Keenan takes up the contemporary interest in understanding democracy in paradoxical terms, though without reference to Plato (2003: 13).

[4] Markell 2006: 11.

between these democratic distinctions, however, emerges strictly and strikingly through a language of performance: Socrates speaks in a series of couplets that imagine people with statuses in specific, oppositional relation to each other becoming, through the performance of their roles, indistinguishable. There are significant political and theoretical implications to casting relations of naturalized difference in such an idiom. Only a concept like mimesis could conjure the regulatory fiction that insists a permanent distance separates two terms – model and copy, privileged and abject, citizen and metic – while serving as the very practice that spans and threatens that distance.

What concerns me in the pages that follow, then, is the sense that Plato's picture of democratic instability, figured as a series of mimetic acts, demands a closer look in the particular context of classical Athens and that resituating the passage in this way will yield new critical insights about democracy. It is not coincidental that in the fifth century of the text's dramatic setting, a blurring of distinction should be cast in mimetic terms or, more to the point of the passage, that mimesis should be figured as the culminating *practice* of democratic freedom. In the Funeral Oration, Thucydides has Pericles suggest that a mimetic relationship between Athenians and non-Athenians is the bedrock of the city's freedom: to serve as a model for the rest of Hellas, Athens famously opens itself to all and bears the (curiously unspecified) risks that come from courting strangers. The city's freedom and expansion – let us call this Athenian exceptionalism – depend on the always-inadequate approximation and affirmation of its ideals by noncitizens. And so the democracy's exceptionalism rests on an idea of "mere" mimicry, stressing that, no matter how fine a copy, the metic stands at an infinite and evident distance from his autochthonous model.

Yet in Book VIII, I argue, Plato reenvisages Periclean mimicry as mimesis, a concept far more dangerous to democracy's autochthonous self-conception because it foregrounds what Thucydides' Pericles would rather keep concealed: the disconcerting proximity between two "naturally" differentiated figures. What Socrates witnessed at the Bendis festival in Chapter 3 finds renewed expression here in Book VIII: democracy insists on – at the same time that it unsettles – the notion that political difference is an internal attribute that can be ascertained reliably in practice. Once again, though in a different sense, the *Republic* shows democracy making visible the ambiguity of its distinctions and exposing the fragile artifice that underlies its own democratic-expansionist order.

However tempting it might seem, then, to conclude with John Wallach that Book VIII depicts "imposters" running around democracy "arrogating power" to themselves and "misleading the *demos*,"[5] such a negative evaluation forecloses the historical-political import of the status-blurring scene because it obscures the conceptual heterogeneity of mimesis. What is more, as an orientation to the text, that angle fails to take stock of the bidirectionality Plato assigns to his mimetic examples. If metics act like citizens and citizens act like metics in democracy, the *Republic* renders all status a performative achievement, however "right" or "wrong" it seems. Plato's dialogue permits a reading in which democracy cannot maintain the notion of an internal identity constituted in advance. What this means is that Book VIII offers less the articulation of a regime's constitutive rebelliousness than a meditation on political difference that confounds the political (here, Athenian and democratic) logic that thinks of some actors as imposters, renders some political activity passing, and casts membership as an effect of (mis)identification – that is, remove a citizen's mask and you will find a metic lurking underneath. In the *Republic*'s depiction of democratic politics, there is no surefire way to tell that difference or make that call, but there are certainly attempts to do so.

It is worth keeping in mind that the emergence of the metic as the proximate counterpart to the autochthonous citizen coincides in the fifth century with a discourse, political and dramaturgical, for naming and exploring the threatening powers of disguise and passing. I raise this observation as an invitation to look carefully at the relationship Plato constructs between political difference and mimesis in Book VIII. For the problem of what Froma Zeitlin calls "reading the other" is not only "a continuing obsessive concern in Greek tragedy."[6] It is also a critical subtext of Plato's political theory, in which it appears, however unassumingly, as both the expression and the effect of democratic taxonomies and membership dynamics. Yet readers have been slow to consider that mimesis might serve as a language of democratic-imperial self-fashioning in the setting of the *Republic*. Despite persistent interest in mimesis as a Platonic index of theatricality and emulation, they have generally failed to address how this idiom might be generating specific political theoretical meaning in a dramatic context of shifting conceptions of Athenian identity. If, as Karen Bassi argues, "Plato bases his critique [overall] on the possibility that social and political structures can be destabilized by bodily or visually manifested impersonations,"[7] Plato's rendering of democracy as a mimetic

[5] Wallach 2001: 295. [6] Zeitlin 1996: 362. [7] Bassi 1998: 19.

regime is more than a pronouncement of democracy's constitutive allergy to distinction. It is a reckoning with democracy's investment in naturalized distinctions and their unstable effects. Democratic politics looks like mimesis in the *Republic*, then, not only because human activity is always a form (or effect) of impersonation but also because autochthonous power expresses itself in Athenian discourse through a language and logic of mimicry.

The picture that materializes from this reorientation to the *Republic* reconfigures what critics have long identified as the central problematic of Book VIII and compels us to rethink the theoretical tradition in which this story of democratic change – as an enduring paradigm for the analysis of political regimes – might be considered an exemplary tale. As I elaborate in the pages that follow, the tendency to see a complete dissolution of natural and political distinctions in Book VIII's portrayal of democracy rather than their ambiguous performance depends first on reading the passage outside of the city's citizenship realities and second on overlooking the key role mimesis and its cognates play in Greek. Taken together, these occlusions comprise an interpretive strategy for maintaining that the *Republic*'s admiration for ontology extends to its analysis of how political and social roles work.

The rest of the chapter proceeds by introducing Book VIII's portrait of democratic disorder in some detail. I then analyze two interpretations of the scene that I take to be representative of political theory's engagement with the passages on democracy. Specifically, I track the widely shared critical habits that lead the theorists Arlene Saxonhouse and Jacques Rancière to turn away from crucial matters of language, idiom, and historical context so that they can situate *Republic* VIII at the origins of an essentialist, antidemocratic plea for fixed order and whence it can secure an emancipatory democratic ideal (in spite of Plato). Notwithstanding important differences in emphasis and approach, their accounts ultimately converge in domesticating the dialogue's explorations of political difference because they presuppose that the *Republic* endorses something like "essence" or "identity" in its reflections on democratic politics. I contend that the readings mistakenly commit the Book VIII passage to a belief in kinship for deciding, and cognition for discerning, democratic status. Their inattention to the language of theatricality and performativity in the passage leads both thinkers to miss that the *Republic* is challenging, not endorsing, the necessity and naturalness that democracy gives its (own) distinctions.

The conclusion to the chapter advances a new reading of the passage in light of the role mimesis plays in Greek. I demonstrate first that scholarship's tendency to evaluate mimesis as a "negative" concept in Plato's ontology has effectively displaced it from the passage (when it sits in plain view). I then explore the new political-theoretical possibilities that a focus on performativity and theatricality opens up. To figure democratic freedom as an act of mimesis, as Plato does, is to explore democratic anxieties about the instability of naturalized distinctions. I end the chapter by establishing a deeper intertextual context for this position with a reading of the Funeral Oration. I cast the Book VIII scene as a rejoinder to this famous Periclean pronouncement of democratic exceptionalism. Whereas Pericles suggests democratic freedom depends on an act of "mere" mimicry, Socrates insinuates that democracy fails to keep the dangers it courts at bay. I argue that the *Republic* prompts us to consider whether democratic equality is undone not by its openness but by the nature of its exclusions.

Democracy's Topsy-Turvy World

It is late in the evening when Socrates and Glaucon finally resume their conversation where Polemarchus' whispering had previously interrupted them.[8] They return to the four main types of unjust constitutions to claim that each is brought into being by the character of its inhabitants (445a–449b, 544a, 544e). Democracy, the third, is born from violence. The desperate and disenchanted rise up against oligarchs in a civil war that buries some and exiles the rest (557a). In response to their oppression, the free men grant themselves equal share in the city's constitution, public office, and speech (557b). But this political freedom (357d) quickly encourages an attitude of *exousia*, Socrates says, the "license" to be whoever and do whatever they want (557b, 558d). The citizens are drawn to spectacle

[8] The precise substance of Polemarchus' interruption remains a mystery to Socrates, who goes out of his way to describe the strange exchange in detail. He tells us that, drawing his cloak to his face, Polemarchus whispered in Adeimantus' ear and conveyed what we might conclude is a preoccupation with kinship's earlier retooling. Biological relations between parents and children will not suffice as a criterion for caretaking or membership status in the callipolis. At Polemarchus' provocation, Adeimantus thinks Socrates needs to elaborate—to air an argument for this rethinking. Whispering is an appropriately metic mode of expression: it falls somewhere between speech and silence and has productive (and pointed) effects: the whisper incites the Socratic elaboration of his redrawing of the city's kinship lines and thus implicates *metoikia* directly. That Plato has the metic host attempt to conceal himself in the act of asking for an argument about the artifice and political utility of kinship criteria is striking: the scene draws attention to the metic as, on the one hand, the figure whose kinship bars him from political speech and, on the other, the figure whose constitutive exclusion provokes the rethinking.

and consumed by excess. Eventually they are unwilling even to hold the offices that give their political freedom meaning. If the city's democratic institutions start to feel like a burden, you do not have to obey the people you have appointed to office "if you don't feel like it," Socrates explains; "nor go to war when the city is at war, nor to be at peace when everyone else is, unless peace is what you want" (557e). Noncitizens in the polis may stand formally outside the boundaries of full membership, but in democracy, even citizens fail to actualize their privileges and responsibilities. Book VIII's depiction of democratic indifference contrasts sharply with the iconic picture of the self-actualizing Athenian demos. The autonomous men of the earth are nowhere to be found in this account. Here heteronomous men of appetite roam a topsy-turvy landscape in which the freedom to participate fails to engender political activity and might even preclude it. In the short term, Adeimantus concedes, this is a delightful way to live (558a). But in time, even the call to participate will feel restrictive and citizens will take no pleasure in public life.

Democratic concepts and values appear to undergo a crisis in meaning, a transformation that will find eventual expression in the rampant transgression of political and social roles with which I began the chapter. Once the colorful, tolerant democracy rejects moderation and economy, traditional democratic principles lose their power. People privilege insolence as they had sophistication. They think of shamelessness as though it were courage and pursue extravagance with an ease that only generosity would have previously warranted (558b, 560d). A shared impulse to defy people in leadership leads citizens to usurp power even from those whose positions they had originally sanctioned by vote. For what democracy defines as "good," its "insatiable desire for it" leads the city to neglect all else (562c).[9] A love of freedom makes the citizenry's practice of ruling over itself – the very condition for that freedom – impossible. The distinction between rulers and ruled is the first to fade. This "anarchy" then spreads, like a plague, to people's households:[10]

[9] This is Rowe's translation in Plato 2012b.

[10] Ober writes that *anarchia* in the classical Greek context would describe "a condition in which the magisterial offices of the government are vacant, generally due to civil strife over who is to occupy them" (Ober 2008: 4n3, 6). This is the case in Herodotus (9.23), who uses the word to describe a military situation in which there was no one to give orders. The term is used in an indirect speech attributed by Thucydides (6.72.4) to the Syracusan general Hermocrates, who deploys the word to describe the disorder of troops. At this point in the history, the Athenians have yet to be defeated. Xenophon (*Hell.* 2.3) says that Athenians used the term *anarchia* to describe 404 as the archon-less year—the time that the Thirty Tyrants chose Pythodoros as archon (a chief magistrate). A fourth-century association of anarchy with that year makes the application of anarchy to democracy here

> A father, for example, gets accustomed to being like (*homoion*) a child, and being afraid of his sons. A son gets used to being like his father. He feels no respect for his parents. All he wants is to be free. The metic is made equal to (*exisousthai*) the citizen (*astos*), and the citizen to the metic. And the same with the foreigner (*xenos*) . . .. In general, the young *resemble* [*apeikazontai*] their elders and challenge them in speech and action. The old descend to the level of the young. They pepper everything with wit and humor, imitating [*mimoumenoi*] the young, because they don't want to be harsh or dictatorial . . . But the high-water mark of mass-freedom in a city of this kind comes when those who have been bought as slaves – whether male or female – are no less free than those who bought them. As for the relationship of women to men and men to women, I all but forgot to mention the extent of *isonomia* and *eleutheria* between them. (562e–563b)[11]

The *Republic* leaves little doubt that democratic freedom produces a contagion of transgression that eventually, in the figure of tyranny, comes to threaten freedom itself. On the face of it, democracy cannot help but disregard the laws, conventions, and distinctions it needs to safeguard its ability to rule.

Plato depicts democracy in the throes of a self-defeating operation. Less clear are the reasons democratic freedom produces this particular kind of unsettling.[12] Why should freedom take the form of an imitative practice in Socrates' account?

Plato's Lament?

In a careful reading of Book VIII, Arlene Saxonhouse seeks an answer for this demise. She locates the source of collapse in democracy's apparent

striking: Plato's scene describes the movement from democracy to tyranny, and it suggests the anarchic behavior associated with the Thirty Tyrants is already taking root in democracy.

11 The italics here are mine. I have combined Griffith's translation with my own throughout this passage. In particular where Griffith's English word choices do not accurately capture the multiple and repeated mimetic relations between statuses, I have chosen standard English translations of Plato's Greek terms that illuminate this often overlooked and critical dimension of the passage. I find that translations frequently mislead when they suggest Plato's language is one of equivalences of identity. Nowhere does Plato indicate that one *is* the other; rather, his examples in Greek suggest a much more complex and equivocal relation.

12 Chris Emlyn-Jones and William Preddy introduce the recent Loeb translation of the *Republic* with the curious evaluation that the passage's narrative mode betrays a shortcoming of argumentation. Assuming a heuristic hierarchy that would classify the dialogue's range of dramatic styles in a descending ladder of philosophical prowess, they write that "the markedly vivid rhetorical style which marks Books Eight and Nine masks (was perhaps designed to mask) further problems with the state/soul analogy" (Plato 2013: xxxi). I contend that Plato's prose style is a device that does not conceal the failures of demonstration or logical speech but, in its capacity to show, makes possible (new) thought and experiences for the reader.

aversion to recognizing difference. Attempts to identify a person's membership standing, gender, or class, she argues, are contradictory to democracy's spirit. If democracy "means that nothing and no one is imprisoned in a form," freedom consists in "not being forced into a shape."[13] Without the "capacity to categorize – to recognize similarities and differences so that we can distinguish one person or object from another and recognize as well what unites them," we cannot "define equal and unequal."[14] On this capacity rests not only "the foundation of mathematics" but also "our capacity to distinguish the good from the bad, the noble from the base, *the citizen from the noncitizen*."[15]

The blurred social and political distinctions of Socrates' portrait, on this view, appear to be symptoms of the "epistemological and theoretical problems posed by the absence of forms (*eidē*)" in democracy. If "freedom and equality lead to formlessness," says Saxonhouse, democracy cannot or is unwilling (she says both) to typologize people. Being "true to [democracy's] principles of equality and freedom" means resisting "the tyrannizing of *eidē*, the boundaries and limits that define citizenship and the relations of parts. [Democracy] must resist the typologies and forms that are part of a Platonic philosophical order."[16]

The identitarian logic that takes membership to issue from a pregiven status is apparently neither Athenian nor democratic in Saxonhouse's account. It belongs to "Plato." To the extent that the *Republic* endorses this view, Saxonhouse explains, "Plato does not *merely* favor hierarchy and reject equality as a political principle; he does not *merely* assert the preexistence of *eidē* waiting to be forcefully stamped on individuals to set them into an ordered world. Instead, inquiring into the principles of a democracy, he explores the premises of a fluid nature, of a world without *eidē*."[17] The *Republic* sees no foundation in democracy "for recognizing those who are equal and unequal," Saxonhouse maintains, and so there can be no "hierarchy" in democracy, "whether of male over female, humans over animals, or Greeks over barbarians."[18] There are, or should be, preexisting identities for Plato. It is just that democracy manages to withstand them all.

Let me bracket the question of whether the democracy of Plato's scene is indeed constituted by an allergy to (or lack of) hierarchy in order to consider first how Plato's passage acquires the epistemological assumptions of an identity politics that acknowledges but moves steadily away from the

[13] Saxonhouse 1998: 279. [14] Saxonhouse 1998: 274. [15] My emphasis. Saxonhouse 1998: 273.
[16] Saxonhouse 1998: 274. [17] My emphasis. Saxonhouse 1998: 282. [18] Saxonhouse 1998: 280.

possibility of a "fluid nature." Saxonhouse is upfront about her decision to give pride of place to the concept of identity in her reading of Book VIII. Identity politics provides a kind of missing link between the freedom and status disorder that I suggested Socrates evokes but does not theorize fully. From there, Saxonhouse is able to envision democratic freedom evolving into, and eventually becoming tantamount to, a practice of resisting identity formations (i.e., expressive status). The reason? Democracy cannot or does not want to tell difference. It is the *politeia* that rebels against an identity complex of gender, class, and culture in neat opposition to the callipolis, which is assumed not only to desire the discovery of such formations but also to ensure it by recourse to a "Platonic philosophic order." So long as Plato's primary problem with democracy concerns its inability and unwillingness to recognize difference, Book VIII is vested with a familiar strain of antidemocratic and essentialist polemic best exemplified by the premises of the callipolis.

What is the textual support for this view? Although Saxonhouse is careful to qualify that her interpretation reaches for the "forms" not as "a vision of the Good" but as a general "mechanism for categorization,"[19] it is worth asking whether the use of this terminology introduces an ontologizing gesture that it is meant simply to convey. The convoking of democracy and the forms (*eidē*) is supposed to be motivated by Plato's own language. Noting that the text employs the word for "forms" in a different discussion of regime types and their corresponding human characters (though, for the latter, it also employs words like *psychē*), Saxonhouse brings the forms into the Book VIII passage about democratic performance as a way of patterning the problems that she thinks plague democracy in Plato's dialogue.[20] Thus the forms function as a kind of a theoretical shorthand for designating a range of activities that Saxonhouse assumes that the callipolis rulers will be good at and the democracy's rulers (therefore) bad: identifying similarities and differences, discerning them in people (and things), and categorizing them accordingly. So positioned, how could democracy not self-destruct? The polis lacks the forms that "enable us to order what we experience and enable us to live in this world."[21]

I linger on Saxonhouse's reading because there are significant political and theoretical implications to presupposing that Socrates introduces

[19] Saxonhouse 1998: 273.

[20] In order to cast people as the reified "human counterparts" to the forms, Saxonhouse quotes from passages that expound on dispositions of the *psychē*. For the relationship between city and soul as an analogy, see Ferrari 2003.

[21] Saxonhouse 1998: 276.

"democracy's incapacity to assess who rules, to decide who – metic, slave, women, Cyclops, horse – is inside or outside the city" as an "epistemological problem."[22] The view attributes to democracy's social and political categories a pregiven status for the *Republic*, which is to say it holds that they exist for "Plato" independent of democracy's "inability (or unwillingness) to engage" them.[23] Identities are assumed, for Plato, to precede the moment in which they unfold performatively. If this is right, then the metic's invocation in Book VIII – the singular explicit reference to metics in the dialogue – would imply that Athenian statuses like *metoikos* have something like corresponding forms in and for the *Republic*. And yet we know from previous chapters that this idea is better seen as a democratic fiction that would be difficult to square with the critique of Athenian membership the *Republic* has offered thus far.

In the end, the Book VIII that emerges from Saxonhouse's reading assumes that membership is a question of cognition for Plato rather than Athens, a democracy that tries to isolate "true" parentage and bestow citizen and metic status accordingly. If one's loss of distinction in democracy is really a forgetting of the forms, as she suggests, then membership in the *Republic* is a conscious identity not a spectrum of behaviors and democratic rule an exercise in recognizing, however poorly, what is "already" there. The last chapter maintained that the capacity to assign people in the callipolis to their apparently pregiven classes depends on the application of a philosophical knowledge that the demos lacks. But even in the callipolis, acts only ever approximate the idealized, formal categories that are propagated by the myth of the metals. The semblance of their perfect correspondence occurs after the fact, as it were, through a risky practice of interpretation and judgment. Hence the necessity of the noble lie, which teaches the politically convenient falsehood that political statuses express an internal attribute. What I have been calling the identitarian reading of Book VIII, then, assumes that the *Republic* exhibits a preoccupation with discerning statuses as fixed types *even as* it reveals their performativity and fluidity, and it takes for granted the *Republic*'s investment in the naturalness of particular Athenian categories. The main difficulty with this view is that the *Republic* does not actually present

22 Saxonhouse 1998: 282.

23 Although people are distinguished according to an idea of natural aptitude in the callipolis, the shapes of people's souls are largely the *effects* of institutions, practices, and discourses. These are the dimensions of material culture (*paideia*) the dialogue spends its duration investigating and imagining. Hence, mimesis's ubiquity in the *Republic*. For an excellent discussion of *paideia*, see Burnyeat 1997.

democratic politics as a crisis over (knowing) who people are. As previous chapters indicated, the need to know who someone "is" is an Athenian problem: it would certainly be difficult to know who a citizen is in the democracy Socrates describes, just as it could be difficult to tell a citizen from a metic in Athens, but the Book VIII passage never mentions distinguishing or categorizing, successful or failed, in a democratic context. What it does explore are the things people in democracy do: act like, resemble, and imitate.

To see how the democratic trouble in status might be better read as an effect of the regime's own foundation in a logic of natural difference, I want to turn now to Jacques Rancière's reading of Book VIII. For when Rancière sets out to trace a similar tradition of antidemocratic polemic, he finds reason to conclude from the passage that democracy is not a form of rule but a rupture from the logic of foundation (*archē*) altogether. In *Hatred of Democracy*, Rancière provides an extended interpretation of the Book VIII scene that dovetails in striking ways with Saxonhouse's view that democracy's status trouble is an epistemological problem for Plato. He too reads the passage outside the context of its Athenian membership politics and overlooks the language of mimesis (the acting like) that runs through the examples in the text. His reading concludes that Socrates' remarks are more than secondary evidence of democracy's love of freedom. Through the series of "inverted" relations, the *Republic* furnishes the apparently perennial insight that democracy is actually definitively explosive of kinship. Rancière writes of the passage,

> Everything here is of course upside down. But this disorder is reassuring. If all the relations are inverted at the same time, then it seems that they are all of the same nature, that all these subversions express the same inversion of the natural order – and hence it appears that this order exists and that the political relation also pertains to that nature. The entertaining portrait of the disorder of both democratic man and society is a way of putting things in order: if democracy inverts the relation of the governing and the governed in the same way it inverts all other relations, then it confirms *a contrario* that this relation really is homogenous to the others, and that governors and governed can be distinguished by means of a principle of distinction that is as certain as the relation between those who beget and those who are begotten, those who come first and those who come after: a principle that assures continuity between the order of society and the order of government, because it firstly assures the continuity between the order of human convention and that of nature.[24]

[24] Rancière 2006: 38.

The *Republic* lumps political and biological relations together as a way of claiming their simultaneous, neat, and complete inversion. Here Rancière faults Plato, seducer par excellence, for trying to order democracy's messiness, a structure that Rancière will nevertheless find useful for his own theoretical purposes. I will come back to the question of who is really doing the ordering here. I want first to look at how Rancière reads the *Republic* so as to cast democracy's penchant for confusion in terms of an inevitable drive toward rebelliousness.

The image of orderly democratic disorder, according to Rancière, serves a normative argument for a politics grounded in nature. When Plato has Socrates denigrate democracy's "breaking with the power of kinship," the philosopher is actually revealing his own investment in "the power of birth." The problematic excess Socrates observes in democracy, then, is not the sign of "a supposed consumptive madness." For the *Republic*, says Rancière, democracy's "scandal" actually lies in its "disjoining of entitlements to govern" *from* "the order of nature."[25]

To find this symmetry in the *Republic*'s account reassuring and ordering, however, Rancière must look past another kind of mirroring. This is the performance of social and political roles that would actually further the sort of anxiety – the unpredictable disorder of democracy – Rancière thinks Plato tries so hard to inoculate the reader against. If Rancière neglects to see the role mimesis plays here, it is because he too presupposes that the referents of Socrates' examples (men, women, metics, slaves, citizens, old, and young) have an extrapolitical foundation for Plato.[26] This (mis)judgment licenses and finds reinforcement in a range of interpretive moves in *Hatred of Democracy*, including the claim that Book VIII comprises a list of inversions.[27] Rancière reads Plato's acts of imitation as violent disorders in and against nature in order to construct a conception of politics as "rupture" both through and against a Plato who holds that democracy is not a political regime precisely *because* it signifies a break with "the order of kinship." Indeed, democracy is not a regime, says

[25] Rancière 2006: 40–41.

[26] There is particular irony to Rancière's overlooking mimesis and its related ideas in this section of the dialogue. Mimesis is a recurrent theme in Rancière's thought, including in his engagements with Plato, where he interprets the *Republic*'s "one artisan, one craft principle" as a way of restricting, if not combating, the mimesis that plagues democracy (Rancière 2003). In Athens, the worker is not (just) in his workshop but also in the space of public discussion, performing the additional role of the demos (see Rancière 2006a: 43) and thus, like the poet, theater, and mimetician, assuming more than one form.

[27] Rancière 2006b: 36, 40–41, and 45.

Rancière.[28] But, he adds against this "Plato," only once the "principle of government is separated from the law of kinship" can (democratic) politics possibly emerge.

As an original site for a contemporary democratic tension and under the weight of this problem's concomitant binarisms (e.g., philosophy/politics; democracy/callipolis; order/disorder), Socrates' picture could seem to do little but express the aforementioned view that democracy, the abstract regime, is characterized by formlessness. From Rancière's particular angle, Book VIII suggests democracy's promising fatal flaw is its rejection of kinship or, as it is sometimes recalibrated, its rejection of any foundation whatsoever. This Platonist reading of the *Republic*'s disorderly and disordering democracy depends, as the identitarian account also did, on a particular understanding of the callipolis as a "reordering project." For Rancière, explains Samuel Chambers, philosophy "arrives on the scene" with Plato in order to "supplant the *kratos* of the *demos* with the *archē* of the philosopher king."[29] In this rendering of political philosophy's origins and principles, Plato's text appears indifferent and irrelevant to its own Athenian context, in particular to its notions of democratic difference.

I vowed earlier to return to the question, provoked again here by the language of rupture, of whether Book VIII presents democracy as un- or antihierarchical, as Saxonhouse suggested. It is a question that both theorists sidestep because they read democracy "back" from a callipolis they hold to be singularly invested in hierarchy rather than revelatory of hierarchy's various iterations, machinations, and indeterminate effects. And for different reasons, as we have seen, each reader takes up the democracy of Book VIII as an abstract ideal, not a historical-political regime, that is constituted not by the boundaries a democratic regime draws but by the totalizing resistance it exhibits to such distinctions.

The callipolis aims for rigidity, but it is not immune to mistaken judgment or interlopers. It is also not the only hierarchical regime the *Republic* explores. The rhetorical structure and figurative temporality that comprise Socrates' narrative also give us reason to doubt the antihierarchical characterization of democracy on which Book VIII's identitarian and essentialist portraits depend for both their salience and their persuasiveness. Socrates' story of political and social transgression does not indicate that democracy is characterized by a simultaneous collapsing of all

[28] Although the *Republic* calls democracy a *politeia*, as it does all the other political arrangements it explores in Book VIII, Rancière sets democracy apart and maintains that, for Plato, it is distinguished from the other regimes by its lack of grounding.

[29] Chambers 2012: 135.

distinction. Socrates never says that democracy emerges *as soon as* "inversions" of social roles occur.[30] Democracy, as a *politeia*, precedes this anarchic movement, though even anarchy occurs in time and is marked by a gradual movement toward the perceived convergence of people's behavior.[31] Rancière reads the compressed time conjured by the passage, however, to imply that "all the relations are inverted at the same time" and makes democracy's appearance in the narrative appear synonymous with absolute, sudden, orderly, and complete collapse, as if democracy were constituted by this chaos.[32]

What if we paid more literal attention to the vague open-endedness connoted by the lines (562e), with their string of present infinitives in Greek (e.g., *ethizesthai; gignesthai; phobeisthai; aischunesthai; dedienai; exisousthai*)? The passage would suggest something different, not totalizing disorder but the recurrent violability of all naturalized status. A great deal hangs on this ability to see that the democracy of Book VIII precedes the moment of transgression with which it is aligned in the readings I have been criticizing. The shift in perspective helps us appreciate that distinctions of kinship and law, which is to say, distinctions of "nature," are *native* to this democracy. The identities that are (eventually) hard to keep straight make up democracy's own constitutive oppositions.

Seen in in this light, the *Republic* gives rise to a rather different set of concerns about the logic of difference that democracy employs. The social and political boundaries of democracy stand in danger not of being unrecognized merely but of betraying a particularly dangerous similitude, precisely because they do not have the solid foundation in nature the democratic city claims them to have. I say "in danger" because in spite of the flattened and hurried character of Socrates' dramatic allegory of political change, there is no reason to conclude that democratic categories cease to mandate conduct altogether or exert force simply because they are indeterminate. The city's distinctions are preceded and enabled by a compulsory political discourse, like autochthony, like the myth of the metals, even if, when, and although the performance of these ideals fails consistently to command belief in the correspondence between a person's status and performance. That is what noble lies do. Thus, the passing that democracy enables here need not render the city's hierarchical order of

[30] In Socrates' story, democracy inherits some of its political categories (from oligarchy) and generates others, distinctions that are formalized in the democratic polis and thus peculiar to that regime.

[31] As Saxonhouse points out (1998: 274), no word for "decline" appears in the Book Eight passage. We read instead of changing (*metaballei*) and moving (*kinēthēsetai*) at 545Id and 54Id5.

[32] It is not clear that anarchy should flatten; we might instead think about how unpredictable it is.

inclusion wholly inefficacious, just as Cephalus' being like a citizen does not render the metic-citizen distinction unimportant or theoretically unilluminating.[33] As I suggest in the final section, the status trouble in Book VIII indicates not a total absence of, or even a resistance to, hierarchy but the constant and inevitable possibility of status transgression – an uneven, unpredictable, and strategic instability.

Equipped with this alternative understanding of the temporality Plato's language affords and the sense of unpredictability it conjures, I return briefly to Rancière's reading. In addition to assuming a scene of complete collapse, his interpretation notes that the list of upside-down social roles – fathers act like sons; slaves seem like their masters; foreigners and immigrants are made equal to citizens and vice versa – are grouped alongside other instances of inversion (e.g., the old and young) as "trivial examples of the same kind" (*kai smikra toiade alla gignetai* [563a3]).[34] What are they examples of? Rancière's account of the political theoretical import of the passage turns partly on his answer to this question. We saw that Rancière locates the common feature of the distinctions in their source, which he posits in nature, an assumption that depends on a prior interpretive move: the privileging of relations of kin. Nature grounds convention in the *Republic*, he says, and therefore should also ground politics, since for Plato nature is the only criterion for political rule. Democracy disrupts this neat correspondence and is therefore distasteful to Plato.[35] Yet there is orderliness even in Plato's portrait of democratic self-subversion, Rancière says, which makes it not as threatening as it might otherwise be. Plato privileges the father–son relation because of its "certainty," Rancière adds, and assumes the ontological and interpretive priority of a kinship status (e.g., father) rooted in facts of birth.

Anxieties over paternity, however, pervade extant classical Athenian literature, especially tragic poetry. As Ion showed, the father–son relation may be the least secure, in biological or epistemic terms. Not only is the father–son relation indeterminate of membership status in the *Ion*, the

[33] We find this insight elsewhere in Athenian thought. Consider, for example, the anonymous fifth-century author of the *Politeia* of Athens. The "Old Oligarch" emphasizes the significant legal privileges enjoyed by citizens in democracy at the same time, however, that he laments the woefully intemperate conduct and appearance of citizens, metics, and slaves, which makes it easy to confuse them in practice—to treat them differently from what their juridical status says they are (Ps-Xen., *Const. of Athens*, 1.10).

[34] This is Griffith's translation in Plato 2000.

[35] Rancière 2006b: 38. Elsewhere, as the myth of the metals suggests, the *Republic* does propose that in the callipolis, membership responsibilities should accord with one's natural and virtuous capacities. It is not clear that Socrates would find democracy's social and political distinctions natural.

metic–citizen relation emerged as the "natural" political distinction most illuminating of how classification works.[36] The *Republic* also presents kinship as a willfully constructed relation that need not and should not serve as a criterion for caretaking or membership status in the callipolis.[37]

To invest the *Republic* in the power of birth, then, one would need to hold that in its discussion of different regimes, the dialogue is concerned, as Saxonhouse also suggested, with showing that like models of truth, categories of identity – including those based in ties of blood – exist even in the absence of any activity. One would need, in other words, to claim that the passage on the blurriness of distinction emphasizes the importance of "being" (a father) not "acting" (like one) when it permits just the opposite. Even Rancière may ultimately be unable to manage the determinism he puts into play here: "[a]s certain as the relation between those who beget and those who are begotten" may not be very certain at all.

The aforementioned stress on Plato's investment in nature and kinship is important to Rancière's theoretical project: it enables him to maintain that in place of an economy of kinship, democracy posits the "law of chance" and the "absence of every title" to rule, which manifests itself most clearly in the practice of drawing lots. But insofar as Plato's text registers that classical Athens did not actually throw off all entitlements to rule, there is reason to doubt whether the democracy of Book VIII ought to stand for a rupture with the order of kinship rather than the equivocal productions that can result from a democracy's kinship order. My disagreement with Rancière, then, is not over his historical (in)accuracy, however telling its contours may be. Nor do I think his occasional or inconsistent use of democracy as a specifically classical Greek preoccupation poses a challenge to his theorization of democracy, which is not contained in his writing by any particular historical example. Rather, my interest in the Athenian context of Plato's text is intended not as a claim about the possibility or merits of unmediated access to this reality but as a claim about the theoretical toll this sort of decontextualizing exacts. What appears to readers like Rancière as a recurring, abstract formulation about disorder comes at the expense of a *Republic* that intervenes in specific

[36] In the *Republic*, the exchange of roles between father and son seems like an extension, if not an effect, of their equal citizen standing in the polis.

[37] On the particular issue of fathering or parenting, see Book V of the *Republic*. Socrates does not assume a correspondence between begetting and caretaking. In fact, he argues that children in the callipolis may be separated from their parents and raised by people of their own metal class (459d–459e; 461d–461e). In short, there is no "kinship" in the ideal city, Saxonhouse (1998: 277) notes, because there are no kin.

historical debates about membership and exclusion; it comes at the expense of finding in Plato an ally for a certain (resonant) democratic self-criticism.

Hatred of Democracy's reading of Book VIII derives much of its rhetorical force from inverting what it casts as Plato's original inversion so as to locate a Platonic, which is to say originary, ground for a theory of democratic politics as rupture. It would thus seem worth asking, as Kirstie McClure does, "So – what about those Greeks?" Could there be "some historical sense irreducible to invocations of 'the beginning' of the Western tradition of political philosophy?"[38] In what ways is Plato's political theory (not) read so that it can speak without fail of order and essence? Do the sorts of invocations of Plato and democracy we find in Rancière's reading actually depend on not seeing the *Republic* as a situated text?

Rancière is "careful to distinguish the demos as a theoretical concept from its historical origins," as McClure points out. "For him the demos is not necessarily 'the poor,' much less the poor of fifth-century Athens. In fact, the demos has no positive qualities at all; it is, rather, the 'unqualified.'" That may be one reason Rancière's own thought frequently depicts the demos "rub[bing] shoulders with the people, the citizens, the workers or proletarians."[39] If historically specific terms serve as interchangeable placeholders here, it is because this rhetorical strategy serves a deeper theoretical claim in which "the people" is by definition always "an abstract supplement," "an empty, supplementary, [sic] part," a "void" in relation to "any actual (ac)count . . . of the qualifications for part-taking in the community."[40] "Differentially located in time and place," McClure notes, "they do not do so in the same way – yet each appears as something like an exemplary instance of political invention in which the part of the unaccounted for is successfully identified with the political community as a whole."[41]

But however self-conscious or indiscriminate this use of historical examples, the "demos" emerges as an *exemplary* example in Rancière's text.[42] Fifth-century Athens, writes Richard Halpern, "has an important

[38] McClure 2003: paragraph 27. [39] McClure 2003: paragraph 29.

[40] Rancière (2001: paragraphs 14 and 15). Samuel Chambers has suggested to me, however, that this decontextualizing may be an intentional blindness that enables Rancière to engage in his own political context of 1980s and 1990s French republicanism (personal communication, September 4, 2015).

[41] McClure 2003: paragraph 29.

[42] From time to time, the specifically Athenian demos does turn up, as in the "Ten Theses on Politics" (Rancière 2001), where the Cleisthenic reforms serve to illustrate a democratic break in the police logic that runs from the principle of birth to the principle of wealth. But what of Pericles' Citizenship Law, which would suggest a democratic investment in kinship?

foundational standing in Rancière's thought" in part because of the position occupied by Plato, who "in founding political philosophy" reveals the ongoing complicity between that discourse and what Rancière calls the "police."[43] To say, however, that Athens has a special status in Rancière's thought because of the series of "fundamental connections" Plato draws between aesthetics and politics is to make even clearer Rancière's investment in a certain Plato, the supposed author of a philosophical tradition rather than the writer whom Pierre Vidal-Naquet describes as the "witness to the changes, or what some would call the crisis, that affected the Greek city in the fourth century BC."[44] And yet Rancière's critical approach implicitly acknowledges that Plato's dialogues emerge through and against Athenian practices and discourses. According to Jason Frank, a historically sensitive approach would "risk fixing the experiences and actions of historical agents within an unquestioned field of categories and identities" for Rancière.[45] Yet its eschewal has the ironic effect of sealing Plato's text in amber even as it trades on the symbolic weight of the *Republic*'s cultural accretions.

How can the *Republic* on the one hand be *of* Athens, weaving stories out of historical places and faces, and, on the other, constituting meaning (only) by effacing the very historical specificity that runs through it? This is, as Chambers notes, precisely what "political philosophy," as identified with Plato, seeks to do in Rancière's estimation. Through a series of universalizing moves, philosophical thinking "identifies politics with the deployment of the properties of a type of man or a mode of life," as in the constitutional types of Book VIII, the membership classes in the callipolis, and the city–soul analogy that dominates the *Republic*. In Rancière's understanding, then, Plato uses a "theory of 'man' in the service of a philosophy of order: to provide a framework into which each person, with his or her proper role, can be made/forced to fit."[46] The callipolis is a reordering project, in other words, because Plato is responding to democracy's eventuality. But the form this reordering takes in the mode of political "philosophy" is assumed to foreclose an interpretation of the *Republic* within the very historical context of its provocation. The democratic conditions that are said to inspire the callipolis are somehow only secondarily illuminating of the text's political theoretical meanings and concerns.

[43] Halpern 2011: 565. [44] Vidal-Naquet 1995: 21. [45] Jason Frank 2015: 250.
[46] Chambers 2012: 107.

There is something curious about assuming that the *Republic* is most legible or theoretically meaningful at the doctrinal register in which its ideas are supposedly postulated. According to Linda Zerilli, this sort of critical posture imagines that "the theorist stands above the disorder he purports to describe and is a master of the signifying structures he employs."[47] Yet it masks a prior sleight of hand, by which the theorist's meanings are made accessible and univocal (i.e., the way Plato supposedly wanted them to be). The Plato or Platonism this interpretive strategy produces (in control, straightforwardly knowable, benignly transmitted) enables and is enabled by the *Republic*'s historical decontextualization.[48] The act of dislocation prepares the dialogue to serve as a model for such enduring problematics as the paradox of democratic rule with which I began this chapter. Insofar as this hermeneutics necessarily abstracts as it attends to the text, however, it finds affirmation in the very practices of abstraction it generates but attributes to the *Republic*.

The universalizability of Plato's portrait of democracy – its ability to speak across time and space to late-modern concerns with democracy's formlessness – turns in part on figuring Book VIII's trouble in status as a strictly conceptual rather than historical-political problem. It is hardly clear that Socrates' own narrative efforts at "typologizing" necessitate a reading of Book VIII's transgressions outside time and place, however. The references the narrative makes to specifically Athenian categories of difference are one obvious reason to consider that the typology that precedes the story of regime change is fruitfully read as an empirically informed project, but it is not the only one. Before Book VIII describes democracy in any detail, Socrates insinuates that the project of schematizing *politeiai* is akin to conducting a series of case studies. After deciding on four types of constitutions, he asks Glaucon to think of "another idea of a *politeia* with a distinct type of its own" (544c6–544d1).[49] But he immediately cautions that the dynasties and bought kingships they observe around the world will probably find a place in the categories they have already adumbrated. And in a small but telling wager, Socrates adds that these regimes exist as much among non-Greeks as Greeks (544d).

I pause on these remarks because they help us think differently about what it means for the *Republic* to typologize. Note, in particular, that the schema Socrates proposes is revisable because it emerges in conversation and, perhaps most important for our purposes, in observation of the

[47] Zerilli 1994: 7. [48] On "Platonism," see Derrida 1981. [49] This is my translation.

(shifting) geopolitical relation between Hellas and its *barbaroi.* Considerations of range and groundedness give the typology its explanatory power, and only then do they make worthwhile the subsequent work of fleshing out the typology as a narration – as the tragic and alarming story of political change in which the mimesis passage finds expression. Glaucon's reply is characteristically underwhelming ("There are certainly lots of strange regimes that people talk about" [544d]) but manages at least to highlight the contingency of the enterprise.[50] The democracy these characters consider is not only or merely an ideal. It is also a historical, cultural, and discursive space.

The telescoped story of subsumed and subsuming polities that follows from this short exchange between characters lends important traction to the *Republic*'s exploration of democracy by focusing on the appetites of the polity's archetypes. Though hot on the trail of "typology," the account that proceeds actually evokes little in an analytic mode. Socrates lingers on experience, and he narrates society's dissipations as a series of psychic metamorphoses. More tragedy than elenchus, this account is a loosely temporal tale of political movement that stops short of offering an explicit argument about the relationship between democratic freedom and the conduct that follows (from) it. Plato's prose may not explain the mimicry that characterizes and menaces democracy in these moments, but it invites us to consider and even to feel that the political problems bedeviling democracy may be best theorized along affective lines.[51]

I suggested in Chapter 4 that readers typically displace the nativism of Athenian membership politics from the *Republic*'s world so that pregiven political difference can re-appear more safely as the wishful and original notion of an antidemocratic thinker. This angle emerges from a *Republic* that somehow fails to comprehend the democratic nativism it otherwise goes out of its way to stress (even if casually), as Chapter 3's discussion of the Piraeus setting showed. If, as I have been suggesting, this failure of comprehension is less a problem of the *Republic*'s than of its interpretation, it is a highly generative oversight. For the much-beloved contemporary democratic ideal of the agonistic, socially mobile, egalitarian ancient polis that cannot help resisting its own taxonomies comes into view as the product and flipside of this dialogue. It is born of a Platonist lament about democratic flux and of a longing for an earlier time when polities

50 This is Rowe's translation (Plato 2012b).

51 Rancière (2001: paragraph 28) writes that Plato's tendency to theorize regimes according to a "type of man" or a city's "ways of life" is a form of "concrete" sociological analysis that only aids the political philosophical project of reducing democracy to a sociological phenomenon.

left "nature" alone to do its distinguishing work. In looking past the ways Athenian democracy did not simply erase but also produced "natural" divisions, readers unwittingly enlist the *Republic* in the reproduction of a chauvinistic status quo: the categories of woman, metic, and citizen appear on behalf of this text to preexist and determine their use in democracy, much as an autochthony politics claims they do.[52] As a critical tendency, this way of reading impedes the *Republic* from shining a light on how politics operates in practice.

We saw earlier that the *Republic*'s myth of the metals is designed to close the (Athenian) gap between membership assignment and its practice, a gap we now see Book VIII staging in its description of democracy. (Recall that passing in the callipolis is conceptually impossible; the "wrong" performance will necessitate a status reassignment.) The democracy of Book VIII, however, does much more than figure a problem for the callipolis to solve. It positions democracy as the constitution that establishes and menaces its own borders. Its narrative structure also invites us to draw our own political conclusions about what this operation really means. Let us set aside the assumption that Plato's text is either taking for granted or gunning to resecure antecedent democratic identities and have another look at what it says. If nature is not necessarily the thread running through Socrates' examples, what is? The young resemble their elders; the old imitate the young; a father becomes accustomed to being *like* his son. "Psychological and behavioral assimilation is a phenomenon [Plato] acknowledges in various contexts of his writings," writes Stephen Halliwell. "It appears ... for example, in the fascinating claim in *Republic* 8 that the pervasive freedom of a democratic culture leads to a kind of psychological (and specifically 'mimetic') exchange of roles between fathers and sons."[53]

Mimesis and its cognates set the terms of Socrates' comments about democracy. If the acts of imitation to which democratic freedom amounts, in Socrates' story, do not evince a struggle against an identity politics, as others conclude, could it be a sign of that politics and its ambiguous effects?

Mimesis, a Political Concept

Mimesis is a difficult concept to translate or delineate in the *Republic*, because while it refers to a complex of related ideas such as imitation and

[52] Saxonhouse (1998) concedes that the "forms" through which a democracy fails to recognize its "parts" may not be natural, but this prompts a question: in what would democracy's distinctions be based?

[53] Halliwell 2002: 76.

representation, neither term fully captures the ground mimesis covers in the dialogue's explorations of human action, learning, culture, making, and discourse. Halliwell parses mimesis according to what he sees as its two operations in the text: "one fixes on the complex relationship of 'likeness' between mimetic images and the features of the world they (purport to) represent, the other on the psychological implications and consequences of mimesis for its audiences." But, he cautions, Plato presents "exploratory, shifting, and inconclusive arguments on the subject, not at all the monolithic 'doctrine'" that is one of the "supreme myths of modern histories of aesthetics."[54] Indeed, one of the things that complicates the standard negative valuation of Platonic mimesis as a "decline from truth" is the text's narrative style, according to Philippe Lacoue-Labarthe. The *Republic* takes up the philosophical goal of "circumventing mimesis" by "[mimesis'] own means." Plato, after all, "does not speak one word of the *philosophical discourse itself*" but employs mimetic tools – a "mixed" narrative, a character called "Socrates" – to figure philosophical propositions about the dangers and inadequacies of such impersonating enterprises.[55] Insofar as the *Republic* is parasitic on forms of imitative discourse its characters criticize, it exposes its own need for (figuring) foundational, non-mimetic truth. This means the *Republic* reveals not only the dependence of philosophical truth's comprehensibility on mimesis but also the dependence of all argumentation on rhetoric. It would therefore seem necessary, as Derrida suggests, to dismantle the interpretive juggernaut that presents "the truth of adequation" produced by mimesis as "simply," which is to say, merely secondary to another, "more original truth."[56]

The reductive verdict on mimesis nevertheless suggests the concept is a "negative term in Plato's ontology."[57] While this widely held position tends to discount the productive and rhetorical uses of mimesis in the *Republic*'s fictional framing, it has also, if less obviously, steered readers away from exploring its political theoretical implications as an idiom of performance. This section takes up the injunction to think more affirmatively about Plato's use of mimesis by resisting the temptation to treat its diverse emanations as merely privative, which is to say, as signaling a failure to secure or reveal truth, and asking instead what its operation in Book VIII might contribute to the explorations of membership I examined in previous

54 See Halliwell 2002: 25. Dramatic enactment, Halliwell reminds us, is a particularly intense mode of mimesis.
55 Lacoue-Labarthe 1998: 95, 123.
56 Derrida 1998: 27. This approach is implicit in my reading of the noble lie as an open secret.
57 Ford 2002: 95.

chapters. Accounting for the generative and performative dimensions of mimesis, this section shows that the *Republic* mobilizes the concept in Book VIII not to secure but to reveal the workings of democratic difference.

Let us note first that while the contours of the *Republic*'s exploration of mimesis are clearest when Socrates discusses "making" (*poiēsis*), before Plato, making does not seem to have referred to arts of representation; it designated primarily "the production of something material, especially in an artisanal context."[58] The *Republic* aligns crafts like painting and sculpture with arts like singing, music, and dance. In treating them all as mimetic, the dialogue suggests they perform a similar function. Whereas earlier thinkers like Gorgias explored the deceptive power of poems and paintings without invoking mimesis, Plato employs the term to impart that poetry and images, like sound effects and mimicry, are capable of creating "a particular kind of pleasure without necessarily embodying or expressing philosophical truth."[59] In this spirit, poetry, painting, music, and verbal accounts are mimetic modes for expressing both good and bad ideas about the world (394e–403c; *Crit.* 107b). These views and attitudes press themselves on the minds of their audiences, especially, but not only, those of the young.[60] In most cases, people mistake "likenesses" or "copies," which can only *seem* to be, for "models" (*paradeigmata*) of true knowledge. This is one reason Socrates argues for the careful regulation of arts in the callipolis but famously not for their wholesale elimination: stories (*mythoi*) have a significant role to play in shaping the right *paideia* of the callipolis's citizens.[61] The philosopher's childhood, the myth of the metals, and the proposals for the callipolis are all examples of mimesis done right. "Used with knowledge," as Richard McKeon puts it, "there is no danger in imitation."[62] But knowledge, we know, is hard to come by. And so mimetic arts seem simply to falsify, or at least only to resemble, what is true and real.[63] From painter to poet, a *mimētēs* (imitator) has no knowledge of truth, only appearances (601b–601c), and yet there are better and worse instances of mimesis, depending on what (truth or appearance) is being modeled.[64] For these reasons, critics tend to believe that the *Republic* subscribes to an evaluative truth–illusion matrix.

[58] Ford 2002: 134. Acton 2014 explores the meaning of production (*poiēsis*) in an artisanal context.
[59] Ford 2002: 95. [60] Halliwell 2002: 49, 50. [61] Consider, for one, the "noble lie."
[62] McKeon 1936: 14. [63] For an overview of this issue, see Diamond 1997 and McKeon 1936.
[64] To buttress his argument about efficiency, Plato uses mimesis to think through the principle of social specialization in Book II (394e), which argues that the same person cannot do more than one thing well because, as parsed by Halliwell (2002: 51), "no one can engage in effective mimesis, or dramatic representation of 'many things.'" Only the philosopher-ruler is allowed to do more than one thing—to tell myths or, in effect, to lie. See Rancière 2003: 3–30.

Since there is implicitly much at issue for the *Republic*'s political theory in these views, a further point about the *Republic*'s mimetology is worth raising. Plato draws on the resources of a "derivative, probably fifth-century meaning of a word for 'mimicking' or imitating" when he constructs these new mimetic distinctions.[65] What this means is that the *Republic* appropriates a term for "using the body and voice to copy human and animal behavior" and extends it to art, a subject that was until then understood to be distinct from behaviors and phenomena.[66] With this move, Jean-Pierre Vernant points out, Plato directs attention away from the salutary simulation that is achieved between the *mimos* and the one whom the mime copies toward the *mere* "resemblance that joins and yet distinguishes" the image and the thing of which it is the image.[67] No longer capable of actualizing what it represents, images acquire a sort of gaping distance from reality.[68] These observations raise important, albeit familiar, issues about Plato's intervention into the meaning of mimesis. Yet if there is anything like a shared habit of thought constructing the background of this concept's reception as an unequivocally idealizing and hierarchizing term in Plato's thought, it is the ironic tendency to fixate on what is most original in Plato's engagement with mimesis and to look past the traces and performativity of the notion that he is reaching back to the past to use.[69] It is on this dimension that I will now focus.

The *Republic* develops its account of mimesis by exploring and evaluating a range of imitative operations according to the truth value of their models, but the truth–model axis, as Elin Diamond highlights, is only one piece of classical mimesis. Just as important is the concept's duality, its meaning as both guaranteeing "'the objective nature of the work of art, its truth value' (and, by extension, the truth of the represented) and representing, as generative, as performance."[70] Put differently, mimesis denotes both a doing (*mimeisthai*) and a thing done (*mimēma*);[71] it involves the act

65 Ford 2002: 94. "Explicit comparisons between poetry and the visual arts cannot be traced back further in Greece than Simonides," but Simonides (who is invoked in the first book of the *Republic*) never uses *mimeisthai* or related words, argues Ford. Mimesis designated copying (not representing) behavior in the *Homeric Hymn to Apollo*, a work compiled in Simonides' lifetime. See Ford 2002: 97–98.

66 Ford 2002: 94; Potolsky 2006: 16–17. 67 Vernant 1991: 166. 68 Potolsky 2006: 16–17.

69 Just as Book III uses mimesis to describe behavioral modeling rather than artistic or media-driven reproduction (as in Book X), so does the passage in Book VIII.

70 Here Diamond (1997: iv) draws on Lyons and Nichols 1982.

71 Diamond 1997: v. This bidirectionality is clear in Aristotle's idea of *poiēsis*, which is "both the making and thing made"; this making is, for Aristotle, also a kind of mimesis, which he links explicitly to all activity—not just dramatic performance: "Insofar as all human action is always already an imitation of action, it is in its very nature poetic," says Davis (2002: xvi, xvii). Tragedy, for

of imitating as well as its effect, the imitation. This means that the *mimētēs* imitating or upholding the "truth value" of a model also becomes a copy in the act of imitation. (When Ion imitates a metic, for instance, he is not only an Athenian imitating a foreigner but the imitation of a metic.) Writing on the history of Greek practices of theatricality, Edith Hall explains that archaic choruses, as precursors to Athenian dramatic actors, "long played with alternative identities, expressed fluctuating and mutating subjectivities, and incorporated mimetic elements into their gestures." The theatrical, she notes, was constituted by the moment an actor masked his identity and spoke in the voice of another.[72] Even the earliest uses of the word "mimesis" that mean something "approximating 'representation,'" Hall adds, "still retain the early connotation of dressing up in order to act a theatrical role.'"[73] When subsequently "Plato's Socrates evicts theatre from his *Republic*, he objects less to the narratives retold in dramatic plots than to the idea of theatrical impersonation" because "acting goes beyond the idea of role-playing to the *shaping* of nature itself."[74] There is no such thing as merely assuming a role for Plato, Hall suggests, because mimesis, as an act of impersonation, generates what we would call "identities." Book III argues for the careful regulation of upbringing and education on the basis that imitation produces habits that sediment.

Commentators on the *Republic* tend to acknowledge that Plato's mimesis takes the form of a fundamental and vulnerable practice of role-playing and emulation, by which all learning and character formation occurs. But they also retreat from the larger political theoretical possibilities that are implied by the protean character of "identity," as we saw in the previous section, so as to reinvest the text in the supposedly identitarian policies the callipolis pursues. Karen Bassi thus argues on the one hand that "[bodily] impersonations pose an inherent threat to the notion of a core" identity in the *Republic* by "presenting the possibility that this core may only be an effect of bodily acts, and not their cause"[75] and on the other that the "repudiation of the effect of bodily impersonation – overt and political in Plato" nevertheless "functions in the service of creating and maintaining the integrity and stability of the masculine subject."[76] So long as the

Aristotle, is illuminating on this point: "By presenting an alternative to the real as real, all poetry in saying what is not true has as its nature to conceal the true nature of the poet who created it," Davis writes. "Drama, then, by making the poet invisible in its imitation of action is in a way poetry at its most pure" (Davis 2002: xixn8). In other words, the truth that is obscured is the maker behind the deed.

[72] E. Hall 2006: 21. [73] E. Hall 2006: 23. [74] E. Hall 2006: 21, 38–39. [75] Bassi 1998: 23.
[76] Bassi 1998: 30–31.

Republic is read as both fearing and disavowing the troubling insights it provokes, any acknowledgment of the centrality that impersonation and resemblance are accorded in Book VIII's discussion of democracy would seem simply to further support to the expressiveness of pregiven political distinctions, including ones that are said to belong to an "unjust" regime like democracy. Whether readers choose to interpret Book VIII's invocations of mimesis as essentializing or to avoid them completely, they nevertheless occlude the concept's heterogeneity and, more specifically, to foreclose the question of what the meaning of mimesis as impersonation might have to tell us about how democratic difference and sameness operates.

Keeping in mind that mimesis is an established idiom of impersonation and reenactment in and before Plato's present, we are now in a position to attempt a close reading of Book VIII's discussion of democratic disorder and see how this new emphasis on theatricality might open up its political meanings. In freeing mimesis from the static language of the truth–model axis, we can more easily appreciate that what characterizes and constitutes life in democracy is a pluralizing operation of imitation. When it comes to mimesis, one generates or becomes an imperfect copy of a model. What does it mean, then, that Socrates' observations about democratic citizenship are cast as mimetic instances?

Recall that the remarks in Book VIII conjure a series of comparative performances all expressing the same kind of operation. Fathers and sons get used to being "like" (*homoios*) each other. "The metic is made equal (*exisousthai*) to the citizen, and the citizen to the metic. And the same with the foreigner (*xenos*)." The young "resemble their elders and challenge them in speech and action" and vice versa. In their levity, the old end up imitating (*mimoumenoi*) the young. Slaves act as free as their owners. The same goes for men and women, who act like each other (562e–3b).

Four points emerge immediately. (1) Every example takes the form of a dyad. Each dyad expresses an opposition between a privileged and an abject term that in Athens are institutionally and ideologically opposed to each other by the polis's order of inclusion. (2) In every example, the terms are related by a mimetic operation that works two ways. The bidirectionality calls into question the supposed internal stability of the terms and suggests they exist in an uncomfortable relation of interdependence. It is not just that the deprivileged act like citizens. Citizens act like them, too. The doubling of mimesis exemplifies the generative, pluralizing, multidirectional – and potentially endlessly mirroring – operation I suggested earlier is an integral part of the concept. (3) Each relation expresses approximation achieved in practice, not identification. The Greek does not tell us that a citizen *is* a metic but that a citizen is *made equal to* a metic.[77] (A difference in juridical standing would persist.) Approximation implies that no copy will be a perfect iteration of its model, and the bidirectionality of each example belies the possibility that there is any original in the first place. (4) Each comparison is presented as the effect of a performance of particular acts, gestures, and discourses. In portraying the "wrong" categories of identity, the examples reveal the dependence of all identities on performance. The same idea of performance therefore holds for portrayals of the "right" identities, too.

Impersonations may pass as authentic. Rancière concluded from this that people in democracies have a tendency to subvert their own *nature*, to act differently from who (Plato thinks) they really are. But in the passage, there is no status that is not already a mimetic performance and therefore an impersonation. The increasingly frequent and consequently noticeable discord that emerges in democracy between, say, a person called *metoikos* and whatever the autochthony ideal says about *metoikia* affords us a view of the tenuousness of status differentiation. In approximating but never fully realizing what it is to be a metic – there is always the chance one might actualize one's political capacity – the metic risks exposing this and the citizen's status as constructed not natural. As we will see in the next chapter, because little more than one non-Athenian (unoriginal) parent was needed to justify a metic's exclusion from the demos for most of the classical period, metics could resemble citizens in terms of birth as well as in their lived experiences of membership. But the city insinuates that metics are the inadequate copies of citizens, who are the original models. One startling and critical implication of Socrates' application of mimesis, however, is that no original truly exists in democracy. By suggesting one is the other's copy, Socrates' description of the citizen as a *mimetic* copy of the metic troubles both the imitation/original opposition and the metic/citizen opposition. The passage reveals the dependence of Athenian status on being (re)performed or (re)made in certain ways. Plato's depiction of democratic disorder is therefore not about inversion, as Rancière insisted, but about copying. From an autochthon's perspective, its effect is not "reassuring" but disturbing. If being a citizen is really a seeming that results from a performance, then, as Ion showed, the citizen is always in danger of becoming a metic and vice versa.

[77] This does not mean Socrates thinks the law does not maintain a difference.

This reading of the *Republic*'s exploration of democracy takes membership out of a discourse of truth and falsity in which the central question is one of cognition (whether one knows or, as Saxonhouse puts it, "remembers" one's own status or someone else's). Citizenship is not an independent status, detectable and prior to practice, but a performance of indeterminate meaning. The stress this places on the generative effects of mimesis suggests that in every making of a citizen, the citizen is simultaneously involved in a doing that *makes* one into a citizen (i.e., a copy). The semblance of a citizen's originality, then, is a matter of artifice and an effect of public practices of regulation that make it seem so, not unlike the activities explored in Chapter 4's reading of the noble lie.

This angle onto mimesis may not preclude Saxonhouse's and Rancière's conclusions. We could accept the central role mimesis plays in Book VIII and still argue that democracy suffers from a lack of distinction, as Saxonhouse contends. Likewise, Rancière could consider the disturbing quality I ascribed to status' dependence on performance as alternative support for the view that Plato thinks democracy is dangerous. Indeed, both views permit Socrates' interest in describing a mimetic boundarylessness. The difficulty lies not with the plausibility of their accounts but rather with their inability to encompass the full thrust of the passage's political significance and its theoretical relationship to the rest of the dialogue, in particular to the activities of myth-making and status assignment we saw in Chapter 4.

****

When democratic freedom threatens its own social, political, and symbolic boundaries, it reveals the vulnerability of its own distinctions. If this vulnerability is not a sign of democracy's anti-identitarianism, of what politics is it born? Assuming, as I have, that the *Republic* does not take for granted the disjoining of kinship and democracy other readers have implied, the dialogue invites us to consider mimicry as the *effect* of their joining. These issues can be helpfully explored by turning finally to the insights of another theorist of democracy, Thucydides. Like the *Republic*, Pericles' famous *epitaphios logos* sets out to construct, if ostensibly just to convey, what the democratic citizen and his freedom entails. What makes the Thucydidean rendering of democracy especially relevant for my purposes is that the speech is uncompromising in its claim that democracy and its hegemony in the Hellenic world (both conditions for Athenian freedom) are predicated on a mimetic relation between the Athenian citizen-soldier and his other, whom Thucydides variously casts as a metic spectator-soldier, colonized subject, non-Athenian ally, and Spartan enemy. Athens is a model for the rest of Hellas, according to Pericles, because its copies aspire to be but can never really be Athenian. The Funeral Oration invokes the dynamics of imitability and inimitability we find in Book VIII and links them to a specifically Athenian self-conception; Thucydides helps us see Plato's portrait of democratic flux in this new light.

Inimitable Imitable Athenians: Plato Responds to Pericles

The Funeral Oration constructs an idealized Athenian self-conception by explaining Athens' difference from the rest of the Hellenic world. Thucydides has Pericles begin the eulogy with the familiar claim that an unbroken line of successive generations has inhabited Attica. But the autochthony reference is so pat that, for some readers, the eulogy seems to displace, if not reject, the role blood plays in the logic of Athenian exceptionalism.[78] To be sure, the speech intimates that the mythical, inherited landedness that distinguishes Athenians from their transient neighbors is inadequate to guarantee, on its own, either a practice of citizen freedom or its corollary practice – the imitation of Athenian ways by nonautochthonous spectator-actors. The early lines of Pericles' speech suggest democratic freedom is a condition dependent on a curious, even paradoxical notion. Neither entirely earned nor entirely pregiven, Athenian citizenship (and the freedom and equality it guarantees) appears to be a kind of inherited achievement. The citizenry's ancestors transmitted freedom (*eleutheria*) to subsequent generations by performing their *aretē*. Recent Athenians maintain and augment this bequest by performing additional acts of greatness. In particular, Pericles points out, they established an *archē* (empire).

The Funeral Oration charts this ambiguous terrain further in a series of comparisons with Sparta. Pericles submits that Athenians do not undertake the sort of repetitious training (*meletē*) the Spartans need to in order to fight well. And yet they reveal themselves to be just as brave as the men who are always preparing. So unlabored is the courage that springs from Athenian souls that it actually comes about from "taking things easily" (*rathumia*, 2.39.4).[79] Athenians possess a quasi-natural bravery, which

[78] For instance, W. Robert Connor (1984: 66) hinges the rhetorical innovativeness of this funeral oration at one point on its "pass[ing] over the customary survey of Athenian history, real and mythic" so that it can concentrate "instead on those habits, civic arrangements, and dispositions that stand behind Athens' growth to greatness."

[79] This is my translation.

requires no behind-the-scenes effort but depends for its value nevertheless on being actualized. Athenians perform this bravery and ensure the witnessing of their performance. Pericles suggests that doing so produces a desire in non-Athenian spectators to imitate and approximate Athenian greatness. This desire is not unlike the appetites that drive democratic assimilation and mimicry in *Republic* VIII. The noncitizen's longing to be Athenian produces the desire for imitation and attests to the hierarchical relation on which the city's exceptionalism and citizenship depend.[80]

What are we to make of a democratic freedom that alternates in Pericles' speech between a language of inheritance and a language of accomplishment? If freedom, or the membership on which it is frequently predicated, is inherited, why must it also be (re)performed?[81] At times the oration draws the reader into resolving this tension, to conclude that Pericles, despite this equivocating, really emphasizes the importance of one (activity) over the other (nature) for securing a privileged status in the Greek world. This may be one reason commentators interpret the brevity of autochthony's invocation as a sign of its insignificance, both to Pericles' rhetorical strategy and to the speech's conceptualization of Athenian hegemony. As we learned from Xouthos' speech, however, this downplaying can also function as a political strategy: it draws immigrants to the metropole. The hardworking metic who believes money can render autochthonous difference insignificant affirms the ideal that democracy values deeds, like military service, over blood. To approximate Athenianness through acts of valor and speech, in other words, is supposed to be enough to secure a life of wealth and power.

It is tempting to take the speech's exceptionalist claims at face value and conclude, with Dimitris Vardoulakis, that the Athens of Thucydides' *History* has transitioned out of "a politics of kinship toward a democratic politics" insistent on participation, the very thing that "binds the citizens together."[82] But I think it would be a mistake to dismiss the invocations of ancestral ties as mere, or already undercut, convention without considering

80 This idea emerges again in a speech the general Nicias makes to a group of deflated sailors (7.63.3). Hoping to encourage the apparently metic members of the fleet, he goads them to consider the pleasure they will find in continuing to preserve the Athenian way of life that empire brings and in which they, "though not really Athenians," have shared *as if they were*, emulating habits, dialect, and deeds, including the pursuit of autochthonous expansion. In her reading of the passage, Greenwood (2016) discusses a concept of imperial mimesis that requires a shared Athenian cultural identity at the same time that it posits an unbridgeable difference between Athenian and metic.

81 This is particularly apparent from Pericles' injunction to his listeners to act as daily spectators and lovers of the city's power (2.38).

82 Vardoulakis 2013: 46.

why the argument calls on a figure of autochthonous birth to support a democratic ideal of praxis in the first place. To examine, further, how Pericles' eulogy puts the subtexts of ancestry and mimesis together, we might ask not, "Why isn't blood enough to secure democratic citizenship?" but the very question the speech almost conceals: "Why aren't deeds?" What are the particular needs of this democracy such that the speech's rhetorical structure demands a series of quiet but no less constitutive and introductory references to a politics of autochthony?

Pericles gives us an oblique answer to these questions when he says with pride that Athenians open their city to all despite the risks entailed (2.39). These dangers are worth courting because migration and mobility attest to the city's exceptional standing, which, though not perfectly imitable because also inherited, ensures that any unclear foreign contamination, passing, or status trouble is conceptually impossible. The speech can, indeed, it must, concede that a metic can be like a citizen since an Athenian, as the model, can never be like a metic. Pericles presupposes that the lines between Athenians and non-Athenians are permanently invulnerable. Despite what we saw at the Bendideia, Athens does not emulate other cities; other cities emulate Athens (2.37). So long as the mimetic operation that underlies imperial expansion is, unlike the operation in Book VIII, always only one way, democracy can secure the citizen as an unattainable ideal and insist that the city's hierarchical order is expressive of determinative and discernible political difference.

Through a series of practices – loving beauty, loving wisdom, thinking, acting, educating, and speaking in public – Athenians display their *aretē*, show their *andreia,* and so appear to earn an exceptional status that is, as it were, already there (2.40–2.41).[83] It is perhaps ironic, then, that in the midst of so much comparing, Pericles should conclude that every Athenian body (*sōma*) is able to prove itself "self-sufficient" (*autarkes*). Self-sufficiency is a truth (*alētheia*) in deed (*ergon*), he says, signified (*sēmainei*) by the power (*dunamis*) of the city, a power, we ought to recall, that is simply a consequence of those qualities that made Athenians self-sufficient in the first place (2.41). Thucydides has Pericles repeat this circular logic several lines later, in the context of the funeral oration's ostensible occasion: "And it seems (*dokei*) to me that such death as these men died gives proof enough of manly courage (*andros aretēn*), whether as first revealing it or as affording its final confirmation" (2.42).[84] Democracy's

[83] Loraux (2006: 213) notes that in his comparisons with Sparta, Pericles presents "Athenian courage" as a "fact of nature." This is the quasi-bravery I referred to earlier in this section.

[84] This is Smith's translation of Thucydides (1919): vol. 1.

exceptionalism acquires its self-sufficiency from its citizens, who are said to possess it by virtue of the univocal meaning of their deeds.

How exactly does Pericles manage to give the authority of self-evidence to these hierarchical relations? Consider again the early lines of the oration, so prosaic they might read as a "digression," in Vardoulakis's term, Pericles' "quick, almost forced gesture toward the ancestors."[85] Noting the curiousness of this "diminution" of democracy's forefathers, Vardoulakis argues that the reference to ancestry serves to distance democratic Athens from its earlier aristocratic formations, which were governed by an ancestral order. The passing reference to previous generations produces "an agonism," he thinks, between democracy and a "politics of kinship" in order to demonstrate that Athenian democracy "enacts the agonism toward the politics of *kingship*" of a now-foregone era.[86] As neat as this parsing sounds, however, the interpretation does not account sufficiently for the speech's rhetorical structure and, in limiting kinship politics to monarchical rule, may actually facilitate rather than undercut Xouthos' romantic presumption that the imperial and blood-based dimensions of Athenian politics are merely incidental to its democratic ethos.[87] From the perspective of less elite immigrants and their Athenian-born children, who enjoy a practice of freedom but no citizen status, democracy's blood-based taxonomy would seem only to complicate the city's participatory membership politics.[88]

It is not clear, then, why the quick summoning of Athenian forebears should reveal democracy's oppositional relation to kinship rather than its ambivalent dependence on it. For although the oration does not play up the significance of autochthony, the Athens it constructs is everywhere haunted and enabled by its authority, which Pericles calls into motion in the first lines. Is this simply a matter of oratorical custom, as some readers conclude, or could it be a rhetorical necessity? If autochthony's generative effects and symbolic power are hard to pin down in the oration, that slipperiness may have something to do with what Nicole Loraux calls the speech's "strange strategy," which "makes understood what it refuses to say outright."[89] We hear, for instance, of Athenian openness and prosperity but never explicitly about the dependence of these democratic values on empire and subjugation or their euphemistic and compensatory utility as conduits for trade and imported sustenance. Just as the logic of self-sufficiency demands, the oration works to absorb the figurations of

85 Vardoulakis 2013: 49, 51. 86 Vardoulakis 2013: 51. My emphasis.
87 Kingship hardly exhausts all political relations of kinship, and so Vardoulakis' slippage is telling.
88 Demosthenes' client will make this apparent in Chapter 6. 89 Loraux 2006: 131.

foreignness it nevertheless relies on to construct the conditions for Athenian exceptionalism. From the metics listening to the eulogy to the foreign foods flowing into Piraeus, Pericles employs non-Athenian imagery as a sign of the city's already-existing completeness. Like the bravery that needs no preparatory effort but must be actualized nevertheless, Athenian autochthony preexists the manifestations that it also requires others to witness, desire, and emulate. Similar to the logic of imperialism, then, the funeral oration hides the source of its autochthonous authority from scrutiny even as it leaves no doubt, Loraux says, that it "presupposes the existence of an other."[90]

Pericles' figurations of this autochthony politics, contained and indirect, demonstrate that even this practice-oriented democracy is still parasitic on kinship. The speech's argument and the "Athens" it imagines depend for their self-sufficiency on a persistent but persistently disavowed practice of comparison. Whereas the *Republic* suggests this political order is antithetical to, even undermining of, a performative politics of *aretē*, the idealized Athenian self-conception in the Funeral Oration is at pains to disavow the possibility that autochthony could pose or produce any threat to the hierarchical membership order. This is perhaps understandable: members of the demos depend for their standing on the same notion of expressive difference that the empire does.

The oration's conceit of self-evidence and self-sufficiency – the idea that Athenian deeds speak for themselves – must draw on and try to conceal the work of autochthony at the same time that it attempts to evince the power of (the) speech to produce such illusions of necessity as the claim that citizenship is an expressive act. And yet, as Loraux concludes, "Pericles seems in the end to arrive at a praise of the Athenian *nature*."[91] The speech desires to demonstrate that the self-evidentiary greatness of Athenian activity depends on an autochthonous first premise, according to which moving around, imitating, and mixing never end in the kind of ambiguity Socrates describes in Book VIII. However much Pericles seeks to conceal his initial mythical claim, however, it is, much like the self-evident act itself, as unprovable as it is foundational to the demos.

This Periclean political order depends on a desire for and a practice of emulation. Yet it insists nevertheless on the continuity between this performance and the "natural" status that is said to precede it. When Pericles indicates that there is nothing less original, less Athenian, than striving to be *like,* he gives expression to the tension between inherited and

[90] Loraux 2006: 131. [91] Loraux 2006: 221.

earned excellence in Athenian citizenship that the metic also brings into view. What democracy gains from an ideology that oscillates, like the speech, between artifice and nature, becoming and being, practicing and emanating is a politics in which metics evince their underlying, inferior, and permanent difference in their act of being *like*.

Mimesis, in Pericles' telling, is thus decidedly different from the critical, disordering, and practicable version I drew out of the *Republic*'s rendition of this democratic operation. Periclean mimesis is an autochthonous ideal. As such, it enables the excellence and courage that constitutes the democratic *politeia*. This idealizing operation insists that a telling difference exists between the citizens and the metics who can only ever approximate them. Plato's Book VIII, on the other hand, puts pressure on the safe distance between copies and their so-called originals and makes their difference always potentially unrecognizable. The *Republic* challenges the autochthonous premise that Athenianness is self-evident and autochthony always successful. Insofar as metic and citizen are made equal to *each other*, Book VIII counters the democratic-imperial scenario in which mimesis works only one way to augment and attest to the power and invulnerability of the Athenian citizen.

Mimicry may enable an expansionist logic like autochthony, but from the *Republic*'s vantage point, it can never contain the mimesis that this expressive notion of citizenship is predicated on denying. And so there is even more to glean from the hyberbolic Socratic tale that makes citizens into metics and men into women. Even citizen men – the ones who express the inimitable yet imitated ideals of Athenian greatness – would seem only ever to approximate the democracy's autochthonous ideal. Book VIII's rendering has the citizen pointing out the "infinite distance that separates [all] 'performers' from their ideal."[92] If in democracy there is only being *like*, then the being Athenian that Periclean mimesis claims ahead of time for real citizens is also a regulatory fiction. As we will see in the next chapter, this is precisely how an active citizen like Euxitheus could end up vulnerable to accusations of passing.

Ultimately, Thucydides' account of Pericles' Funeral Oration shows us a citizenship of natural difference that claims to manifest itself unambiguously in acts of freedom and *aretē* (i.e., empire, bravery). Plato's *Republic* challenges this model of expressive acts by presenting the democratic and imperial strategy of mimesis that sustains that model as a failure.

92 I borrow this phrasing from Berger (2013: 29), who uses it to discuss femininity and masculinity as ideals. "Seen in this light," she writes, "all other women would be . . . 'failures at being women.'"

The placid confidence with which Pericles' Athenians perceive a person as a citizen presents the education and emulation implied in mimesis as a stabilizing operation that, far from threatening, actually affirms the naturalness of the citizen/noncitizen dyad that regulates life inside and outside the metropole. Periclean mimesis positions the nonautochthonous as "*a subject of difference that is almost the same, but not quite*," to draw on Homi Bhabha's construction.[93] In establishing itself through a mimetic order according to which approximation is possible but equivalence never, Athenian democracy insists on "a not quite" that is necessarily discernible in deed and yet, from the *Republic*'s vantage point, never evidently so. The demos depends for its authority on an idea of the citizen as an authentic, imitable, and expressive category. It casts the city's deprivileged members and subjugated allies as resemblances, figures whose imitative acts claim to secure but therefore also threaten the notion of origins on which democratic distinctions and expansionism depend.

Although persistently overlooked in *Republic* VIII's portrait of democracy, the idiom of mimesis as an index of theatricality, impersonation, colonial standing, and representing and resisting difference is already in place in and around the time of Thucydides' history. Democracy is figured as a mimetic regime in the political context Plato dramatizes. That this expansionist and democratic strategy looms so large in what Loraux refers to as the "authorized voice of classical Greece"[94] suggests the essentialist politics typically attributed to Book VIII's typology of regimes might be more productively read as a *democratic* ideal. Pericles' speech assumes that the expressiveness of Athenian blood reveals itself in a membership performance that follows from it and that inspires, but does not require, emulation. In pointing to the performativity of membership, however, the oration generates the conditions for mimesis and thus for the fiction's strategic undoing. To say that the *Republic* helps us see this, however, is not to claim that it would prefer Athens *could* deliver on its claim that the difference between original and copy is self-evident and conducive to acts of *aretē*. When Pericles maintains that any true Athenian can prove his autarky in deed, he presents the citizen as a category that depends on an interpretation of performance. If deeds were really expressive of a pregiven difference, they would make Euxitheus, the subject of Chapter 6, impervious to accusations of passing.

[93] Bhabha 1994: 126, 128. [94] Loraux 2006: 31.

Postscript: Socrates Imitates Aspasia in Plato's *Menexenus*

As Platonic rejoinders to Pericles' Funeral Oration go, the *Menexenus* would be the more obvious choice. The dialogue repeatedly alludes to Thucydides' text and in particular to the history's fashioning of Pericles and his funeral oration.[95] Among the many complex ways the *Menexenus* establishes this intertextuality, most striking, for our purposes, is the claim that Socrates and Pericles have the same rhetoric teacher: according to Socrates, Aspasia of Miletus, Pericles' metic companion, is the source of his and Pericles' funeral orations.[96] "For an occasion that celebrates *andreia* (manly courage)," observes Madeleine Henry, "Plato supplies the words of a woman, not a man; of a foreigner, not a citizen."[97]

According to Nicole Loraux, the Thucydidean eulogy studiously avoids many of the *topoi* "common to all the orations,"[98] whereas Socrates' speech in the *Menexenus* is appropriately rote. The meandering, clumsy eulogy of the dialogue stands in many ways opposite to Thucydides' compelling and evocative prose. The *Menexenus* speech unfurls like a long list of unpersuasive, if not unusual, assertions. Claims about Athenian greatness swirl around, exaggerated, hard to follow, at times contradictory. Most relevant here is the emphasis the speech places on the citizenry's autochthonous origins (238a, 239a), a notion we saw Pericles' speech invoke quickly and quietly. Christopher P. Long points out that "Aspasia's speech is said to have been stuck together from remnants, from things left out of that speech spoken in 431 BCE."[99] What Pericles almost fails to mention, then, is underscored in Socrates' recounting: Athenian exceptionalism rests on a fictional foundation in nature.[100] For Loraux, the stress the *Menexenus* places on autochthony endeavors to bring out the "implicit reasoning" of Athenian democracy "that deduces political equality from equality of origin."[101]

Before elaborating on how the dialogue's engagement with autochthony relates to its invocation of Aspasia and the preceding discussions of mimesis in the *Republic*, let me note that the *Menexenus* begins with the claim that

[95] Loraux 2006: 224, 244. Monoson 1998: 491, 492.

[96] In her historical account of the real Aspasia, Kennedy (2014: 68–96) is critical of prevailing accounts of Aspasia's life that remain curiously tethered to her (mistaken) figuration as a *hetaira*, which is indebted in part to her figuration in Plato's text and to comedy.

[97] Henry 1995: 35. [98] Loraux 2006: 308.

[99] Long (2003: 50) has *Men.* 236b in mind. See also Monoson 1998: 492.

[100] Monoson (1998, 500) stresses that, by contrast with Pericles' Funeral Oration, Socrates' speech relies on a "family relations metaphor" that suggests "the bonds among citizens and between citizens and city are rooted in material necessity and nature."

[101] Loraux 2006: 245.

Athenian funeral orations bewitch their listeners – even Socrates is vulnerable to their charms – before it offers a most unseductive eulogy.[102] The funeral oration that follows amounts to an exercise in "narcissistic ecstasy," says Loraux, an exceptionalist account that actually tries to make readers invulnerable to the genre's magical powers.[103] It achieves this inoculation in part by recourse to obvious "manipulations of fact and outright untruths," says Monoson.[104] The strategy induces a remarkable critical distance in the reader. As Long observes, the rhetoric and humor of Socrates' oration serves "to challenge the methods of manipulation by which such political ideologies are established, but also to hold the more dangerous dimensions of which [listeners] remain unaware in check."[105] Once seen in this light, the claims about Athenian autonomy, originality, and superiority look suspect as well.

Yet Plato's text undermines the political genre of the funeral oration without providing explicit argumentation (against it) for our analysis. Any challenge his text poses to the political uses of the *epitaphios logos* results from what Long calls the dialogue's "playful parody of the rhetoric itself" and not, I want to stress, through the presentation of claims about its dangers.[106] This means that the *Menexenus* does not simply undercut the city's reliance on these forms of speech and their function of promoting Athenian exceptionalism. The dialogue actually directs our attention elsewhere – to questions of dramaturgy and mechanics, which is to say, to an examination of the speech's artifice.

By "artifice" I have in mind not only the idea that the funeral oration amounts to a mechanism for producing Athenian civic ideology, that it "invents Athens," to borrow Loraux's expression, though this is also true.[107] I mean that this particular funeral oration depends on an artifice for its vocalization. Recall that before Socrates shares his speech about

102 Before he launches into the speech, Socrates ironizes that the wise men who honor the dead at public funerals "cast a spell over our souls" (*Men.* 235a). All translations of the *Menexenus* belong to Griffith (Plato 2012a). Loraux discusses Plato's depiction of the genre as a "piece of sorcery" (2006: 333).

103 Loraux 2006: 332.

104 Monoson 1998: 494. Socrates' account of the Peloponnesian War contrasts sharply with the care and detail in Thucydides' history, according to Monoson. The distortion suggests that such exalting and patriotic recounting of Athenian history cannot but "disregard, paper over, indeed wish away, real vulnerabilities and real causes of adversity" (Monoson 1998: 494).

105 Long 2003: 51. On the *Menexenus* as a parodic text, see also Henry (1995: 32–40), who also discusses the dialogue as pastiche; Loraux (2006 [1986]: 38, 136); Saxonhouse 1992: 111–122; Monoson 1998; Pappas and Zelcer 2015: 77–93.

106 Long 2003: 51.

107 *The Invention of Athens* is Loraux's groundbreaking study of the funeral oration as a genre and civic institution the city used to constitute various idealized self-conceptions. See Loraux 2006.

Athenian exceptionalism, he tells Menexenus that he has learned it from Aspasia. Socrates does more than attribute the origins of his words to a metic woman, however. He assumes the role of one and articulates the exclusionary tenets of Athenian membership entirely in her voice. Socrates pretends to be a metic for the duration of the dialogue, breaking out of character just long enough at the end to reiterate Aspasia's authorship and remind his amused listener not "to betray" (*katereis)* him if he ever wants to hear another speech.

Plato assigns an unmoving speech about democratic difference to a person twice excluded by the city's political membership rules. The speech that founds democracy in this fiction is produced by – made equivalent to – an act of imitation, the very citizen–metic mimesis I have been exploring in this chapter. Where Book VIII described democratic membership in mimetic terms, the *Menexenus* enacts it. Where Book VIII depicted status instability as the undesirable effect of everyday practices of membership, the *Menexenus* employs it as a dramaturgical structure and equates it with – renders it the catalyst of – a foundational practice of claiming political difference. The *Republic* established mimesis as a bidirectional operation. The *Menexenus* exploits this theoretical possibility but by inverting the hierarchical terms of Periclean mimicry and dramatizing only one side of that relation. The dialogue shows Socrates ventriloquizing Aspasia and becoming the citizen copy of the metic original. As if designed to expose what Pericles' speech tried to disavow, the *Menexenus* places the citizen's dependence on the metic front and center when it has Socrates perform this relation. Socrates speaks as Aspasia, and so he dramatizes the idea that the autochthonous and androcentric democracy acquires its definition through the exclusion of metics and women. Aspasia's presence in the dialogue – her invocation – reminds us of the necessary contribution of metics and women to this idealized self-conception.

But why a mimetic act in particular should serve as the conduit for conveying the citizen's pregiven difference from the metic as a political fiction is not immediately evident. In the texts explored thus far, the unnatural truth about democratic membership emerged in moments or figurations of performance. Ion's fluctuating identity, for example, revealed that political status rests unstably on a claim about kinship, the meaning of which was as open to interpretation as any other discursive act. When Plato juxtaposes the hierarchical ideals of the *Menexenus* speech against the status-blurring conditions of their articulation, he performs a similar unsettling between what the city claims about membership and what it enables in practice. It is on this score, however, that the murky matter of Menexenus' betrayal of Socrates seems important to revisit. "The public speech of the dialogue is to be kept private" and, like the woman who has authored it, Saxonhouse observes, kept "out of the *agora* from which Menexenus had just come when he meets Socrates."[108] And yet the text does not tell us what about the speech should stay private. Are we to conclude that the object of Socrates' anxiety concerns the source of his words?

In response to the request for secrecy, Menexenus promises Socrates that he will be discrete and offers his gratitude "to the woman or man who recited [the speech]" (249e). According to Tom Griffith, this statement "implies that [Menexenus] takes Socrates, not Aspasia, to be the real author."[109] The gender ambiguity in the passage may have a more straightforward explanation. If it is difficult to settle the question of who – man or woman, citizen or metic – really "said" (*eipōn*) this *logos*, that is because Socrates has played both parts, and mimesis blurs lines of distinction. To assume that the real secret to keep is the speech's true source, as Griffith does, is to presume that Aspasia's authorship signifies little more in this dialogue than a titillating cover for the speech's authentic origins. To understand Aspasia's role in this way is to interpret Plato's dramaturgical use of mimesis not as an enactment or exploration of how membership works (unstably and to ambiguous effects) but as a problem of origins for the reader (or the city) to solve. Any confusion about identity, on this view, appears as a joke or, perhaps worse, a mistake in need of fixing.

The reading of the *Republic* offered in this chapter points us to an interpretation of the *Menexenus* that would underscore the importance of mimesis as a critical political idiom. The preceding readings suggest that the (open) secret Socrates asks Menexenus to keep is not who the original speaker is but rather what Socrates has done. The secret is Socrates' impersonation. This is the mimetic act that confounds the very attempt at identification and makes the difference between metic and citizen impossible to settle once and for all.

108 Saxonhouse 1992: 117. 109 See Griffith in Plato (2010: 136n41).

PART III

Evading Detection

CHAPTER 6

Citizen Passing in Demosthenes 57
The Oration of Athenian Blood

Besides, in an over-populous state foreigners and resident aliens will readily acquire the rights of citizens, for who will find them out?
– Aristotle, *Politics* 1326b21–1326b23

A man called Euxitheus risked enslavement in the middle of the fourth century by appealing his deme's decision to strip him of citizenship. He argued boldly to a jury that the deme's sudden and wrongful accusations of his foreign lineage reflected the citizenry's prejudices and the personal enmity of his accuser. Apart from working a menial job in the agora, he had not done "any of the things that men improperly made citizens are *seen doing*," like paying the metic tax or seeking membership in any deme that would have him (my emphasis, 57.55).[1] He was a man known for doing what citizens do.

For a person already found guilty of masquerade, Euxitheus' remarks sound ignorant, even willfully naïve. Spoken as though the basic machinations of a blood-based regime were still opaque to him, the question – How could I be a metic when no one has seen me act like one? – sets before us, by way of circumvention, what cannot be said outright: a citizen with an accomplished political record has been disfranchised; his appearance in court as a newfound metic bespeaks the overriding value of kinship. In Athens, blood would seem to trump deeds.

We have seen this rule of exclusion before. The Athenian tendency to extol origins above participation was Ion's reason for staying in Delphi, at least at first. Socrates invoked it, too, along with its political utility, when he archly repurposed the idea of Athenian *eugeneia* for the hierarchical organization of the callipolis. But when Euxitheus insinuates that people need to have seen him act like a metic before calling him one, he is doing

[1] Unless otherwise noted, I rely on Bers's translation in Demosthenes 2003. The speech is usually dated to 345 BCE.

more than criticizing the blood-based logic that has ousted him. He is skillfully deploying the argument provided by the architect of the citizenship law itself.

I argued toward the end of the previous chapter that Pericles (whose law linked citizenship to dual Athenian parentage) suggests in the Funeral Oration that citizen acts reveal a pregiven Athenianness. As Susan Lape observes, Euxitheus "adduces the fact that neither he nor his mother ever paid the taxes imposed on noncitizens as prima facie evidence that they are citizens."[2] He stakes his innocence on a version of the Periclean claim. Euxitheus asks the jurors to infer his Athenianness from the absence of any metic act (he has not done the things metics *qua* metics do). And yet, Lape adds, "Athenians clearly believed it was possible to get these performances wrong – either because one was not actually a citizen or because a genuine citizen failed to learn or properly perform his part."[3]

We might go further. In light of the foregoing readings of the *Ion* and the *Republic*, I propose instead that the idea of citizen masquerade, a "wrong" performance or a mistaken judgment about the difference that is supposed to underlie it, are possible precisely because the city tasks blood with securing a lived practice that it is inadequate to decide. In the last chapter, Pericles' Funeral Oration figured Athenian acts as inimitable and expressive deeds that follow implicitly from a claim of autochthonous birth. We saw that Pericles draws on practices of display and spectatorship to construct an exceptionalist narrative in which citizen acts must be seen by others to be admired and approximated. But these spectators, whom the oration frequently imagines as non-Athenians, are only "mere" witnesses. They do not bestow the meaning of Athenian acts, at least not officially, since the value of citizen deeds is said to be inherent in their doing. Thus *nearly* displaced from a space of inherited birthright onto one of heroic, autonomous action, Athenian acts are positioned by Pericles' speech to establish and maintain the hierarchy of the city without what Pierre Vidal-Naquet describes as "recourse to either proof or investigation,"[4] or even the myth of autochthony. Foucault's language further illuminates the point: the function of Athenian deeds is "nothing more than to develop . . . and dramatize an order of truth that is given from the beginning."[5] Thus, at the same time that Pericles famously dismisses the city's need for poets like Homer to sing Athens' glory, he tries his own hand at the role, mobilizing an archaic notion of poetic meaning to make citizen acts, like his own *epitaphios logos*, appear as performative not expressive truths, the sorts of

[2] Lape 2010: 210. [3] Lape 2010: 197. [4] Vidal-Naquet 1999: 16. [5] Foucault 2014: 38.

pronouncements, in Marcel Detienne's phrase, that "were never challenged or demonstrated."[6]

The dependence of Athenian exceptionalism on a notion of noncitizen mimicry, however, produces serious problems for – indeed it provokes – Pericles' insinuation that imitative (metic) acts do not function to verify an autochthonous regime (which is given in advance and self-evidently great). The way to guard against the dangers associated with the mobility and intermingling brought on by immigration, then, is to advocate the solution of a mimetic ideal. Such an ideal creates the conditions for passing by reassuring and perhaps threatening the city not only that an act of citizenship might be fraudulent but also that true imposters always have a tell. It is in this sense, I have been arguing, that the Funeral Oration endeavors to keep at bay the unsettling implications of mimesis we found in the *Republic*'s argument. On my reading, Plato's dialogue uses the idiom to represent acts of democratic membership and exposes the "natural" and rigid lines of difference on which the democracy's accusations of masquerade depend as a fragile noble lie. Seen this way, the *Republic* permitted a rereading of Periclean mimesis as mimicry, an operation that betrays the dangerous similitude between metic and citizen acts and suggests this instability is an unavoidable and sustaining feature of Athenian democracy.

So far in this book, then, passing has operated as a crucial but subtle fulcrum of Athenian reflections on the ambiguous effects of democracy's membership rules. In this chapter, however, passing is the ostensible crime and, as such, it generates a new set of questions and insights for us about the city's blood-based citizenship order. Euxitheus' case "is a basic dispute about the criteria of citizenship," as Robin Osborne asserts.[7] And while there are certainly legal and institutional explanations for Euxitheus' predicament, this chapter contends that it (also) provides a political theoretical reflection on the reasons Euxitheus seems "so vulnerable" and finds his citizenship in question.[8] The pages that follow attend carefully to Demosthenes' rhetorical invocations of genealogy and *metoikia* in light of the preceding discussions of mimesis and status flux. I find that the orator explores the city's uncertain and indeterminate citizenship criteria

[6] Detienne 1999: 52.

[7] R. Osborne 1985: 147. In the estimation of Osborne (1985: 151), "Euboulides' interests are not so much with the infiltration into the citizen body of foreigners, but with Athenian outsiders interfering in local affairs." Euxitheus was unknown by his own deme members (hence his reliance on kin from other demes), which suggests to Osborne that the charge of foreignness is a ploy for policing a different (citizen) line between inside and outside.

[8] These are R. Osborne's words (1985: 150).

through a series of political analogies that bring us face to face with the sometimes harrowing democratic need to account juridically for a "natural" difference that gains so much of its symbolic power by claiming to evade proof.

That democracy courts the mimetic risks Pericles would prefer we discount may be clearest in this speech. The dangers the membership order poses to citizens of lower socioeconomic standing – the ones whose enfranchisement it is meant to secure – appear particularly acute. On my reading, *Against Euboulides* picks up exactly where the Funeral Oration left off. This is the point at which the aspirations of an autochthonous membership order confront the demands of a democratic politics that entreats its citizens, as the Eumenides do (*Eum.* 432), to judge not by use of oaths or liturgical-like truths but by arguments and inference.[9] The jury in this case is tasked with reopening the gap between the authentic Athenian and his indistinguishable copy, a breach the client Euxitheus threatened to close the moment he was accused of masquerading. The jurors are charged with affirming mimesis as "mere" passing. And so we would do well to ask, as Euxitheus has, just what are the signs of this citizen masquerade. If not through metic acts, exactly how does the truth about a citizen's *metoikia* manifest itself?

Making Blood Work

Demosthenes presents his client Euxitheus as a sympathetic, luckless victim of a *sykophantēs* out for revenge – Euboulides is apparently still bitter over an unrelated trial at which Euxitheus testified against his interests.[10] The orator casts Euxitheus' accuser as a familiar Athenian type. He is the litigious parasite who abuses his citizen privilege of prosecution by targeting vulnerable, innocent Athenians for personal gain. And while he may be the officiating demarch in the deme of Halimous (a position even Euxitheus has held), he is the real fraud, we are to understand, an unscrupulous citizen who reportedly fixed the vote against Euxitheus because he knew deme protocol well enough to disregard its strictures.

9 Detienne characterizes the shift (1999: 105): "The technicality of the swearing of the oaths, which carried a definite religious force, gave way to discussion that allowed reason to put forward its arguments and thereby gave the judge a chance to form an opinion based on these arguments."

10 A *sykophantēs* is a professional denouncer who targets innocent people through judicial institutions in exchange for payment or favors. On the abusive connotations of the term, see R. Osborne 2010: ch. 10.

Under Euboulides' watch, that deme is said to have committed a dazzling number of injustices to ensure Euxitheus' citizenship was overturned procedurally. The decision to strike him from the official register of members occurred at a hearing so sparsely attended that the few citizens present did not know (or like) Euxitheus well enough to identify him as a member of their own deme.[11] Only thirty people were left by the time the vote was called, and among them were all the men Euboulides had set up (57.10). The accuser provided no witnesses to support the charges he leveled against Euxitheus' family, no evidence of a paid metic tax. But he did not need to, Euxitheus intimates. The hearing was so well orchestrated that the vote took place in the growing darkness (*skotos*) (57.9), a ploy to guarantee that the remaining citizens could be counted two or three times each.[12]

And yet Euxitheus does not rest his appeal on a complaint about procedural machinations. The accusations of his non-Athenian parentage are false, he says, whether they were properly pursued. The only "just" (*dikaion*) thing now, he says, is for him to "show" (*deixai*) (57.17) the jury his dual Athenian parentage, and so he sets out to destroy the abusive innuendo that has turned him into a metic. Where Euboulides originally failed to do so, Euxitheus will perform what Susan Lape calls "a kind of *dokimasia* within the trial, identifying his parents, their parents, and their tombs, and providing witness testimonies deposed under oath."[13] Rather than discount all the unfortunate family details that were used against his client, Demosthenes has Euxitheus demonstrate their polysemy. He will suggest that to accuse a poor, working Athenian family of fraudulent citizenship is not only unsupportable in this instance. It is undemocratic.[14]

[11] Following their expulsion from Thrace in northern Greece by Philip II of Macedon, a large number of Athenians (or people claiming to be Athenians) migrated to Athens. This may have been the impetus for 346's assembly decree, instructing demes to check on and clean up their members' lists. See Bers's introduction to his translation of the speech in Demosthenes 2002: 108. See also Plut., *Life of Pericles* 37.4.

[12] This is Usher's reading of the episode (1999: 261).

[13] Lape 2010: 204. On the practices involved in *dokimasiai*, see Aristotle's *Ath. Pol.* 42.1 and 55.2–4. James Fredal explains that a *dokimasia* ("examination" or "scrutiny") was a legal and political process that gauged the "fitness" of a citizen to perform his political duties. One was likely to experience a few in a lifetime. "An initial *dokimasia* was held for all young men nominated for membership to the rank of citizen. A more intense level of 'scrutiny' was held for men entering office . . . Any citizen could challenge the nomination of the candidate . . . The examination was performative: It declared authoritatively the citizen's fitness to fill the position for which he was nominated" (Fredal 2006: 159).

[14] Ober notes that this speech is unusual for suggesting the "use of slanderous topoi" based on birth or past occupations "unjust in principle." Speeches that do take up this sort of rhetoric concern attacks on the orators themselves, and their responses tend to argue that they are living "in accordance with

Was the Western Greek accent his father possessed a sign of his un-Athenian origins, as Euboulides claims, or the years Thucritus spent as a loyal Athenian soldier, captured and sold into slavery while fighting abroad in the Peloponnesian War? As for the work Euxitheus and his mother Nikaretē do selling ribbons in the agora, it is a job not exclusively done by metics, and so it is indicative only of their economic standing. "If we were rich, we would not be selling ribbons, nor would we be in such dire straits," Euxitheus says. "But what does this have to do with our ancestry (*genei*)?" (57.35).[15]

It is a rhetorical question worth pondering. How does one citizen point to another one's *work* to expose a counterfeit citizenship?[16] Through what chain of specifically Athenian signifiers could a marker of economic standing become a sign of passing in a city that has legally eliminated economic barriers to membership? We might note, for now, the striking lack of "natural" facts for inferring Euxitheus' political difference and the need to rely on a series of performative enactments – not only speaking and working but also (their) witnessing, interpreting, and testifying – to establish his bloodline. If Euxitheus is any measure, the practices Athens uses to judge ancestry are apparently ambiguous in their meanings and effects. This means, however, that a lived practice of membership can stand just as easily for authentic citizenship as it can for passing. That is one reason the initial case against Euxitheus had to presuppose some (additional) signs of foreignness to mark the distance between two ways of living in the city, one authentic and the other counterfeit. To make that difference apparent to his deme, Euboulides could not simply point to Euxitheus' family tree. He

the highest standards of the old-fashioned aristocratic code of behavior," a tactic that would not work in Euxitheus' situation. See Ober 1989: 281.

15 Whether Euxitheus himself was poor is not clear, given that he could afford to hire Demosthenes to compose a speech for him. Christopher Carey goes as far as to wager that Euxitheus was "evidently rich, while his parents were by his own admission paupers." Even so, Euxitheus' wealth would not necessarily discredit the other claims he makes in the speech, since "we cannot rule out the possibility that Euxitheus increased the family wealth by his work in the market" (Carey 2007: 243). Worth stressing is that regardless of how lucrative they could be, some forms of work left a person vulnerable to accusations of foreignness in Athens. Cecchet (2015: 216–217) provides a brief but focused discussion of the rhetoric of poverty in Demosthenes 57.

16 The procedure by which one citizen charges another for performing citizen privileges fraudulently is the *graphē xenias*. This speech, however, is not a response to this legal act – "no extant speech by the Attic orators was delivered for a *graphē xenias*" – but rather to the *diapsēphesis* (a deme's review and purging of the citizen rolls) that nevertheless implies the fraudulent exercise of citizen privileges has been committed (Kapparis 2005: 81). Regardless, *Against Euboulides*, like *Against Neaera* (another speech that revolves around accusations of alienage), "can provide some insights into how the prosecution and the defense could be built when someone's citizen status was in dispute before a court" (Kapparis 2005: 81).

had to organize accusations of *metoikia* around the social meanings of work.

The anxiety over Euxitheus' appropriate place in the city, however, can hardly be understood apart from the "rather loose relationship (and getting looser all the time) between hierarchies of wealth, status, and power" in classical Athens or the "inefficient perpetuation of these advantages from one generation to another."[17] Demosthenes' speech skillfully demonstrates that all the family details Euboulides has deemed metic actually reflect the range of hardships that could befall any Athenian family living through the political and economic upheaval of the late fifth and early fourth centuries.[18] During and after the Peloponnesian War, "fortunes came and went with alarming rapidity."[19] The "city's generally depressed financial condition" also pushed citizen women into paid work despite the heavy stigma their visibility apparently carried in Athens.[20] We learn, for instance, that after Nikaretē's first husband chose to marry her off to Euxitheus' father so that he could pursue a more profitable match, she was in a few years destitute, with two children and a second husband away at war. She turned to wet nursing to support her family and was hardly alone in doing so: Euxitheus says he could name several citizen women "wet nurses (*tithai*), servants (*erithoi*), and grape harvesters (*trugētriai*)" (57.45).

Euboulides might have been able to persuade his own supporters that only a servile (and foreign) past could account for the unimpressive occupational history of Euxitheus' family, but slavery was really just "one factor in a multitude" to account for "the experience of poverty" in Athens.[21] As Nikaretē's life suggests, economic mobility depended on "family circumstances such as marriage, inheritance, and gender" as well as a person's "social relationships, economic activities, and personal networks."[22] The speaker acknowledges that work is commonly coded as a state of dependency in Athens, but he is adamant that neither ribbon selling nor nursing is proof of anything besides poverty. The evidence Euboulides marshaled against him does not so much attest to as trouble the cleavages typically presumed to exist among citizen, metic, and slave experiences in Athens.[23] None of the practices used against Euxitheus are

[17] Davidson 2011: 234–235. [18] See Lacey, 1980: 57–61, esp. 58–59. [19] Davidson 2011: 184.

[20] Lape 2010: 207.

[21] Taylor 2016: 266. An implication of Euboulides' accusations is that members of Euxitheus' family would have been *former* slaves who, upon gaining their freedom, became metics.

[22] Taylor 2016: 264.

[23] Ironically, Demosthenes' own origins were called into question twice by the orator Aeschines (2.183, 2.22, 3.172) who accuses him of having Scythian (servile) ancestry and therefore of lacking a genuine claim to Athenian citizenship. Kamen points out that the use of slave invective against known free or

enough to *settle* the question of his ancestry, because regardless of what Euboulides had the deme believe, these practices are performed by citizens and foreigners alike.

To the extent that the initial hearing against Euxitheus deployed foreignness as a strategy for modeling not what citizenship is but what it should be, Euboulides suggested a real Athenian is a person who triumphs over adversity and accumulates wealth.[24] The view was hardly novel in Athens (Xouthos represents it in the *Ion*). For while Nikaretē's work helped the family survive, it ultimately "brought no advantage" to them precisely because it was "the source of all the slander" about them (57.42).[25] If it was slander that succeeded in persuading the deme to disfranchise him, the accusations against his mother were not only false but illegal.[26]

Under the presumption that the initial case against Euxitheus depended on mobilizing Athenian prejudices against the working poor, Demosthenes' speech attempts to expose the deeper citizen anxieties this bias may be working to manage. Although "Solon's prohibition on debt-slavery guaranteed a free citizenry as one of the cornerstones of democracy," notes Victoria Wohl, "Athenians recognized that extreme poverty could render that civic freedom meaningless."[27] Euxitheus fastens to this instability in his speech as a way of inciting the jurors' sympathies and raising concerns about their own vulnerability. "Poverty forces free men (*eleutherous*) to do many servile (*doulika*), humble (*tapeina*) things," he says, and "it would be more in keeping with justice (*dikaioteron*) if they will be pitied for that, men of Athens, than if they are pushed further into ruin" (57.45).

Having thus demonstrated the uncertain meanings of work and poverty, Demosthenes would seem to have rescued his client from a narrative in which this citizen is really an outed metic. The expressive capacities of

freed men was not infrequent and wages that it reflected Athenian anxiety over the increasing use of manumission and naturalization, which revealed the fluidity and, we might add, the artifice of the city's "natural" political distinctions. See Kamen 2009: 55. Cf. Demosthenes 18, which mobilizes these prejudices to his advantage when it invokes the slavishness of Aeschines' parents (18.128–18.129) and deploys their occupations vituperatively (18.258–18.265) to cast doubt on Aeschines' heritage and citizen standing.

24 Ironically, such mobility and materialism are best exemplified by wealthy metics like Xouthos and Cephalus. Indeed, what Ober calls "lust for gain over honor" was typically "ascribed to metics" (Ober 1989: 275).

25 Censuring a man or woman for working in the marketplace was significant enough to deserve legislation – the city deemed it "evil speaking" (*kakēgoria*). Even if "Athenians did not think such reproaches were fair in a court of law," writes Ober, "at some point in the past . . . slander based upon occupation had been common enough to spark the concern of the lawmakers" (Ober 1989: 276).

26 Lape 2010: 206, citing 57.30.

27 Wohl 2010: 194.

work should dissipate in a democratic regime with no wealth qualification for citizenship, after all. And while Euxitheus may appear to evoke this celebrated democratic axiom, it is, crucially, not what he says. "We did nothing wrong, after all, if we were poor," he explains, "but only if we were not citizens (*mē politai*): and the present trial now is not about our luck or our money but about our descent (*genous*)" (57.45). As metonyms for economic standing, ribbon selling and nursing are irrelevant to questions of citizenship in a regime in which only ancestry counts.

There is much at stake in these seemingly simple lines with their admonishing reference to the criminalization of poverty and their autochthonous emphasis on the singular and egalitarian importance of blood.[28] The remarks aim to direct the jury's attention away from work, which is unrevealing, back to kinship, which is what the law counts for citizenship. Justice in Demosthenes' estimation would seem to consist in pulling apart two distinct forms of difference (political and economic) that have been unfortunately and unfairly intertwined, as if the symbolic integrity of one form of difference did not depend on the other, as if Euxitheus' ancestry really could speak for itself without the signifying help of his labor.

The problem, as we know from Euboulides' own prosecutorial strategy, is that while genealogy counts, it is elusive, uncertain in its effects, and in this case insufficient. At first glance, the speech suggests the link between work and foreignness does not hold up (in court) because in addition to violating the spirit of a demos, whose members come from all economic strata, it contradicts the political realities of Athenian life: the jurors deciding Euxitheus' fate would have known firsthand that citizens worked in the agora.

Such considerations of law and fact would seem like good reasons to conclude, with Victor Bers, that the evidence against Euxitheus is "flimsy and mean-spirited"[29] – were it not, however, for the significant matter of

[28] In Plato's *Republic*, both poverty and wealth can "corrupt" artisans. Without claiming, however, that poverty leads to crime, the text nevertheless prepares the ground for this idea when it figures the transformative power of poverty over character. Like wealth, it has "a damaging effect both on what craftsmen produce and on the craftsmen themselves" (421d–421e).

[29] Bers 2003: 108. On this point, Lape writes that Euxitheus reframes "the legal issue, shifting it from possible allegations of his mother's servility to the question of his opponents' slanderous speech, an offense that in this case also constitutes a harm to democratic ideology," and in so doing plays "on the sympathies of the democratic jury" (Lape 2010: 209). Lape is right to suggest the speech seeks to "point out that [his mother's employment history] has no bearing on the matter of either his own or her citizen identity," but her evaluation cannot address the pressing question of how one comes to depend on the other rhetorically, which I address later in the chapter. Lape, who reads the speech more as forensic practice than forensic rhetoric, neglects to consider – despite her interest in the "racialized" ideology of democratic Athens – how the symbolic politics of class and foreignness work

the city's symbolic order, which ensures that it is precisely this sort of "trifling" proof that is charged with endless potential for political manipulation.[30] We could speculate from the inconclusive nature of the evidence brought against him that Euxitheus is really an Athenian. The problem is that this indeterminacy is exactly what the charge of passing depends on exploiting, too. Important to remember is that the case for Euxitheus' original disfranchisement depended, among other things, on a rhetorical association of work with foreignness. That dimension goes underappreciated in readings that focus on evaluating the strength of Euboulides' evidence and conclude it is proof of little more than a personal feud. If the speech enables this juridical reading, it also permits one in which the indeterminacy of the evidence brought against Euxitheus carries a deeper meaning: the democracy's symbolic economy, according to which a citizen, or his accuser, is tasked with producing the *signs* of a counterfeit citizenship, necessitates the representation of work as a criminal act so that poverty can stand in for the ostensible crime of citizen passing – where ancestry should but as an internal attribute cannot. To take this different route into Demosthenes' speech is to begin to see how a citizen with a background like Euxitheus' is not simply protected by the blood-based criterion that guarantees citizen standing to the "earth-born" but also uniquely endangered by it.

Euxitheus implies that his accuser drew on prevailing tropes of the working poor to render his and his mother's lives abject.[31] Athenian discourse frequently links trade to noncitizenship by representing such work as servile and feminine.[32] "The underlying assumption of the rhetorical attack upon the occupation of one's opponent," as Josiah Ober notes, is that "working as a hired laborer limited the personal freedom of the hired man."[33] The figuration of work as a condition of dependency on an employer and thus on someone like a master or a husband serves an idealized portrait of the democratic citizen as an autonomous, free

together to produce Euxitheus' predicament. On "the desire to render the rhetoric of forensic oratory transparent," see Wohl 2010: 13. As I address briefly in the second section, Wohl argues that this scholarly tendency "has its roots in forensic oratory itself, as it seeks to deny its own status as a self-interested and potentially deceitful *logos*." To avoid that interpretive complexity is to fall prey to one of the genre's rhetorical conceits, but it is also in this particular case to buy into the logic of Athenian exceptionalism.

30 The word "trifling" comes from Carey 2007: 104.

31 In the fifth and fourth centuries, there were a number of terms for the "poor" to designate the destitute as well as those who worked for a living. See Taylor 2016: 238–239.

32 For more on slavish occupations and their associations in oratory, see Ober 1989: 272–279.

33 Ober 1989: 277. See also Aristotle, *Rhetoric* 1367a32–1367a33.

man.[34] Within this social discourse, explains Claire Taylor, work like nursing could be cast as a "shameful response to financial hardship" in spite, or rather on account, of the fact that it provided women with "networks of relationships, primarily with other women, which could be drawn on when necessary" to make them more not less self-sufficient.[35] Wet nursing might lend itself particularly well to castigation insofar as all work can be construed as an act of using the body for profit, but ribbon selling had its own overdetermined associations with the body. Aristophanes (*Thesm.* 400) seems to use it as a euphemism for prostitution, labor for which both men and women lost their citizen privileges.[36] What is more, the ribbon trade that renders Euxitheus' background so self-evidently foreign is itself in the business of producing status signs (Pl., *Sym.* 212e).[37] Ribbons were worn primarily by women and male victors. Here it is their selling that is made to do a kind of distinguishing work.

Whatever their specific occupations, citizens who work alongside slaves and foreigners in the agora are always potentially guilty (of passing) by association. Yet symbolic connections among work, poverty, and noncitizenship do not rest exclusively on figurations of dependence. The Athenian legislation of property also helps ensure that wage work can operate as a sign of political difference. Although classical Athens did not restrict landless Athenians from citizenship or rule, it barred metics, who did not share in ruling, from owning land.[38] So long as property-less-ness characterized some citizen lives but constituted all *noncitizen* experiences in

[34] In the *Politics*, Aristotle draws a fine line between artisans and slaves, arguing that those who perform necessary tasks for an individual are slaves, but those who perform them for the community are craftsmen and laborers (1278a). He argues for the exclusion of craftsmen from citizenship in the best city on the grounds that, while they are essential to its functioning as a city, they lack the time to hold office and run the risk of growing disaffected.

[35] Taylor 2016: 271.

[36] I am grateful to Laura McClure for pointing me to this possible connection to Aristophanes' *Thesmophoriazusae*, where the character of the garland seller is a widow and, like Euxitheus' mother, must support her children by working in the agora. She weaves garlands in the myrtle district (443–458). See Roselli 2011: 172. Fredal (2006: 160), drawing on Halperin and Winkler, explains that "prostitut[ing] oneself was to become the slave of something over which one ought to be master, including especially one's own passions – desires and fears."

[37] As Roger Brock (1994: 340) notes, "Both ribbons and garlands can be seen as luxury goods, principally for the symposium." See also Davidson 2011.

[38] However, as Akrigg (2015: 6) points out, the metic restriction on land ownership does not mean all metics were disconnected from land. Metics (and citizens without land ownership) could still engage in agricultural work by renting land. (See also Lysias 7.10.) This suggests that even when legislation on land ownership attempts to make the distinction between metic and citizen clear, it is once again undercut by economic mobility – the ability for metics to rent and farm land without owning it. This possibility does not undo servile associations with trade but makes them less revealing and therefore more ambiguous.

Athens, landed property could be aligned with citizenship and employment with foreignness. Such restrictions might be read as the traces of an older, aristocratic association between citizenship and landed money, but they reveal more than the familiar class bias Euxitheus invokes in his speech.[39] For in a genealogically stratified city, blood-based rules on property seek to make the difference between Athenians and metics more, not less, apparent – to address, perhaps even to solve, the conundrum produced by a legal regime that asks for proof of what isn't or shouldn't be seeable. The land limits that aspire to make metic status more legible, however, are ironically the very ones that produce a degree of ambiguity and openness around claims of citizenship. In fact, they make a trial like Euxitheus' inevitable; for, so long as landless employment can be called on to signify a counterfeit citizenship, the link between work and foreignness makes poor citizens particularly susceptible to accusations of passing, disfranchisement, and in this case enslavement.

Euxitheus' predicament is for these reasons not adequately explained by readings that follow his lead in casting his expulsion from the demos as a matter of aristocratic envy or class division. The many references to ancestry in the speech are just one indication that the premise for this trial – Euxitheus' illegibility – could only emerge under the specific symbolic conditions first enabled by Pericles' Citizenship Law, that is, within a democratic membership order that claims blindness to wealth at the same time that it delimits membership by blood. In a polity where assimilated, even native-born "foreigners" may live as free persons, permanently excluded from membership and thus with the potential to pass as citizens, how could employment not excite a particularly charged anxiety? Consider the mingling between citizens and noncitizens at work in the well-known Erechtheum inscriptions: descriptions of the payment, job, and membership status of workers who constructed the Acropolis temple, as Richard H. Randall notes, reveal that "[s]laves, metics, and citizens received identical wages and worked side by side at the same tasks."[40] It is partly in and through the practice of work that the "natural" difference between citizens

[39] As mentioned in Chapter 1, the argument made by Ober (1989: 288) that "the enduring influence of aristocratic ideology led the Athenians to believe that some people really might be better or worse than others by virtue of their birth" does not attend sufficiently to the "autochthonous" reasons for the persistence, or resilience, of aristocratic arguments about inherent nature, birth, and virtue in democratic Athens. This is curious in part because later on Ober makes the brief but striking point that the divisive language used to distinguish among the citizenry now worked instead primarily to separate "noncitizens – especially metics and slaves" (Ober 1989: 291).

[40] Randall 1953: 209.

and metics will be sought, only to be found fundamentally indeterminate and in need of further policing.

The speech's exhortation to the jury to disentangle Euxitheus' poverty from his ancestry seeks to establish some degree of certainty for the litigant and his case at the same time that it also reveals the precariousness of this task. For in attempting such a wishful disentanglement of the economic and the political, the speech lays bare a rhetorical strategy not wholly dissimilar to the scholarly habit I mentioned in Chapter 1. I suggested there that readers tend to understand the Athenian achievement of expansive citizenship in predominantly socioeconomic terms (i.e., egalitarianism) without thinking simultaneously about its exclusionary blood-based dimension. As important as this aspect of democracy is, the critical impulse to privilege the city's disaggregation of citizenship from economic status may inadvertently work to conceal the index of blood difference to which citizenship is, at least by the time of Pericles' law, simultaneously tethered and thus to obscure the extent to which the full membership of the poor remains potentially precarious. To read Demosthenes' figurations of the (citizen) poor primarily as references to citizens, then, may be as idealizing as Euxitheus' invitation to decouple his ancestry from his economic standing.[41] It is to think descent apart from work. Although they approach the issue from opposite directions, both the speech and the critical habit I outlined in Chapter 1 risk simplifying questions of Athenian citizenship by attempting to isolate their supposedly determinative feature (class or blood) and thus by masking the extent to which, as the accuser in this case knows, such issues must be considered in tandem.

Some historical studies have emphasized that naturalized differences between citizens and non-citizens helped Athenians avoid *stasis* and preserve democratic unity above and beyond the fissures of class.[42] As we saw in Chapter 4, a similar focus on solidarity is frequently the focus of discussions of autochthony as well. Euxitheus' case reminds us that there may be more to the story: the mandate to preserve the integrity of the metic-citizen distinction makes it justifiable, perhaps even necessary, to pursue "class" antagonism. The Athenian poor gained an unprecedented privilege with the establishment of democracy, and yet it is important to consider how with the metic's invention they became newly, if differently,

[41] As Steven Johnstone notes, "[A]ny account of Athenian democracy that considers only the relations between citizens is less an account of power in that society than a recapitulation of an interested ideology of power" (Johnstone 1999: 141n50).

[42] See, for instance, Davidson 2011 and Lape 2010, especially 202.

construable as uncitizenly precisely because blood could not speak for itself.

To see more clearly how an autochthonous membership order can betray some of the citizens it promises to protect from exclusion, I want to go back to the speech's characterization of Euxitheus' parents. Consider again the Peloponnesian War in which Euxitheus' father Thucritus fought and is said to have acquired a foreign accent. "Whereas in Solon's time Athenians had been sold into slavery owing to poverty, Thucritus was reduced to slavery as an unfortunate consequence of performing his duty as a citizen soldier."[43] In the speech, the Athenian exceptionalism that justified imperial expansion and war and required Thucritus' military service is the same autochthonous logic that makes it possible to see an Athenian soldier as a counterfeit citizen. What is more, the military activity that puts Thucritus' nativity at risk is the very reason Nikaretē sought her employment, the activity that is used within the same symbolic order to suggest her disqualification from citizenship. The autochthonous politics that simultaneously requires these citizenly acts might also render them impossibly Athenian.

If empire and war exacerbated economic instability in Athens, they are also what make economic mobility the sign of a more malignant kind of movement – a political mobility between membership categories that is secretive and unnatural and therefore necessary to expose. The seemingly foreign but ultimately indecipherable behavior of Euxitheus' parents troubles the coherence and stability of the metic–citizen dyad. Their illegibility was originally mobilized to exclude two Athenians from citizenship. This status confusion is presented as the consequence of fraud. I am suggesting the predicament might be better read as the effect of a democratic membership order that depends for *its* salience on oppositions it cannot stably uphold. The more Athens seeks to actualize its autochthonous exceptionalism, the more it seems to endanger the incorrigible status that the founding myth promises to secure for Athenians regardless of wealth. The city's efforts to maintain the difference between citizens and metics (on which the demos depends for its definition) appear to put its own democratic ideal at perpetual risk.

Signs of Being a Metic

Did Euxitheus walk away from court a reinstated citizen or slide further down the membership hierarchy into slavery? There is no record of the

[43] Lape 2010: 205.

jury's vote, and this uncertainty may be one reason scholarship on the speech tends to read juridically, preferring to decide Euxitheus' fate as a jury might to drawing out the theoretical insights of its engagements with kinship and wealth. David Whitehead, for instance, arrives at Euxitheus' innocence through a faith in the Athenian democratic system as Cleisthenes had imagined it.[44] If Euxitheus had really been a metic, he concludes, the people of Halimous would have noticed his imposture sooner and blocked him from reaching his position of prominence (57.48). "Athenians assumed that a citizen's birth identity would be common knowledge in his (or her) local neighborhood," and so we might say the same about Euxitheus'.[45] After all, "[i]t was the duty of citizens to remain on guard against surreptitious infiltration by outsiders."[46] Athens would seem to withhold rightful membership only in exceptional cases, when sycophants prove too persuasive or clever to resist.

At first glance, Demosthenes' speech provokes this conclusion. The orator sometimes presents Euboulides' pursuit of Euxitheus as a clear-cut case of corruption, motivated by class prejudice, solvable by recourse to the city's egalitarian and judicial ideals. "I have been clearly acknowledged, men of Athens, all along, by all my current accusers, as a citizen," Euxitheus says (57.47), registering his faith in their previous decisions. Indeed, how could a democracy place overarching importance in a single one of its practices – the *diapsēphisis* that produced his noncitizen status – while discounting a host of others (such as his or his father's appointments to magistrate), which yielded the opposite conclusion? By disavowing Euxitheus' citizenship, the deme disagreed with a number of its own previous judgments. It would seem more sensible to call into question the single one that has excluded him.

So important is it to Demosthenes' argument that his client stake his innocence on the integrity of the city's institutions and *vice versa* that at times the speaker finds himself in the curious spot of suggesting that even his accuser is mostly law-abiding: "Euboulides would not have allowed this alien, as he now says I am, to serve in magistracies or to be selected to draw lots for the priesthood alongside him," Euxitheus proposes. "And as my enemy from long before, he would not have waited until this opportunity now, which no one anticipated, if he had known such a thing about me

[44] Whitehead's belief in (or acceptance of) the demos's ability to detect the autochthonous with certainty leads him to disregard the ways the speech treats the notion of membership as a conscious epistemological identity with suspicion. See Whitehead 1986: 85. For a critique of the idea of Athens as "a face-to-face society," see Vlassopoulos 2007: 36; see also Johnstone 1999: 2.

[45] Lape 2010: 210. [46] Ober 1989: 266.

then. But he did *not* know (*ou sunēdei*) it" (57.48–57.49). Euxitheus' closing reference to knowledge, a kind of bearing witness in Greek, begs for a layered reading. Does Euboulides not know it because he lacked the information, as readers tend to assume, or because such facts of blood are not absolutely knowable? To suggest his accuser would have acted on information about his foreignness if he had possessed it, that he would have acquired the information if there were any to have is, as Foucault reminds us, to mount a defense of (im)plausibility, a "typically" sophistic strategy.[47]

Athenian forensic oratory tends to construct a world of "legal agents" in which all, even criminals, are said to "commit their crimes with an eye toward the defense they will make in court."[48] By presupposing that "the entire *world* works like the law," Demosthenes' speech is able to make "the people just and the laws democratic" even as it sets out to prove they are engaged in deception and corruption. Oratory finds a way around this apparent contradiction by constructing an opposition between "the honest, transparent oratory of the speaker and the deceitful oratory of his opponent."[49] In other words, it is to the litigant's advantage to make a predictable, litigious actor out of a *sykophant* like Euboulides. The gesture works to augment the power of the law and, more specifically, the juridical discourse of the orator. Here it has the specific effect of restoring faith in the institutions that more often than not attested to the authenticity of Euxitheus' citizenship.

The extent to which readers may be pulled into deciding Euxitheus' innocence or ascertaining the intentions of his accuser may reflect the seductiveness of this sophistic strategy, which works to "conceal its status as rhetoric."[50] Demosthenes involves his client in laying out the political events of his life in a procedural story. But Euxitheus also speaks of the ambiguous quality of the law's citizenship criteria, and he does so to such rhetorical excess that he manages to introduce a degree of undecidability into his otherwise reassuring juridical-institutional account. This sort of doubling produces a number of interpretive effects. The speech evokes the greatness of the law courts and the litigiousness of the citizens not, or not only, to resecure the institutions that granted him citizenship but also to point out their limits. This means that Demosthenes' oration facilitates our discernment of how the very problem of kinship that readers are tempted to solve (for the jury) takes on the shape of an aporia.

[47] Foucault 2014: 73. [48] My emphasis. Wohl 2010: 22. [49] Wohl 2010: 25.
[50] Johnstone 1999: 3.

Such irresoluteness comes out in the speech in several ways, most obviously when Euxitheus describes his political status as a fact that, though apparently natural, might nevertheless be rendered false by the same acts of swearing and judging that had previously demonstrated its truth. Yet few lines can begin to capture the orator's concern with accenting the difficulty of the task before him as the sentences we find near the end when, following a list of exasperated questions – Am I a *xenos* then? Where did I pay the tax on metics? Who in my family ever did? – the speech suddenly gives way to desperation of a frightfully contagious because democratic kind:

> Now, how could anyone show (*epideixeien*) you more plainly that he has a share in the city (*meton tēs poleōs*)? . . . So let each of you, men of Athens, think how he would show that his relatives were the same from the start using another method (*tropon*) than I have: by having them give testimony under oath. Feeling confidence in myself for these reasons I have turned to you for refuge (*kataphugon*). (57.55–57.56)

We saw earlier that Euxitheus begins the appeal announcing that the only just thing for him to do is show (*deixai*) the jury his Athenian parentage (57.17). Nearing the end, he claims to have done so using the only method available to a citizen in Athens. Just what is entailed in this democratic demonstration of an antecedent status, however, is not as obvious as it first appears. For although Euxitheus believes in his own display, he ends the line in trepidation, pleading for the jurors' protection as a supplicant would.

Josiah Ober interprets the line as indicating that Euxitheus' appeal uses the "same tokens" all Athenians had at their disposal: phratry members, relatives, demesmen, and members of the *genos*.[51] And yet the list Ober has in mind is given earlier (57.24) in a context that may open up more questions about the demonstration (and the speech) than it actually resolves. Following the reading aloud of testimonies deposed by kin and demesmen at an earlier date,[52] Euxitheus rattles off that list in order to – and this is key – head off the jurors' worries about the impostures of his

[51] Ober (1989: 263) is quoting from the early parts of the speech. The question is how the demonstration *of* the speech differs from what Euxitheus says it entails.

[52] As David C. Mirhady explains, the practice of "committing evidence to writing was completed sometime in the 370s, when it appears that witnesses were no longer required actually to give testimony in court at all. While their presence was still required, they did not speak: their prerecorded testimony was simply read aloud to the court by the court secretary." Demosthenes, he adds, was the first orator to "be able to exploit the full ramifications of the shift" to written evidence, which he calls "documents." See Mirhady 2000: 184.

witnesses. "How could I manage to rig all these pseudo-relatives?" he asks plaintively (57.24). That question is not "merely" rhetorical. For while the length of the list is meant to eradicate the jurors' doubts, it also airs a concern with the authenticity not of his Athenian parentage but of the testimonies he needs to establish that fact. The legal requirement to have people give testimony under oath in this case is suddenly subject to the same suspicion that adheres to Euxitheus' identity.

Athens relied on live witnesses to attest to a person's Athenian descent or citizenship, above and beyond any available documentation, at a number of communal events. From a "modern perspective," comments Adele Scafuro, the fact that Athens had "no central or local archive" for preserving "a written record of the births of polis inhabitants" seems "startling in view of the strict requirements of citizenship."[53] But, as S. C. Humphreys explains, "[a]n Athenian could not even imagine relying on official registration procedures [or] written documents." Questions of identity "were phrased in relation to persons, living and dead." That structure, she maintains, had to do with Athens' evolution from "a small community" to a large city with an "urban court" and "a loss of knowledge."[54] If, by the period of the Cleisthenic reforms, "Athens had ceased to be the sort of face-to-face society in which members knew each other by sight (if it had ever been) and could judge character on the basis of firsthand knowledge," it was, as James Fredal puts it, "difficult or impossible, even given the importance of rumor and common report, to know the character, or *phusis*, of every citizen." Nevertheless, "citizens' claims for leadership status and public influence made it important to know just what sort of men they were . . . "[55] Amid urban expansion and mobility from the countryside, witnessing techniques aspired to "recreate in court the social context from which the litigant had been detached," not to "establish the facts."[56] Yet disputes "concerning the identification of citizen and familial status were so significant – and so liable to error – they warranted the privilege of retrial," Scafuro argues.[57] The promise of future trials did not guarantee "the testimony of a truthful witness" but "a stage for [further] witness testimony," an opportunity for more talk and presumably further accusation.[58]

Commentators on the speech have occasionally noted that *Against Euboulides* is an unusual case because, by contrast with other extant forensic speeches, its witnesses were made to take an oath. If the hearing

[53] Scafuro 1994: 156. [54] Humphreys 2007: 200. [55] Fredal 2006: 161.
[56] Humphreys 2007: 144–146, 141. [57] Scafuro 1994: 179. [58] Scafuro 1994: 180.

that originally disfranchised Euxitheus was carried out by people under "an oath of special solemnity," then it might have seemed best to appeal the decision with sworn witnesses, to fight oath with oath.[59] Beyond binding jurors and witnesses, however, oaths also provided for citizen status in Athens in several ways. Thucritus would have sworn an oath when he claimed Euxitheus as his legitimate child and, eventually, like all citizens, Euxitheus would have taken one to join his deme at eighteen. A juridical reading that sees the task of proving Euxitheus' citizenship as a matter of following the right procedure, then, cannot fully account for the foreboding and suspiciousness that permeate this speech. It cannot make sense of why every move Demosthenes makes and each marshaling of evidence still leaves us wondering not so much about the client's innocence or the functioning of the court system in Athens but about the political and symbolic conditions under which a citizen like Euxitheus is asked to tell the truth about his parentage, again.

Anxieties about Macedonian political ambition, expansion, and dominance lurk behind the scenes of this case. Indeed, the question of citizen masquerade is just as, if differently, urgent as it was in the imperial fifth-century world of Plato's *Republic*. The polis of Demosthenes' speech, as Susan Lape explains, had placed "renewed emphasis on Athenian-ness."[60] Just a few years before the trial, Philip II of Macedon had expelled a number of people claiming Athenian descent from Thrace. They immigrated to Athens and joined the citizenry by claiming Athenian blood ties. Concerns about the legitimacy of their incorporation may have precipitated the *diapsēphisis* that disenfranchised Euxitheus.[61] In his recounting of the vote that turned him into a metic, Euxitheus chooses not to pin the injustice of the decision exclusively on fraud but reports that he is "fearful of the city's current keen excitement over the disenfranchisement of citizens" (57.2). He claims his accuser chose a time of civic strife and unease over the composition of the citizenry to make the move against him.[62] Euboulides' *sykophancy* was in some larger sense opportune. The rightful expulsion of some, he says, has justified the detection of all and rendered "victims of plotting" like him guilty by association (57.2).

Whether the doubts about Euxitheus' disfranchisement are disingenuous and whether they were motivated by personal enmity is not so important from this vantage point. When the oration demonstrates the

[59] Sommerstein and Bayliss 2012: 87, 88. Note, however, that after the 370s, witnesses did not testify in court but confirmed, by speech, the validity of a deposition drafted ahead of time.

[60] This is Lape's phrase (2010: 143). [61] Bers 2003: 108.

[62] Usher emphasizes this point (1999: 262).

indeterminate meaning of work or when it recalls the grave economic flux that characterizes life for most Athenians, it draws our attention to a deeper question about the precariousness of Athenian citizenship and the political moments in which this precariousness becomes acute and apparent. If this is part of its persuasiveness as a court speech, then it is also one of its strengths as a political theoretical text. For the critical purchase of Demosthenes' oration lies in its ability to articulate in a new way what I have tried from the start of this book to bring into view: the blood-based division that is supposed to secure equality, mobility, and exceptional standing for the demos also makes it possible to contest the authenticity of a lived practice of membership. Demosthenes does more than provide us with a real-life dramatization of these machinations. He shows us the political urgency of (recovering) their theorizations.

To see better what I mean, consider something Euxitheus says much earlier in the speech when defending his father's reputation against the accusation that he was also a fraudulent citizen. Charges that "no one brought against [my father] while he was alive" (57.27), Euxitheus says, have been effective at casting doubt on his own citizenship. Euxitheus thinks the new claims about his father are unfair because they were never proven and will stay that way: Thucritus has died and cannot defend himself. These may seem like unique circumstances for revoking citizenship. On closer inspection, however, they bring together the indeterminacy, status flux, and suspiciousness that *Ion* first tethered to this autochthonous regime.

Until this case, Euxitheus' own citizenship seemed established on sworn ancestral claims, and yet, from his current perspective, his citizen status is perhaps best described as having been only temporarily secured by an absence of suspicion. (Apparently, even death does not make Athenianness impervious to doubt.) Ion prepared the ground for this possibility when he made (his) Athenianness a secret, took on *metoikia* as a fake role, and justified ahead of time, as it were, the democratic city's preoccupations with passing and exposure. It is telling, then, that Thucritus' *metoikia* has the status of a suspected crime rather than a criminal act and that Euxitheus would acquire his (new) political status by inheriting, just as one does *metoikia*, the potential criminality that now adheres to his father. What are we to make of this connection – in the speech it is more like an allegory – between blood and suspicion?

The matter of an inherited *potential* crime invites us to consider that the "natural" difference between the citizen and the metic may in fact always be tied to an idea of potentiality. That Thucritus was never accused or found guilty of passing does not eliminate the possibility that he did pass as a citizen. The idea of potentiality figured by Thucritus' suspected *metoikia* is thus different from the sort we found in the *Republic*, where metics were described as actualizing their capacity to be citizens and citizens as actualizing their potential not to be in the *act* of being "like" each other. In the oration's notion of potentiality, we find negativity and apprehensiveness, the sort of foreboding I was less willing to grant Book VIII's mimetic blurrings. For recall that in the *Republic* the potential to be (a citizen or a metic) is actualized (or not) in the doing of mimesis. In court, the doing of citizen acts should be enough to actualize Euxitheus' and Thucritus' potentiality to be citizens, once and for all. The reason it is not, however, is that these particular citizens cannot seem to escape the possibility (the potentiality) of being or doing *falsely*. The potential to be or do falsely is not the same as the potential to not be (a citizen). The latter formulation refers to the unsettling but nevertheless emancipatory idea I found in Plato's *Republic*, where the metic has the potentiality to act as a citizen "but does not," as Mary G. Dietz puts it, "(because disallowed)."[63] If we conceive of the danger that adheres to Euxitheus in terms of the potential to be (a citizen) or do (citizenship) falsely, we can begin to account for the shroud of suspicion under which people actualize their potentiality to be citizens in Athens. Here is Euxitheus again:

> Now please, gentlemen of the jury . . . let no one shout, let no one get angry at what I am about to say. I think of myself as an Athenian, just as each of you does; I thought my mother was from the start, the woman I have been describing to you, and I was not pretending to be her son while really the son of another woman. And the same thing, men of Athens, goes for my father. So if you rightly take it as a *sign* (*sēmeion*) of people being aliens (*xenoi*) that they are exposed as hiding the identity of their true parents and pretending they are someone else's children, then surely the opposite should show that I am a citizen. I would not, after all, claim to have a share in the city, while inscribing myself as the son of an alien woman and man. Instead, if I *knew* this was the case, I would have searched for people to claim as my parents. But I did not know any such thing, and so, sticking with my real parents, I claim my rightful share in the city. (57.50–57.51, emphasis added)

Euxitheus' argument appears to rest on a claim about intentionality and performance. Regardless of who his parents really are, he has lived thinking of them as Athenians. He has acted as if he were an Athenian by blood. A metic on this logic is someone who knowingly conceals a secret.

[63] Dietz 2012: 286.

Euxitheus is not guilty of hiding his *metoikia*, he says, because he has known of nothing to hide. Like an inverted Oedipus, he is innocent because he does not know he possesses the wrong parentage. If he is guilty, then he is guilty only of mimicry, that is, of unintentionally acting like a citizen but not of passing.

When Euxitheus says he interprets (*hupolambanō*) himself to be an Athenian the same way all Athenians understand themselves to be, he appeals to what he knows about his parents, details that previously evaded any stable interpretation not simply because the meaning of an accent depends on the context in which it is understood. Had he known his parents were not Athenian, he says, he would have found others who were. Much is at stake in the curious admission that he would simply have chosen other parents. It poses the possibility that it is not parentage *per se* but the act of claiming Athenians as parents that counts for citizenship. The utterance stands for the bond that is decreed to secure blood-based citizenship (or not), much like Cephalus' appeal to kinship in *Republic* I.

And yet Euxitheus insinuates that the sign of being a metic is not being a metic but to have been exposed as one. He acquires his *metoikia* only once he has been accused of bearing the secret of having noncitizen parents. There exists, on this account, no expressive, unequivocal foreignness that precedes the act of exposure. What produces *metoikia* and makes it appear as a pregiven difference, or in this case a hidden truth, is an accusation. The claim calls us back to the *Ion*, in which the taking on of a secret not only established Ion as a metic but also laid the foundation for a democratic membership order of suspiciousness and detection we find playing out for real in this case. Read in this light, Demosthenes' lines take on additional meaning. Everyone is a secret bearer and potential metic in Athens so long as what separates a citizen from a noncitizen, what turns one into the other, is the charge of lying, an act that keeps actualization, which is to say, membership practice, looking like potentiality – the potential to be and do *falsely*. It is in this sense that Thucritus' suspected crime helps us figure not simply Euxitheus' *metoikia* as an inherited suspicion but democratic membership more generally. Every citizen is a potential metic in Athens, as Ion ensured, because every citizen is potentially guilty of pretending, of being caught in the act of masquerade.

We are now in a better position to return to the question I posed earlier, when I asked what might be entailed by the method for demonstrating parentage that Euxitheus invokes and says he shares with all Athenians: how could anyone show (*epideixein*) the jurors more plainly that he has a share in the city? What does it mean that in the space of one line, the invocation of this method shifts in tone from confidence to desperation? Why is it that Euxitheus' many acts of citizenship, for which there is, in point of fact, ample proof, can do nothing to save him here? Euxitheus ends his demonstration in an act of pleading. He seeks safety in the jurors' ability to understand his precariousness as their own potential condition, to see the threat this blood-based order might pose to the poor in particular. The danger is not only that each juror stands at risk of accusation but that, once under suspicion, the mode of demonstration available to "all Athenians" turns its practitioners into supplicants.[64]

[64] Johnstone (1999: 15) notes that litigants engaged in "rituals of weeping and supplication" during their appeals to the jury and concludes that this was a way of "enacting the democracy's power." This interpretation of the ritual, however, does not begin to address what supplicating in particular reveals about the law or, more specifically, about the law's demand for proof of that which belies it. The city's demand for acts of avowal and disavowal positions the citizen, ahead of time, as a potential criminal and, as such, he can be endlessly challenged.

CONCLUSION

Political Theory from the Edges of Athenian Democracy

The distinction between historian and poet... consists really in this, that the one describes the thing that has been, and the other a kind of thing that might be.
– *Aristotle*, Poetics 1451a39–1451b2[1]

In 1983, Michael Walzer published *Spheres of Justice*, a much read and widely cited work of political theory that argued for the full political inclusion of immigrants, refugees, guest workers, and resident aliens in the countries in which they lived. What draws me to Walzer's argument is the moment he interrupts his discussion of contemporary alienage to draw a historical parallel. Before confronting the question of today's "guest worker," he writes, we ought to consider an "older example" of a figure that also resided in democracy without a path to citizenship. The ancient analog of the contemporary "live-in servant" is the metic of Athens who, though free to come and go, was like the guest worker, neither enslaved nor ruling, free yet barred indefinitely from citizenship.[2] Striking about Walzer's turn to the metic is how on second glance it serves an argument not about the enfranchisement of immigrants *per se* but about the lack of concern Athenian political thought showed this population. Walzer wagers that there must have been a "conceptual barrier to the extension of citizenship" in Athens.[3] Theorists at the time did not think to recommend a path to citizenship for people lacking the right parentage, he speculates, because it was difficult for them to see the metic's inclusion-exclusion as a matter of contestation. "The dominance of birth and blood over political membership," Walzer comments, "was part of the common understanding of the age."[4] No sooner does *Spheres of Justice* open a chasm between ancient and modern theoretical sensibilities than it attributes a special perspicacity to

[1] This is I. Bywater's translation (Aristotle 1984).
[2] Walzer 1983: 53, 55, 58. Walzer's engagements with Athenian political thought are mostly based in the interpretations of Whitehead (1977), whom Walzer cites repeatedly in his notes.
[3] Walzer 1983: 55. [4] Walzer 1983: 55.

the contemporary moment. "The question that apparently gave the Greeks no trouble," Walzer writes, "is both practically and theoretically troubling today."[5]

The call to see the disfranchisement of the immigrant as an urgent matter for political theoretical reflection depends in the aforementioned account on telling a progressive story of Western political thought in which late modern thinkers are uniquely capable of grasping the boundaries of membership as a question rather than a given for democratic politics. But to present this picture, Walzer must divest Athenian texts of their critical potential at the same time that he draws on their symbolic value: Athenian political thought plays a critical role in his argument not by disputing a hegemonic and essentializing status quo but by expressing that arrangement as a form of antiquated parochialism – its residual hold on contemporary democracy emerges as the trace of a tribal order in need of overcoming.[6] The "rule of citizens over non-citizens, of members over strangers," he adds, "is probably the most common form of tyranny in human history."[7]

If *Spheres of Justice* is unable to find allies in these "Greeks" for defending the full political inclusion of immigrants, however, it is in part because Walzer seeks prescriptions for making citizens out of resident aliens or, as he puts it, for "distributing" citizenship.[8] What his discussion takes as a lack of concern for the metic, in other words, is really the absence of programmatic political theorizing in Athenian texts. Walzer deduces from the absence of explicitly normative arguments about the metic not only that Athenian thinkers fail to grasp the democratic and theoretical significance of their own nativist realities but also that they are conventional in their chauvinism and for this reason blind to the political artifice and social construction of the city's "natural" divisions. Read in this way, Athenian texts appear complicit in establishing the citizen's difference from the metic as an essential truth.

I draw on Walzer's brief remarks about the metic because his discussion illustrates a persistent tendency in the contemporary interpretation of

[5] Walzer 1983: 55.

[6] *Pace* Rosenblum (1984: 587), who criticizes Walzer for using examples like "Periclean Athens or the Jewish community in Christian Europe" when neither was "a heterogeneous or differentiated society." Athens is an important example for Walzer, as I read him, precisely because the polis is heterogeneous *and* differentiated.

[7] Walzer 1983: 62. However, as Stevens points out, Walzer's argument eventually shifts from renouncing an "aristocratic order that 'rests upon birth and blood'" to adopting what she calls "modern conventions of birthright and kinship" (Stevens 1999: 5, 6).

[8] Walzer 1983: 32.

Athenian political thought that this book has sought to contravene. In the foregoing pages, I have argued that *metoikia* is a central but persistently occluded matter of investigation in the political thought of classical Athens. The metic's recovery as a site of theoretical meaning in texts by Euripides, Plato, and Demosthenes focuses attention on democracy's strategic investments in nativism, the shifting meaning of the citizen, and the precarious membership that a blood-based order effects for those eligible and ineligible to claim it.

But there is another reason at this juncture to reflect on *Spheres of Justice*. Walzer proposes that the metic bears analogies with contemporary membership categories. Whatever he makes of the metic's interest for Athenian thinkers, his argument implies, though it does not fully pursue, that possibilities for contemporary critique might be sought in political theory's relations to its self-appointed origins in classical Athens. In the remaining pages, I take up this provocation but starkly reimagine its terms. For when Walzer casts the connection between present and past modes of theorizing about immigrants as a site of antagonism and wishful overcoming – contemporary democratic theorists find objects of analysis and possibilities for change where Athenian thinkers see only a celebratory status quo – he on the one hand glimpses the critical promise of the metic and on the other restricts this potential to the empirical register: that Athenian law delineated citizenship in terms of descent. And yet the convergence Walzer locates between these two disparate political contexts is not altogether insignificant for political theory. Like Jacqueline Stevens after him, Walzer is writing against the disciplinary grain when he draws a line connecting ancient and modern "democratic" societies over their wrongful exclusion of residents on the basis of birth and blood. Most of the time, as Stevens explains, political scientists would have us believe the "modern fiction" that "a real state has separated the logic of kinship from citizenship" because "it is in primitive societies, and not states, that political communities and kinship structures overlap."[9] Against the standard account, Stevens maintains that "the paradigmatic membership structure for all political societies derives from invocations of birth and ancestry"; even territorial citizenship, she notes, constitutes a birth-based form of membership.[10] In the views of both these political theorists, then, the grounding of political societies in myths of genealogical and therefore "natural" difference is a political fact that stretches back to classical Athens. Its critical accounting and theoretical exploration, however, are

[9] Stevens 1999: 99, 51. [10] Stevens 1999: 51, 61.

strictly modern affairs. Plato may have "politicize[d] the family," Stevens observes, but there is no evidence that "the question of political membership" was a "seriously contested concept" before modernity.[11]

The following conclusion explores some reasons and interpretive avenues for moving beyond *this* modern fiction by asking what is at stake, finally, for political theory and contemporary democratic politics in bringing the discursive site of the metic out of the shadows and using it to activate a series of ancient contestations over democracy's investment in nativist political exclusion. I approach this question with some caution, however, for I did not intend the previous interpretations as solutions to a normative question about how a democracy should treat the persons it deems nonnative, nor do I think the value of studying the past lies in its straightforward application to contemporary problems. "When the past speaks, it always speaks as an oracle," Nietzsche writes. "You will have enough to ponder and to invent when you reflect on the life of the future, but do not ask of history that it should show you the How? and the Wherewith? to this life."[12] If there is heuristic value in the preceding interpretations, it therefore lies in the critical potential of these readings not to show us what to think, as Nietzsche clarifies, but to show us how to see differently some present ways of thinking.

The complex question of how and to what effects political theorists forge links between modern and ancient iterations of democracy in their readings of classical Greek texts has already drawn some attention in this book: part of exploring the metic's critical power often meant unsettling commonly held assumptions about Athenian politics and its theoretical legacies. My argument went a step further, however, to envisage metic figurations as a strategically "forgotten" segment of the past,[13] an orientation inspired by Nietzsche that presses us to ask what political investments the metic's undertheorization has helped maintain and what new ways of seeing its recovery might open up. I present the question of the metic's contemporary significance this way to suggest that there is nothing inherently critical about bringing the metic to bear on exigent questions of democratic exclusion, immigration, or blood-based membership. The critical potential of the encounter depends on (opening) the horizon in which the question "what is a democratic citizen" has been put to Athenian texts for generations without serious attention to what represents the citizen's most menacing, because proximate, counterpart. Exploring the metic's critical promise for contemporary democratic thought and

[11] Stevens 1999: 63, 62. [12] Nietzsche 1997: 94. [13] Nietzsche 1997: 70.

politics therefore means elaborating first on some of the claims of this book and then using them to open paths for future exploration.

****

The standard verdict that finds Athenian texts unresponsive to the descent-based membership order of its political realities is partly symptomatic of what Chapters 1 and 3 called a doctrinal strategy of interpretation. On this approach, readers, not unlike Walzer, look primarily for recommendations or sustained systematic arguments about the boundaries of membership and fail to see how Athenian texts figure, in ways that assay, the democratic discourses, institutions, and cultural practices that were working in Athens to conjure the metic and assign it a pregiven, stable, and hierarchical meaning. One effect of mobilizing these figurations, I maintained, was that Athenian political thought appears newly alert to dynamics of inclusion-exclusion typically considered outside its scope of concern, and helps us make sense of how these dynamics are constitutive of, not merely coincidental to, a democratic order.

Against the predominant view that sees Athenian texts as either indifferent to or invested in a blood-based democratic citizenry, then, the preceding chapters illustrated the ways in which they make creative use of metic figurations to mount a series of immanent democratic critiques. Each reading attempted to inhabit the particular, dynamic, and fluctuating identity of the metic so as to achieve a kind of kaleidoscopic shift in reader perspective. I use the term "kaleidoscopic" to suggest that while some of the objects of the preceding study will have seemed familiar to the reader, a metic lens has the power to open up new and complex patterns between them. Within this different perceptual field, I could give expression to the observation, explored variously in Euripides, Plato, and Demosthenes, that the blood criterion Athenian democracy uses to draw its membership boundaries does not secure, permanently or reliably, a lived experience of citizenship for those eligible to claim it. Athenian thinkers show us membership criteria failing to make good on the democracy's civic purpose: metics act like citizens and citizens like metics. The freedom, assimilation, and membership activity of the metic is thus figured in ways that call into question the democracy's political distinctions and reveal the artifice of this "natural" division. But as the reading of Euripides' *Ion* illustrated, it would be a mistake to assume that instances of passing and status flux are simply the results of the city's failure to police the boundaries of membership. These identity confusions emerge instead as the strategic effects of the membership order itself. In a context of interpolis flows, the inadequacy of blood to determine performance might reveal autochthonous citizenship as a regulatory fiction, but it might also license a politics of nativist retrenchment – the sort of suspiciousness about citizenship contamination that, in Demosthenes' speech, gains traction in moments of political crisis and leads a polis to double down on the expressive power of blood.

In these ways, the foregoing argument has attempted to enlarge our sense of the political theoretical concerns of Athenian texts to include democracy's competing investments in openness and nativism. Throwing light on the complexities of this democratic dynamic, however, also required creating a space for discovery and exploration. This involved pondering why readers have been inclined to see membership questions in Athenian texts posed in terms of gender, class, and slavery but not with regard to the large and integrated presence of metics in Athens and therefore to the blood-based rules for citizenship that defined the demos. I suggested that several interpretive tendencies have lent support to the presumption that Athenian texts have little if anything to say about the metic or the blood-based exclusion it represents. The parsing of theoretical arguments in isolation of their rhetorical structures is one. Another is the binary character of frameworks that dominate the study of Athenian citizenship. The metic, I maintained in Chapter 1, cuts across or fails to emerge within the oppositions (e.g., free/unfree, citizen/slave, native/foreigner, mass/elite, male/female) scholars typically use to explore the meaning of membership in democratic Athens and its texts. To place the metic's political and theoretical meaning at the center of our analysis of Athenian politics and thought is thus to expose some of the limits and obscuring effects of standard membership frameworks.

An additional interpretive assumption impeding the metic's theorization takes the paucity of literal textual references to metics as "metics" to designate their absence from Athenian political thought and the practical unimportance of this status distinction to (contemporaneous analyses of) democratic life. To counter this notion, I argued throughout the book that the metic's presence both in the polis and in the Athenian imaginary circulates in the texts of Euripides, Plato, and Demosthenes in a range of discourses, practices, historical personages, and figurations – from the mythologizing of natural difference and the policing of Athenianness to the power of suspiciousness, apathy, and mercantilism to shape the meaning of citizenship – that do not always name *metoikia* as such.

The preceding pages have for these reasons aimed at demonstrating the political and theoretical importance of reading Athenian political thought in a rhetorically and historically sensitive way. Yet the implications of this approach for political theory and classical studies exceed any particular discussion of democratic exclusion. When I argued in Chapter 3, for example, that Plato casts the problem of democratic injustice in terms of the metic, I was also calling into question a set of common presuppositions about the aims of Plato's political thought and the tradition of "logocentrism" he is said to have bequeathed us.[14] If the metic frames the *Republic* and provokes the discussion of justice, the vital part of Plato's challenge to democratic discourse need not lie exclusively or even primarily in the assertions Socrates is made to speak. They consist in the broader moves of Plato's dramaturgy and narration, which is to say, those features of his writing and theorizing practice that include direct speech, of course, but that also employ framing, dramatic dates, cultural practices, historical characterization, setting, and myth to effect an exploratory, aporetic, and particularized style of critique. This book is hardly the first to attend to the discursive dimensions of Plato's texts, but it has attempted to make a case for the political and theoretical possibilities they can bring into view, in particular for the sorts of unexpected democratic self-criticisms that might spring from a rhetorical reading of passages like the noble lie, which typically elicit a decontextualized and doctrinal reading strategy. At the same time, however, this book's hermeneutic sensibility has not pertained solely to Plato's dialogues, even if its effects might be most evident when applied to such familiar terrain. The interpretations of Euripides and Demosthenes would have been just as difficult to bring forward without some reflection on the generic expectations readers bring to works of tragedy and oratory or some consideration of how these expectations erect interpretive impediments to the examination of figurations of political exclusion.

In short, what counts as "political," "theoretical," or even "democratic" in Athenian texts depends on constructing zones for analysis in which such issues as immigration and inherited exclusion can appear as viable political theoretical questions for the so-called origins of political theory. And yet it is not enough to claim that the metic's undertheorization has been generative of and generated by certain ways of imagining democratic membership and reading Athenian texts without asking pointedly what contemporary political investments might be driving and benefiting from bypassing the metic. We have already seen how readers' retreat from the theoretical significance of *metoikia* serves an impulse, widely shared by political theorists, to abstract some of the concrete (exclusionary) realities

[14] Derrida 1981.

of historical Athens so as to secure an aspirational model of participatory citizenship and inclusiveness for contemporary democratic politics. The problem with this tendency does not concern its accuracy per se. The issue is what political theorists are maintaining and what they are foreclosing when they take classical Athens to exemplify and define an expansive democratic ideal without also posing the always-attendant question of how this inclusiveness is adjudicated and imagined there.

The general interpretive impulse I refer to emerged in the previous chapters whenever scholars failed to discuss the city's blood-based and nativist membership practices in their analyses of Athenian politics, democracy, or Athenian thought and most clearly in Chapter 5's discussion of *Republic* VIII. Political theorists interpreted Plato's deployment of democratic membership categories and his concern with the political utility of claims of nature without noting that Athenian democracy had its own investment in a language and logic of natural difference. Although the *Republic* takes place in Athens and makes discursive use of specific Athenian membership categories, the issue of democratic nativism and the work blood does for the city did not surface, in analyses of the status flux scene, as either relevant or complicating features of the *Republic* argument. Whatever their differences in theoretical aims, Rancière and Saxonhouse both understood the problem Plato figures with democracy – a concept, we ought to note, that shifts in their readings between a historical arrangement and an ideal type – to concern democracy's rejection of natural claims to rule. On the one hand, they conceded that the *Republic* notices, if only to distance itself from, the egalitarianism of its democratic realities. On the other, they presumed that the *Republic* rejects a situated style of political theory, which is to say, the sort of theoretical approach that would make the naturalized divisions of the "real" Athens central to its generalizable analysis of democracy in theory.

This perplexing picture requires some attention. With regard to the exclusionary aspects of Athenian democracy, the celebrated foundational text of political theory is supposed not to register, indeed it seems to reject, the premise that theorizing the paradigmatic (i.e., democracy in general) is inseparable from theorizing the local (i.e., democracy in particular).[15] More precisely, Plato incorporates some features of the local (e.g., Athenian freedom) into his typology but for some reason, we are encouraged to

[15] Some postcolonial studies offer critical discussions of the contemporary tendency to theorize the universal apart from the particular (i.e., the assumption that a universal picture is not in some sense indebted to a particular one). See Chakrabarty 2000; see also Chatterjee 1993: ch. 1.

believe, leaves out the particular calculus and myth of belonging this polis used to naturalize its form of inclusive membership. In other words, the universal definition of democracy as a rebellious form of politics fundamentally allergic to naturalized hierarchy is established in *Republic* VIII by transcending – or instructing the reader to transcend – certain aspects of the political realities in which that definition emerges. Most curiously, Plato enables this transcendence, on the standard reading, despite his framing the *Republic* in a particular (metic) place, or better yet, despite his presenting the relation between abstract ideas and their concrete instantiations for our immediate and persistent consideration.

My quarrel with the approach just outlined does not concern its partiality, which is a feature of any attempt to theorize with Athens or its critics, including my own. The problem is with what this particular vision threatens to elide. When the pull of nativism in democracy falls out of view of a text like the *Republic*, questions of nativism become (i.e., are read back as being) irrelevant to a theorization of democracy in general. Does Plato's text direct us to this conclusion? Or could there be a wider set of critical practices preventing concerns with naturalized exclusion from crossing the border of Athenian politics into Athenian theory, that privileged site for endowing democracy with its universal meaning?

The tendency on the part of democratic theorists to seek animating explorations of political dilemmas in the thought and politics of classical Athens rarely leads them to pose the "prior" question of "who counts as belonging to 'the people' and who does *not*" by way of Athens or its theoretical tradition.[16] The contemporary concern with how a democracy draws its boundaries of inclusion and how these lines produce exclusions emerges persistently instead as a matter of and for the nation-state, bounded territories, and modern multicultural societies, where "the exclusivist tendencies of popular sovereignty" manifests as a conundrum of state politics and as a sign of the uneasy relationships among such modern phenomena as nationalism, cultural and ethnic heterogeneity, and democracy.[17] As Étienne Balibar writes, a "reciprocal interaction" appears to exist "between the *two* notions of the people: that which the Greek language and following it all political philosophy calls *ethnos*, the 'people,'

[16] Cocks 2014: 23, my emphasis.

[17] For a critique of their separation, see Balibar 1991a: 17–27. Cocks (2014: 23–24) raises the important question of whether "the hostility of privileged citizens" to migrants is "an expression not merely, as some critics propose, of a modern form of 'monarchical sovereign power,'" such as the state, but also and specifically of "democratic sovereign power," which she defines as "power exerted via strong popular sentiment."

as an imagined community of membership and filiation, and *dēmos*, the 'people' as the collective subject of representation, decision making, and rights."[18] But if a version of this "reciprocal interaction" already presents itself in Athenian politics, might its interrogation be just as, if differently, alive in Athenian thought?

Where some modern thinkers present the "ethnic" foundation of the demos as a strained relation that would ideally come to an end, the *Republic* depicts the pregiven foundation of a polity as an effect of willful political power, a contingent and unpredictable operation that grounds the boundaries of membership in a claim about nature and is, for this reason, available for our critique and revision. Think back to Chapter 4, in which Plato's "open secret" exposed the natural and hierarchical arrangement of the callipolis as an artifice. On my reading, the *Republic* did this not to recommend the eventual decoupling of the natural from the political or to posit this untethering as a normative ideal but rather to demonstrate that all membership orders, including Athenian democracy, are parasitic on a foundation in "nature." Plato's text, I argued, presents this decidedly unorganic founding as a political machination with strategic effects.

That polities use naturalizing myths to define the limits of the demos seems, from the *Republic*'s perspective, an indeterminate but inevitable feature of political life. This ancient insight is important to confront from a contemporary standpoint. The *Republic*'s dramatization of how origins are made challenges Seyla Benhabib's observation that "[m]odern democracies act in the name of universal principles that are then circumscribed within a particular civic community."[19] The beauty of Plato's dramaturgy is how it conveys these apparently different registers as really one: the scene that depicts Socrates sharing the noble lie counters the contemporary impulse to disentangle permanently the universal from the particular, the democratic from the ethnic.[20] Indeed, a contemporary practice of democratic critique inspired by the *Republic* would seek not the reconciliation of the universal and the particular – Plato presents that operation as a political conceit – but the exposé of their mutual imbrication. If Plato takes Socrates down to Piraeus and if the callipolis takes shape in and through Athens, political change starts with thinking about politics as they already are. This critical practice presupposes that a changing of the status quo involves first casting light on the contingent but naturalized limits of the community one desires to change.

[18] Balibar 2004: 8. [19] Benhabib 2004: 132. [20] Benhabib 2004: 136.

But rather than telling us something vital about how democratic ideals work themselves out in practice (i.e., contingently and to ambiguous effects), the *Republic* is usually interpreted as a series of overhauling normative proposals so as to offer what Danielle Allen has criticized as "a straightforward constitutional blueprint that Plato hoped to see implemented" with little concern for how his "investigations of political questions (whether tending in an anti-democratic or democratic direction) feed back into Athenian politics."[21] To the extent that scholarship does consider Plato's theory a "practical politics," it envisages the *Republic* as an anti-democratic guide for conservative rulers[22] and delimits its examinations of democracy to arguments about the excesses of egalitarianism.

Whatever their interpretive differences, these reading practices conspire to entrench a view of the *Republic* as an abstracting and antidemocratic text of little value for thinking aporetically about democratic politics on the ground. This tendency has immediate implications for contemporary efforts to theorize the pull of nativism in democracy. For the problem is not simply whether Plato's engagements with democratic exclusion can emerge within the standard framings. It is that the *Republic*'s interest in how claims of democratic difference play out in practice drops out of its theorization of democracy, meaning that it vanishes from the so-called foundational vision of democracy that continues to inspire affirmative arguments about contemporary politics (in spite of Plato, as it were). However explicit their engagements with Plato's text, political theorists tend to deploy the *Republic* to fashion a redemptive model of democratic politics according to which immigrant and inherited exclusion are aberrations of democracy rather than fundamental and persistent matters of theorization that are subject to political flux. As a theoretical and interpretive approach, this orientation is not just wishful but also impairing. For it impedes our understanding of how civic promises of inclusion manifest themselves in and as dynamics of subordination both historically and in our own time.[23] This way of thinking hinders us from appreciating how, even in Plato's text, abstract accounts of democracy are always connected to actual ones, which is to suggest, with Nicholas DeGenova, that even models are "produced and continuously sustained by sociopolitical relations."[24]

21 Allen 2013: 14, 15. 22 Allen 2013: 14.

23 For example, Rana (2010) exhibits this theoretical impetus when he argues that the political origins of the U.S. ideal of freedom cannot be understood apart from the country's settler practices of territorial conquest and the dispossession and control of marginalized groups.

24 De Genova 2016: 77.

Approached in this light, my wager that the metic constitutes the unacknowledged provocation of the *Republic* now prompts a more general thought: the metic has not been merely underanalyzed in the reception of Athenian political thought but displaced. The word "displaced" would imply that inattentiveness to the metic's symbolic meaning has not only helped keep blood-based exclusion and nativism outside the domain of classical Greek thought but that it has also helped turn the democracy figured in Athenian texts into the site of a particular contemporary longing. Political theorists may be accustomed to acknowledging that "factual" Athenian democracy (minus its exclusions) constitutes an object of nostalgic desire, but they are much less inclined to consider that the ways they interpret the democracy that is *theorized* by Athenian texts might be working to delimit their own theoretical insights, which is to say that they might read, so as to confirm, the contemporary normative ideal that democracy is a political arrangement aimed at and constituted by a "fully inclusive consensus without exclusion."[25]

Political life always entails "the construction of a 'we'" that "must be distinguished from [a] 'them,'" observes Chantal Mouffe, because politics always involves "establishing a frontier, defining an 'enemy,'" and a shifting one at that.[26] A hermeneutics that disavows the *Republic*'s politically situated character to secure a separation between the theoretical and the political, the ideal and the actual, the normal and the aberrational would appear to deprive us of an enduring Platonic insight: the political drive to hierarchy may be unavoidable, but the specific forms it takes are always open to critique and contestation.

****

This discussion of the *Republic* suggests that long before contemporary thinkers began focusing on the inclusion of the nonnative, the metic was already raising challenges to democracy for political theory texts at the granular level. If foregrounding the politics of *metoikia* has opened a new horizon for interpreting Athenian political thought, it has also, I hope, shifted the interpretive terrain on which membership questions have been formulated by way of "the Greeks" for some time. Where do we go from here?

The interpretations in this book present the metic as an unruly figure, easy to confuse, difficult to pin down, constantly transforming, and therefore indicative of membership politics more generally. From a mythical

[25] Mouffe 2013: 9. [26] Mouffe 2005: 69.

autochthonous progenitor to a mimed and miming citizenry, a politically active ribbon seller to a widowed wet nurse, the "native" Athenians explored in these pages find their citizenship in question, their political standing only temporarily established by a discursive act: the interpretation of a performance, the claiming of ancestry, the taking on of a secret, the analysis of work. Each of these doings attempts to conceal, and so it ends up exposing, the democratic need and daily attempts to fix meaning and impose order on performance, on what is dynamic and in play. The texts I have read in this book remind us of the vicissitudes of political life – regime change, economic collapse, immigration legislation, war, territorial transformations – that suddenly reveal the precariousness of all membership categories.

I began this conclusion by calling into question the "modern fiction" that contemporary theorists are alert to forms of exclusion that Athenian theorists have a strategic investment in not seeing. Let me end by turning that fiction on its head: what if Athenian engagements with the metic actually reveal impasses in contemporary thinking about membership instead? In light of the relations explored earlier between practices of reading Athenian texts and contemporary democratic theories, perhaps what is needed now is to envisage Athens not as a "model" or antiquated ideal but what Cornelius Castoriadis calls a "germ, an index of actual possibilities" that we "engage in discourse" and allow to "question" us.[27]

Thinkers writing on contemporary immigration tend to see the task of political theory to provide prescriptions for or against the extension of citizenship to irregular residents, weighing, for example, whether a country like the United States should provide those living without resident status the "legal authorization to stay."[28] These important discussions often evaluate criteria for citizenship and practices of admission to assess their legitimacy, fairness, or consistency with democratic "principles."[29] But focused on settling questions of (il)legality and immigrant amnesty, as Jacqueline Stevens notes, much political theory "recognizes and endorses clear demarcations between citizens and aliens," and so it upholds "the conventional boundaries between insiders and outsiders" rather than directing attention to their persistent ambiguities.[30]

[27] Castoriadis 2007: 117. [28] Carens 2013: 1.

[29] On the justice or legitimacy of membership criteria, see Walzer 1983; Shachar 2009; Stevens 1999. Carens (2013) applies democratic principles to questions of immigration and inquires into the moral obligations states have to noncitizen residents.

[30] Stevens 2017: 7.

Given this picture, it is not surprising that Athenian engagements with immigration have yet to materialize in contemporary political theoretical discussions. The texts analyzed in this book do not issue recommendations for membership (as Walzer observed), and they do not assume democratic hierarchies are permanently eradicable. But in not doing these things, they do something else. They figure an altogether different way of theorizing that engages the immigrant, no less the citizen, not as a question to solve but as an endless aporia for political life.[31] The readings advanced in this book resist standard notions of the citizen as a fixed status, legal category, or unchanging essence. They offer in its place the metic, a dynamic and shifting concept conducive to political anxiety but also of political contestation and best, though never definitively, imagined along a spectrum of membership rather than on one side of an opposition. They dramatize practices of mimesis to highlight the contingent and performative character of membership categories. They insinuate that the lines between citizens and aliens are impossible to settle once and for all. They denaturalize relations of power so as to reveal their availability for alteration, manipulation, and strategic adaptation.

One may therefore interpret the problem of so-called migrant "illegality" as a peculiarly modern predicament that bears little resemblance to the *metoikia* politics explored in these pages: the physical borders of the nation-state are generally taken to be categorically different from the impenetrable, because interior, borders that divide members along kinship (or ethnic) lines, as they did in Athens or at earlier moments in U.S. history; today exclusion from full political membership appears to rest on a physical and legal transgression not on a pregiven difference – any racialization of juridical inequalities appears, in this frame, as merely coincidental and so on. But to draw these conclusions would be to turn our backs on the metic and the challenges this figure has presented. Democratic difference takes multiple guises, its constituted character is frequently made to vanish, and it mutates tactically. From blood to metal, autochthony to labor, kinship to wealth, political difference has been called forth, figured, or enacted in the texts explored here so as to propagate the semblance of a prior offense (of passing or inadequate blood) that it is supposed merely to evince. Whether we have in mind a border crossing, an invitation from Pericles, or a "mixed" marriage, what classifies the noncitizen, then, is neither nature nor necessity but "a rule of exclusion," as Balibar writes, "of visible or

[31] In a similar vein, Dietz (2012: 289) reads Aristotle to underscore the instability of citizenship and to suggest it is, for Aristotle, "a permanently open puzzlement (*aporia*)" for the polis.

invisible 'borders,' materialized in laws and practices."[32] This was the insight Plato's open secret afforded when it took us behind the scenes of the noble lie's construction. The idea also emerged in Demosthenes 57, where Athenian democracy was shown to produce the terms and conditions for Euxitheus to be a citizen "falsely" much the way modern nation-states present the undocumented as a self-evident fact, as if they were merely chronicling a legal offense.[33]

What this means is not only that present alienage categories are, like *metoikia*, produced and naturalized through practices of policing that render certain forms of human mobility malignant and give them the semblance of facticity and uncontestable meaning. The political effort to distinguish hierarchically among various ways of moving through a space or residing within one turns out to be constitutive of democracy as a political arrangement. Stop-and-detain measures and immigration raids are in their political effects not so dissimilar from the scrutinizing and purging of deme rolls that targeted Euxitheus. As practices of detection and marginalization, they ensure what DeGenova has called the "purported naturalness and putative necessity of exclusion" that "may be demonstrated and verified, validated and legitimated."[34]

To envisage Athens as a germ from this perspective would therefore mean making the metic an analytic tool for troubling the taken-for-granted-ness of any number of contemporary idioms for articulating membership and immigration politics. It would entail questioning the impulse to establish clear lines between geospatial and ascriptive membership boundaries. It would also involve asking whether our conceptual frames for imagining contemporary membership questions are adequate to make sense of current forms of intergenerational democratic exclusion that persist in what Charles Maier has called a "post-territorial world" that lacks a formal category like *metoikia* to capture them.[35]

If the metic resists easy translation into our vernacular, that is not because the concept is obsolete but because it is troubling. The metic spans and inhabits the cleavages of conditions we have long desired to see as dueling and discrete: the foreign and the native; the legal and the illegal; the citizen and the alien; the outsider and the insider. If the metic denotes both an immigrant and its offspring born in Athens, then it constitutes an incitement to name, but also to analyze, the interrelations that might pertain, however informally, between the internal excluded and the

[32] Balibar 2004: 23. [33] For a discussion of migrant illegality in this vein, see DeGenova 2013: 3.
[34] DeGenova 2013: 2. [35] Maier 2016.

external included figures of multiethnic and multicultural democracies. The nearly four million citizen children of undocumented immigrants in the United States today may be fully included juridically, but they are in practice deprivileged variously and unpredictably by their parents' lack of legal documentation. Fear of and susceptibility to deportation circumscribe their education and health care.[36] Though not codified by law, the uneven incorporation, in the form of racial oppression, of citizen minorities in the United States and postcolonial Europe suggests that neither the present nor the recent history of Western democratic societies lacks examples of inherited exclusion. The recovery of the metic might prompt us to avow the always-present, if latent, nativist impulses of democracies. It might provoke us to see connections between various contemporary "crises" today: the uneven inclusion of some citizens, the proliferation of second-class membership statuses, and the anti-immigrant sentiment that rages worldwide. It might incite us to ask whether the figure haunting democracy is not and never really was just the one Derrida calls the "foreigner, from abroad" but also the one Aristotle describes as a "citizen in a qualified sense" (*Pol.* 1274b13–1274b14).[37] It might inspire a new question. What if the metic is the critical figure of our time?

[36] Yoshikawa 2011. [37] Derrida 2000: 3.

Appendix: A Metic Timeline

This timeline includes relevant political events in Athenian history, purported and generally accepted dates of composition, dramatic setting, and performance where relevant. The precise chronology of Plato's dialogues is highly uncertain. All dates are BCE.

c. 480	Birth of Euripides.
460s–450s	Athens establishes *metoikia* as a formal juridical category.
450s–429	Periclean leadership of Athens.
451/0	Pericles' Citizenship Law passes. Citizenship limited to legitimate children of two Athenian citizens. Pericles and the metic Aspasia begin twenty-year relationship.
c. 450	Cephalus immigrates to Athens. His son Polemarchus is born in Syracuse.
431	War declared between Athens and Sparta; Peloponnesian War begins. Pericles' Funeral Oration delivered.
c. 430	Cephalus, Lysias, and Polemarchus return for a time to Sicily as colonists.
431–411	*Republic*'s dramatic setting.
c. 427	Birth of Plato.
413	Athenian expedition to Sicily fails.
c. 412	Euripides produces the *Ion*.
411	Oligarchic revolution of "The Four Hundred" in Athens.
410	Restoration of democracy.
406	Death of Euripides.
404	Spartan victory over Athens leads to oligarchic regime of the "Thirty Tyrants" and temporary end of democracy. Polemarchus is executed by the Thirty.
403	Democracy is restored in Athens.

399	Trial and execution of Socrates.
390s–380s	Plato writes the *Menexenus*.
c. 387	Plato founds the Academy.
c. 384	Birth of Aristotle.
384	Birth of Demosthenes.
380s–370s	Plato composes the *Republic*.
c. 365	Aristotle arrives at Plato's Academy.
360	Philip II begins building Macedonian Empire in Greece.
347	Plato's death.
c. 345	Demosthenes composes *Against Euboulides*.
c. 322	Death of Aristotle.
322	Macedonian hegemony over Athens and end of independent democracy. Death of Demosthenes.

Bibliography

Acton, P. 2014. *Poiesis: Manufacturing in Ancient Athens*. Oxford University Press.

Adak, M. 2003. *Metöken als Wohltäter Athens: Untersuchungen zum sozialen Austausch zwischen ortsansässigen Fremden und der Bürgergemeinde in klassischer und hellenistischer Zeit (ca. 500–150 v. Chr.)*. Munich, TUDUV.

Agamben, G. 2011. *Nudities*. Trans. D. Kishik and S. Pedatella. Stanford University Press.

1998. *Homo Sacer: Sovereign Power and Bare Life*. Trans. D. Heller-Roazen. Stanford University Press.

Akrigg, B. 2015. "Metics in Athens," in C. Taylor and K. Vlassopoulos (eds.), *Communities and Networks in the Ancient Greek World*. Oxford University Press, 155–176.

Allen, D. 2013. *Why Plato Wrote* (2010). Malden, MA, Wiley-Blackwell.

Andrew, E. 1989. "Equality of Opportunity as the Noble Lie," *History of Political Thought* 10/4: 577–595.

Archibald, R. C. 2013. "Dominicans of Haitian Descent Cast into Legal Limbo by Court," *New York Times*, 24 October, A1.

Arendt, H. 1968. *Between Past and Future: Eight Exercises in Political Thought* (1961). expanded ed. New York, Penguin.

1998. *The Human Condition* (1958). 2nd ed. University of Chicago Press.

Aristotle. 2002. *On Poetics*. Trans. S. Benardete and M. Davis. South Bend, IN, St. Augustine's Press.

1996. *The Politics and the Constitution of Athens*. Ed. S. Everson and trans. B. Jowett. Cambridge University Press.

1984. *The Complete Works of Aristotle: The Revised Oxford Translation*. Ed. J. Barnes. 2 vols. Princeton University Press.

Bakewell, G. 2013. *Aeschylus's Suppliant Women: The Tragedy of Immigration*. Madison: University of Wisconsin Press.

1999. "Lysias 12 and Lysias 31: Metics and Athenian Citizenship in the Aftermath of the Thirty," *Greek, Roman, and Byzantine Studies* 40/1: 5–22.

Balibar, E. 2004. *We, the People of Europe? Reflections on Transnational Citizenship*. Trans. J. Swenson. Princeton University Press.

1991a. "Is There a Neo-Racism?" in E. Balibar and I. Wallerstein (eds.), *Race, Nation, Class: Ambiguous Identities*, London, Verso, 17–28.

1991b. "Nationalism and Racism," in E. Balibar and I. Wallerstein (eds.), *Race, Nation, Class: Ambiguous Identities*, London, Verso, 37–67.
Balot, R. K. 2014. *Courage in the Democratic Polis: Ideology and Critique in Classical Athens*. Oxford University Press.
Bassi, K. 1998. *Acting Like Men: Gender, Drama, and Nostalgia in Ancient Greece*. Ann Arbor, University of Michigan Press.
Beardslee, J. W. 1987. "The Use of Physis in Fifth-Century Greek Literature" (1918), repr. in E. Hofman, J. W. Beardslee, and O. Johrens, *Early Greek Thought: Three Studies*. New York, Garland, i–126.
Benardete, S. 1989. *Socrates' Second Sailing: On Plato's Republic*. University of Chicago Press.
Benhabib, S. 2004. "Reclaiming Universalism: Negotiating Republican Self-Determination and Cosmopolitan Norms." The Tanner Lectures on Human Values, www.tannerlectures.utah.edu, 113–166.
Berger, A. E. 2013. *The Queer Turn in Feminism: Identities, Sexualities, and the Theater of Gender*. Trans. C. Porter. New York, Fordham University Press.
Bernal, M. 1987. *Black Athena: The Afroasiatic Roots of Classical Civilization, vol. I: The Fabrication of Ancient Greece 1785–1985*. New Brunswick, NJ, Rutgers.
Bers, V. 2003. "Introduction," in *Demosthenes, Speeches 50–59*, trans. V. Bers. Austin, University of Texas Press, 107–108.
Bhabha, H. K. 1994. *The Location of Culture*. London and New York, Routledge.
Bilsky, L. 2008. "Citizenship as Mask: Between the Imposter and the Refugee," *Constellations* 15/1: 72–97.
Blanshard, A. 2014. "The Permeable Spaces of the Athenian Law-Court," in K. Gilhuly and N. Worman (eds.), *Space, Place and Landscape in Ancient Greek Literature and Culture*. Cambridge University Press, 240–275.
Blok, J. H. 2009a. "Gentrifying Genealogy: On the Genesis of the Athenian Autochthony Myth," in C. Walde and U. Dill (eds.), *Antike Mythen: Medien, Transformationen, Konstruktionen; Fritz Graf zum 65. Geburtstag*. Berlin, De Gruyter, 251–275.
2009b. "Perikles' Citizenship Law: A New Perspective," *Historia* 58/2: 141–170.
Blondell, R. 2002. *The Play of Character in Plato's Dialogues*. New York, Cambridge University Press.
Boedeker, D. and Raaflaub, K. A. 1998. *Democracy, Empire, and the Arts in Fifth-Century Athens*. Cambridge, MA, Harvard University Press.
Bok, S. 1989. *Secrets: On the Ethics of Concealment and Revelation*. New York, Vintage.
Bresson, A. 2016. *The Making of the Ancient Greek Economy: Institutions, Markets, and Growth in the City-States*. Trans. S. Rendall. Princeton University Press.
Brisson, L. 1998. *Plato, the Myth Maker*. Ed. and trans. G. Naddaf. University of Chicago Press.
Brock, R. 1994. "The Labour of Women in Classical Athens," *Classical Quarterly* 44/2: 336–346.
Brown, W. 1998. "'Supposing Truth Were a Woman . . . ' Plato's Subversion of Masculine Discourse," *Political Theory* 16/4: 594–616.

Brubaker, R. 1992. *Citizenship and Nationhood in France and Germany.* Cambridge, MA, Harvard University Press.

Burnyeat, M. F. 1997. "Culture and Society in Plato's Republic." The Tanner Lectures on Human Values, www.tannerlectures.utah.edu.

Butler, J. 2003. "Performative Acts and Gender Constitution: An Essay in Phenomenology and Feminist Theory," in C. McCann and S. Kim (eds.), *Feminist Theory Reader: Local and Global Perspectives.* New York and London, Routledge, 415–427.

1999. *Gender Trouble: Feminism and the Subversion of Identity (1990).* New York, Routledge.

Carawan, E. 2008. "Pericles the Younger and the Citizenship Law," *Classical Journal* 103/4: 383–406.

Calame, C. 2003. *Myth and History in Ancient Greece: The Symbolic Creation of a Colony.* Trans. D. W. Berman. Princeton University Press.

Carens, J. 2013. *The Ethics of Immigration.* Oxford University Press.

Carey, C. 2007. "Artless Proofs in Aristotle and the Orators," in E. Carawan (ed.), *Oxford Readings in Classical Studies: The Attic Orators.* Oxford University Press, 229–246.

1997. *Trials from Classical Athens.* London and New York, Routledge.

1994. "'Artless' Proofs in Aristotle and the Orators," *Bulletin of the Institute of Classical Studies* 39/1: 95–106.

Carmola, K. 2003. "Noble Lying: Justice and Intergenerational Tension in Plato's *Republic*," *Political Theory* 31/1: 39–62.

Castoriadis, C. 2007. *Figures of the Thinkable.* Trans. H. Arnold. Stanford University Press.

1997. "The Greek Polis and the Creation of Democracy" (1983), in *The Castoriadis Reader.* Trans. and ed. D. A. Curtis. Oxford and Malden, MA, Blackwell, 267–289.

Cecchet, L. 2015. *Poverty in Athenian Public Discourse: From the Eve of the Peloponnesian War to the Rise of Macedonia.* Stuttgart, Franz Steiner Verlag.

Chakrabarty, D. 2000 *Provincializing Europe: Postcolonial Thought and Historical Difference.* Princeton University Press.

Chambers, S. 2012. *The Lessons of Rancière.* Oxford University Press.

2009. "A Queer Politics of the Democratic Miscount," *Borderlands e-journal* 8/2: 1–23. www.borderlands.net.au.

Charalabopoulos, N. 2012. *Platonic Drama and Its Ancient Reception.* Cambridge University Press.

Chatterjee, P. 1993. *Nationalist Thought and the Colonial World: A Derivative Discourse (1986).* Minneapolis, University of Minnesota Press.

Clerc, M. A. E. A. 1893. *Les métèques athéniens: étude sur la condition légale, la situation morale et le rôle social et èconomique des étrangers domiciliés à Athènes.* Paris, Thorin & fils.

Cocks, J. 2014. *On Sovereignty and Other Political Delusions.* London, Bloomsbury.

Cohen, E. 2000. *The Athenian Nation.* Princeton University Press.

Connor, W. R. 1994. "The Problem of Athenian Civic Identity," in A. L. Boegehold and A. Scafuro (eds.), *Athenian Identity and Civic Ideology*. Baltimore, MD, Johns Hopkins University Press, 34–44.

1989. "City Dionysia and Athenian Democracy," *Classica et Mediaevalia* 40: 7–32.

1984. *Thucydides*. Princeton University Press.

Cornelli, G. and Lisi, F. L. 2010. *Plato and the City*. Sankt Augustin, Academia Verlag.

Davidson, J. N. 2011. *Courtesans and Fishcakes: The Consuming Passions of Classical Athens (1997)*. Chicago and London, University of Chicago Press.

Davies, J. K. 1977–1978. "Athenian Citizenship: The Descent Group and the Alternatives," *Classical Journal* 73/2: 105–21.

Davis, M. 2002. "Introduction," in *Aristotle, On Poetics*, trans. S. Benardete and M. Davis. South Bend, IN, St. Augustine's Press, xi–xxx.

DeGenova, N. 2016. "The European Question: Migration, Race, and Postcoloniality in 'Europe'," *Social Text* 34/3: 75–102.

2013. "'Spectacles of Migrant 'Illegality': The Scene of Exclusion, the Obscene of Inclusion," *Ethnic and Racial Studies* 36/7: 1180–1198.

2010. "The Queer Politics of Migration: Reflections on 'Illegality' and 'Incorrigibility'," *Studies in Social Justice* 4/2: 101–126.

Demosthenes. 2003. *Speeches 50–59*. Trans. V. Bers. Austin, University of Texas Press.

Derrida, J. 2000. *Of Hospitality: Anne Dufourmantelle Invites Jacques Derrida to Respond*. Trans. Rachel Bowlby. Stanford University Press.

1998. "Introduction: Desistance," in P. Lacoue-Labarthe, *Typography: Mimesis, Philosophy, Politics*, ed. C. Fynsk. Stanford University Press, 1–42.

1997. *The Politics of Friendship*. Trans. G. Collins. New York, Verso.

1981. *Dissemination*. Trans. B. Johnson. Chicago University Press.

Detienne, M. 2009. *Comparative Anthropology of Ancient Greece*. Washington, DC, Center for Hellenic Studies.

1999. *The Masters of Truth in Archaic Greece*. Trans. J. Lloyd. New York, Zone Books.

Diamond, E. 1997. *Unmaking Mimesis: Essays on Feminism and Theater*. London, Routledge.

Dietz, M. 2012. "Between Polis and Empire," *American Political Science Review* 106/2: 275–293.

2003. "Current Controversies in Feminist Theory," *Annual Review of Political Science* 6: 399–431.

Dougherty, C. 1996. "Democratic Contradictions and the Synoptic Illusion of Euripides' *Ion*," in J. Ober and C. Hedrick (eds.), *Dēmokratia*. Princeton University Press, 249–270.

1993. *The Poetics of Colonization: From City to Text in Archaic Greece*. Oxford.

duBois, P. 2003. *Slaves and Other Objects*. Chicago University Press.

Duncan-Jones, R. P. 1980. "Metic Numbers in Periclean Athens," *Chiron* 10: 101–109.

Euben, J. P. 2003. *Platonic Noise*. Princeton University Press.
1986. *Greek Tragedy and Political Theory*. Berkeley, University of California Press.
Euripides. 1997. *Ion*. Trans. K. H. Lee. Warminster, UK, Aris & Phillips.
1996. *Ion*. Trans. W. S. Di Piero with introduction, notes, and commentary by P. Burian. New York, Oxford University Press.
Fausto-Sterling, A. 2000. *Sexing the Body: Gender Politics and the Construction of Sexuality*. New York, Basic Books.
Ferrari, G. R. F. 2007. "The Three-Part Soul," in G. R. F. Ferrari (ed.), *Cambridge Companion to Plato's Republic*. New York, Cambridge University Press, 165–201.
2003. *City and Soul in Plato's Republic*. University of Chicago Press.
2000. "Introduction," in Plato, *The Republic*, ed. G. R. F. Ferrari, trans. T. Griffith. Cambridge University Press, vi–xxxi.
1987. *Listening to the Cicadas: A Study of Plato's Phaedrus*. New York, Cambridge University Press.
Foley, H. P. 2001. *Female Acts in Greek Tragedy*. Princeton and Oxford, Princeton University Press.
Ford, A. 2002. *The Origins of Criticism: Literary Culture and Poetic Theory in Classical Greece*. Princeton University Press.
Forti, S. 2006. "The Biopolitics of Souls: Racism, Nazism, and Plato," *Political Theory* 34/1: 9–32.
Foster, E. 2010. *Thucydides, Pericles, and Periclean Imperialism*. New York, Cambridge University Press.
Foucault, M. 2014. *Wrong-Doing, Truth-Telling: The Function of Avowal in Justice*. Ed. F. Brion and B. E. Harcourt, trans. S. W. Sawyer. University of Chicago Press.
2010. *The Government of Self and Others: Lectures at the Collège de France, 1982–1983*. Ed. F. Gros, trans. G. Burchell. New York, Picador.
François, A. 2008. *Open Secrets: The Literature of Uncounted Experience*. Stanford University Press.
Frank, Jason. 2015. "Logical Revolts: Jacques Rancière and Political Subjectivization." Review Essay. *Political Theory* 43/2: 249–261.
Frank, Jill. 2013. "By Nature and by Design," *Review of Politics* 75/4: 685–687.
2004. "Citizens, Slaves, and Foreigners: Aristotle on Human Nature," *American Political Science Review* 98/1: 91–104.
Fredal, J. 2006. *Rhetorical Action in Ancient Athens: Persuasive Artistry from Solon to Demosthenes*. Carbondale, Southern Illinois University Press.
Gadamer, H.-G. 2013. *Truth and Method (1960)*. Trans. J. Weinsheimer and D. G. Marshall. Rev. 2nd ed. London and New York, Bloomsbury.
1985. *Philosophical Apprenticeships*. Trans. R. R. Sullivan. Cambridge, MA, and London, MIT.
Garland, R. 2014. *Wandering Greeks: The Ancient Greek Diaspora from the Age of Homer to the Death of Alexander the Great*. Princeton University Press.

2001. *The Piraeus: From the Fifth to the First Century B.C.* Bristol, Bristol Classical Press.

Gauthier, P. 1972. *Symbola: Les étragers et la justice dans les cités grecques*. Université de Nancy II.

Geschiere, P. 2011. "Autochthony, Citizenship, and Exclusion-Paradoxes in the Politics of Belonging in Africa and Europe," *India Journal of Global Legal Studies* 18/1: 321–339.

Gleason, M. 1990. "The Semiotics of Gender: Physiognomy and Self-Fashioning in the Second Century," in D. Halperin, J. Winkler, and F. I. Zeitlin (eds.), *Before Sexuality: The Construction of Erotic Experience in the Ancient Greek World*. Princeton University Press, 389–415.

Goldhill, S. and Osborne, R. (eds.) 1999. *Performance Culture and Athenian Democracy*. Cambridge University Press.

1987. "The Great Dionysia and Civic Ideology," *Journal of Hellenic Studies* 107: 58–70.

Gomme, A. W. 1933. *The Population of Athens in the Fifth and Fourth Centuries B. C.* Oxford, Blackwell.

Gottesman, A. 2014. *Politics and the Street in Democratic Athens*. Cambridge University Press.

Greenwood, E. 2016. "Seeing Citizens: Re-Reading Gyges' Ring of Invisibility (Plato *Republic* 359c6–360b2)," *Social Research: An International Quarterly* 83/4: 821–847. Special Issue: *Invisibility*, ed. A. Mack.

2010. "Mimicry and Classical Allusion in V. S. Naipaul's *The Mimic Men*," in S. Stephens and P. Vasunia (eds.), *Classics and National Cultures*. Oxford University Press, 100–120.

Gross, A. 2008. *What Blood Won't Tell: A History of Race on Trial in America*. Cambridge, MA, Harvard University Press.

Gunderson, E. 2000. *Staging Masculinity: The Rhetoric of Performance in the Roman World*. Ann Arbor, University of Michigan Press.

Gündoğdu, A. 2015. *Rightlessness in an Age of Rights: Hannah Arendt and the Contemporary Struggles of Migrants*. New York, Oxford University Press.

Hall, E. 2006. *The Theatrical Cast of Athens: Interactions between Ancient Greek Drama and Society*. Oxford University Press.

1989. *Inventing the Barbarian: Greek Self-definition through Tragedy*. Oxford, Clarendon.

Hall, J. 2002. *Hellenicity: Between Ethnicity and Culture*. University of Chicago Press.

Halliwell, S. 2002. *The Aesthetics of Mimesis: Ancient Texts and Modern Problems*. Princeton and Oxford, Princeton University Press.

Halpern, R. 2011. "Theater and Democratic Thought: Arendt to Rancière," *Critical Inquiry* 37/3: 545–572.

Hansen, M. H. 1991. *The Athenian Democracy in the Age of Demosthenes*. Oxford and Cambridge, MA, Blackwell.

Haraway, D. J. 1991. *Simians, Cyborgs, and Women: The Reinvention of Nature*. New York and London, Routledge.

Henry, M. 1995. *Prisoner of History*. Oxford University Press.

Hesk, J. 2000. *Deception and Democracy in Classical Athens*. Cambridge University Press.

Holmes, B. 2012. *Gender: Antiquity and Its Legacy*. Oxford University Press.

Honig, B. 2010. "Antigone's Two Laws: Greek Tragedy and the Politics of Humanism," *New Literary History* 41/1: 1–33.

2001. *Democracy and the Foreigner*. Princeton University Press.

Humphreys, S. C. 2007. "Social Relations on Stage: Witnesses in Classical Athens," in E. Carawan (ed.), *Oxford Readings in Classical Studies: The Attic Orators*. Oxford University Press, 140–213.

Hurst, H and Owen, S. (eds.). 2005. *Ancient Colonizations: Analogy, Similarity, and Difference*. London, Duckworth.

Irigaray, L. 1985. *Speculum of the Other Woman*. Trans. G. Gill. Ithaca, NY: Cornell University Press.

Irwin, E. 2016. "The Nothoi Come of Age? Illegitimate Sons and Political Unrest in Late Fifth-Century Athens," in P. Sänger (ed.), *Minderheiten und Migration in der griechisch-römischen Welt: Politische, rechtliche, religiöse und kulturelle Aspekte*. Paderborn, Schöningh Wissenschaftsverlag, 75–122.

Johnstone, S. 1999. *Disputes and Democracy: The Consequences of Litigation in Ancient Athens*. Austin, University of Texas Press.

Kahn, C. 1992. "Proleptic Composition in the *Republic*, Or Why Book 1 Was Never a Separate Dialogue," *Classical Quarterly* 41/1: 131–142.

Kamen, D. 2013. *Status in Classical Athens*. Princeton University Press.

2009. "Servile Invective in Classical Athens," *Scripta Classica Israelica* 28: 43–56.

Kapparis, K. 2005. "Immigration and Citizenship Procedures in Athenian Law," *Revue internationale des droits de l'antiquité* 52: 71–113.

Kasimis, D. 2016. "Plato's Open Secret," *Contemporary Political Theory* 15/4: 339–357.

2015. "Greek Literature in Contemporary Political Theory and Thought," *Oxford Handbook to Classical Studies Online*. doi:10.1093/oxfordhb/9780199935390.013.40.

2013. "The Tragedy of Blood-Based Membership: Secrecy and the Politics of Immigration in Euripides' *Ion*," *Political Theory* 41/2: 231–256.

Keenan, A. 2003. *Democracy in Question: Democratic Openness at a Time of Political Closure*. Stanford University Press.

Kennedy, R. F. 2014. *Immigrant Women in Athens: Gender, Ethnicity, and Citizenship in the Classical City*. New York, Routledge.

Kosmopoulou, A. 2001. "'Working Women': Female Professionals on Classical Attic Gravestones," *Annual of the British School of Archaeology* 96: 281–319.

Kurke, L. 1995. "Herodotus and the Language of Metals," *Helios* 22/1: 35–64.

1999. *Coins, Bodies, Games, and Gold: The Politics of Meaning in Archaic Greece*. Princeton University Press.

Lacey, W. K. 1980. "The Family of Euxitheus," *Classical Quarterly* 30/1: 57–61.

Lacoue-Labarthe, P. 1998. *Typography: Mimesis, Philosophy, Politics*. Ed. C. Fynsk. Stanford University Press.

Lambert, S. 1993. *The Phratries of Attica*. Ann Arbor, University of Michigan Press.
Lane, M. S. 2015. *The Birth of Politics: Eight Greek and Roman Political Ideas and Why They Matter*. Princeton University Press.
2001. *Plato's Progeny: How Plato and Socrates Still Captivate the Modern Mind*. London: Duckworth.
Lape, S. 2010. *Race and Citizen Identity in the Classical Athenian Democracy*. Cambridge University Press.
Larsen, N. 2007. *Passing* (1929). New York and London, Norton.
Lefebvre, H. 1991. *The Production of Space*. Trans. D. Nicholson-Smith. Oxford and Cambridge, MA, Blackwell.
Leonard, M. (ed.). 2010. *Derrida and Antiquity*. Oxford University Press.
2006. "The Uses of Reception: Derrida and the Historical Imperative," in C. Martindale and R. F. Thomas (eds.), *Classics and the Uses of Reception*. Malden, MA, Blackwell, 116–126.
2005. *Athens in Paris*. Oxford University Press.
2001. "The 'Politiques de l'amitié': Derrida's Greeks and a National Politics of Classical Scholarship," *Proceedings of the Cambridge Philological Society* 46: 45–78.
Lévi-Strauss, C. 1969. *Structural Anthropology*. Trans. C. Jacobson and B. Grundfest Schoepf. London, Penguin.
Long, C. P. 2003. "Dancing Naked with Socrates: Pericles, Aspasia, and Socrates at Play with Politics, Rhetoric, and Philosophy," *Ancient Philosophy* 23: 49–69.
Loraux, N. 2006. *The Invention of Athens: The Funeral Oration in the Classical City (1986)*. Trans. A. Sheridan. Cambridge, MA, Zone Books.
2001. "Aspasie, l'étrangère, l'intellectuelle," *Clio. Histoire, femmes et sociétés* 13: 2–15.
2000. *Born of the Earth: Myth and Politics in Athens*. Trans. S. Stewart. Ithaca, NY: Cornell University Press.
1993. *The Children of Athena: Athenian Ideas about Citizenship and the Division between the Sexes*. Trans. C. Levine. Princeton University Press.
Low, P. 2005. "Looking for the Language of Athenian Imperialism," *Journal of Hellenic Studies* 125: 93–111.
Lyons, J. D. and Nichols, S. G., Jr. (eds.) 1982. *Mimesis: From Mirror to Method, Aristotle to Descartes*. Hanover, NH, University of New England Press.
Lysias. 2000. *Lysias*, trans. S. C. Todd. Austin, University of Texas Press.
Maier, C. S. 2016. *Once within Borders: Territories of Power, Wealth, and Belonging since 1500*. Cambridge, MA, Belknap Press.
Mansouri, S. 2011. *Athènes vue par ses métèques: Ve–IVe siècle av. J.-C.* Paris, Tallandier.
Manville, P. B. 1997. *The Origins of Citizenship in Ancient Athens (1990)*. Princeton University Press.
1994. "Toward a New Paradigm of Athenian Citizenship," in A. L. Boegehold and A. C. Scafuro (eds.), *Athenian Identity and Civic Ideology*. Baltimore, MD, Johns Hopkins University Press, 21–33.

Markell, P. 2006. "The Rule of the People: Arendt, *Archê*, and Democracy," *American Political Science Review* 100/1: 1–14.
Markovits, E. 2009. *The Politics of Sincerity: Plato, Frank Speech, and Democratic Judgment*. University Park, Pennsylvania State University Press.
Mastronarde, D. J. 2010. *The Art of Euripides: Dramatic Technique and Social Context*. Cambridge University Press.
McClure, K. 2003. "Disconnections, Connections, and Questions: Reflections on Jacques Rancière's 'Ten These on Politics,'" *Theory & Event* 6/4: n.p.
McKeon, R. 1936. "Literary Criticism and the Concept of Imitation in Antiquity," *Modern Philology* 34/1: 1–35.
McNevin, A. 2011. *Contesting Citizenship: Irregular Migrants and New Frontiers of the Political*. New York, Columbia University Press.
Menn, S. 2006. "On Plato's ΠΟΛΙΤΕΙΑ," in J. J. Cleary and G. M. Gurtler (eds.), *Proceedings of the Boston Area Colloquium in Ancient Philosophy*, vol. XXI. Leiden, Brill, 1–55.
Mills, C. 1997. *The Racial Contract. Ithaca*, NY, and London, Cornell University Press.
Miller, P. A. 2016. *Diotima at the Barricades: French Feminists Read Plato*. Oxford.
Mirhady, D. C. 2000. "Demosthenes as Advocate: The Private Speeches," in Ian Worthington (ed.), *Demosthenes: Statesman and Orator*. London, Routledge, 181–204.
Monoson, S. S. 2012. "Dionysius I and Sicilian Theatrical Traditions in Plato's *Republic*," in Kathryn Bosher (ed.), *Theater outside Athens: Ancient Greek Drama in Sicily and South Italy*, 156–172.
2000. *Plato's Democratic Entanglements*. Princeton University Press.
1998. "Remembering Pericles: The Political and Theoretical Import of Plato's *Menexenus*." *Political Theory* 26: 489–513.
Mouffe, C. 2013. *Agonistics: Thinking the World Politically*. London, Verso.
2005. *The Return of the Political* (1993). Rev. ed. London, Verso.
Muller, J. P. and Richardson, W. J. (eds.) 1988. *The Purloined Poe: Lacan, Derrida, and Psychoanalytic Reading*.
Naddaf, G. 1998. "Translator's Introduction," in L. Brisson, *Plato, the Myth Maker*, ed. and trans. G. Naddaf. University of Chicago Press, vii–liii.
Nail, T. 2015. *The Figure of the Migrant*. Stanford University Press.
Nails, D. 2012. "Plato's *Republic* in Its Athenian Context," *History of Political Thought* 33/1: 1–22.
2002. *The People of Plato: A Prosopography of Plato and Other Socratics*. Indianapolis, Hackett.
Nietzsche, F. 1997. *Untimely Meditations (1876)*. Ed. D. Breazeale, trans. R. J. Hollingdale. Cambridge University Press.
Nightingale, A. W. 1995. *Genres in Dialogue: Plato and the Construct of Philosophy*. Cambridge University Press.
Ober, J. 2015. *The Rise and Fall of Classical Greece*. Princeton University Press.
2008. "The Original Meaning of 'Democracy': Capacity to Do Things, Not Majority Rule," *Constellations* 15/1: 3–9.

1998. *Political Dissent in Democratic Athens: Intellectual Critics of Popular Rule.* Princeton University Press.

1989. *Mass and Elite in Democratic Athens: Rhetoric, Ideology, and the Power of the People.* Princeton University Press.

Ogden, D. 1996. *Greek Bastardy in the Classical and Hellenistic Periods.* Oxford, Clarendon.

Osborne, M. J. 1982. *Naturalization in Athens, vol. 2: Commentaries on the Decrees Granting Citizenship.* Brussels, Paleis der Academiën.

Osborne, R. 2011. *The History Written on the Classical Greek Body.* Cambridge University Press.

2010. *Athens and Athenian Democracy.* Cambridge University Press.

(ed.) 2007. *Debating the Athenian Cultural Revolution: Art, Literature, Philosophy, and Politics, 430–380 BC.* Cambridge University Press.

2002. Review of E. Cohen, *The Athenian Nation* (2000). *Classical Philology* 97/1: 93–98.

1985. *Demos, the Discovery of Classical Attika.* Cambridge University Press.

Pache, C. 2001. "Barbarian Bond: Thracian Bendis among the Athenians," in S. R. Asirvatham, C. O. Pache, and J. Watrous (eds.), *Between Magic and Religion: Interdisciplinary Studies in Ancient Mediterranean Religion and Society.* Lanham MD, Rowman & Littlefield, 3–11.

Padel, R. 1990. "Making Space Speak," in J. J. Winkler and F. I. Zeitlin (eds.), *Nothing to Do with Dionysus? Athenian Drama in Its Social Context.* Princeton University Press, 336–365.

Page, C. 1991. "The Truth about Lies in Plato's *Republic*," *Ancient Philosophy* 11/1: 1–33.

Pappas, N. and Zelcer, M. 2015. *Politics and Philosophy in Plato's Menexenus.* New York, Routledge.

Pateman, C. 1988. *The Sexual Contract.* Stanford University Press.

Patterson, C. 2007. "Of Other Sorts: Slaves, Foreigners, and Women in Periclean Athens," in L. J. Samons II (ed.), *The Cambridge Companion to the Age of Pericles.* Cambridge University Press, 153–178.

2005. "Athenian Citizenship Law," in D. Cohen and M. Gagarin (eds.), *The Cambridge Companion to Ancient Greek Law.* Cambridge University Press, 267–289.

1981. *Pericles' Citizenship Law of 451–50 B.C.* New York, Arno.

Pelling, C. 2009. "Bringing Autochthony Up-to-Date: Herodotus and Thucydides," *Classical World* 102/4: 471–483.

Plato. 2013. *Republic*, 2 vols. Ed. and trans. C. Emlyn-Jones and W. Preddy. Cambridge, MA, Harvard University Press.

2012a. *Menexenus.* Trans. T. Griffith. In M. Schofield (ed.), *Plato: Gorgias, Menexenus, Protagoras.* Cambridge University Press.

2012b. *Republic.* Trans. C. Rowe. London, Penguin.

2000. *The Republic.* Ed. G. R. F. Ferrari, trans. T. Griffith. Cambridge University Press.

1963. *The Republic of Plato*. Ed. J. Adam (1902). 2 vols. 2nd ed. Cambridge University Press.

Plutarch. 1916. *Lives, vol. 3: Pericles and Fabius Maximus, Nicias and Crassus*. Trans. B. Perrin. Cambridge, MA, Harvard University Press.

Popper, K. R. 1971. *The Open Society and Its Enemies, vol. 1: The Spell of Plato (1945)*. 5th ed. Princeton University Press.

Potolsky, M. 2006. *Mimesis*. New York and London, Routledge.

Raaflaub, K. 2004. *The Discovery of Freedom in Ancient Greece*. Trans. R. Franciscono. University of Chicago Press.

Rana, A. 2010. *The Two Faces of American Freedom*. Cambridge, MA, Harvard University Press.

Rancière, J. 2007. *On the Shores of Politics*. Trans. Liz Heron. New York, Verso.

2006. *Hatred of Democracy*. Trans. S. Corcoran. London, Verso.

2004. *The Philosopher and His Poor*. Trans. J. Drury. Durham, NC, and London, Duke University Press.

2001. "Ten Theses on Politics." Trans. Rachel Bowlby and Davide Panagia. *Theory & Event* 5/3: n.p.

Randall, R. H. 1953. "The Erechtheum Workmen," *American Journal of Archaeology* 57/3: 199–210.

Reeve, C. D. C. 1988. *Philosopher-Kings: The Argument of Plato's* Republic. Princeton University Press.

Rehm, R. 2002. *The Play of Space: Spatial Transformation in Greek Tragedy*. Princeton University Press.

1992. *Greek Tragic Theatre*. London, Routledge.

Reinhard, K. 2012. "Introduction," in A. Badiou, *Plato's* Republic*: A Dialogue in 16 Chapters*, trans. S. Spitzer. New York, Columbia University Press, vii–xxiii.

Rhodes, P. J. and Osborne, R. 2003. *Greek Historical Inscriptions 404–323 BC*. Oxford University Press.

Roselli, D. 2011. *Theater of the People: Spectator and Society in Ancient Athens*. Austin, University of Texas Press.

Rosenblum, N. 1984. Review of M. Walzer, *Spheres of Justice* (1983). *World Politics* 36/4: 581–596.

Rosenstock, B. 1994. "Athena's Cloak: Plato's Critique of the Democratic City in the *Republic*," *Political Theory* 22/3: 363–390.

Rosivach, V. J. 1987. "Autochthony and the Athenians," *Classical Quarterly* n.s. 37/2: 294–306.

Roy, J. 2014. "Autochthony in Ancient Greece," in J. McInerney (ed.), *A Companion to Ethnicity in the Ancient Mediterranean*. Hoboken, NJ, John Wiley & Sons, 241–255.

Said, E. W. 1993. *Culture and Imperialism*. New York, Alfred A. Knopf.

Saxonhouse, A. 2009. "The Socratic Narrative: A Democratic Rereading of Plato's Dialogues," *Political Theory* 37/6: 728–753.

1998. "Democracy, Equality, and *Eidē*: A Radical View from Book 8 of Plato's *Republic*," *American Political Science Review* 92/2: 273–283.

1992. *Fear of Diversity: The Birth of Political Science in Ancient Greek Thought.* University of Chicago Press.
1986. "Myths and the Origins of Cities: Reflections on the Autochthony Theme in Euripides' *Ion*," in J. Peter Euben (ed.), *Greek Tragedy and Political Theory.* Berkeley, University of California Press, 252–273.
Scafuro, A. 1994. "Witnessing and False Witnessing: Proving Citizenship and Kin Identity in Fourth-Century Athens," in A. L. Boegehold and A. C. Scafuro (eds.), *Athenian Identity and Civic Ideology.* Baltimore, MD, Johns Hopkins University Press, 156–198.
Schofield, M. 2007. "The Noble Lie," in G. R. F. Ferrari (ed.), *The Cambridge Companion to Plato's* Republic. Cambridge University Press, 138–164.
2006. *Plato: Political Philosopher.* Oxford University Press.
Sedgwick, E. K. 2008. *Epistemology of the Closet* (1990). Updated ed. Berkeley and Los Angeles, University of California Press.
Seery, J. 1988. "Politics as Ironic Community: On the Themes of Descent and Return in Plato's *Republic*," *Political Theory* 16/2: 229–256.
Shachar, A. 2007. *The Birthright Lottery: Citizenship and Global Inequality.* Cambridge, MA, Harvard University Press.
Shklar, J. N. 1985. *Men and Citizens: A Study of Rousseau's Social and Political Thought (1969).* Cambridge University Press.
Sissa, G. 2008. *Sex and Sensuality in the Ancient World.* New Haven, Yale University Press.
Sommerstein, A. H. and Bayliss, A. J. 2012. *Oath and State in Ancient Greece.* Berlin, De Gruyter.
Steinberger, P. 1996. "Who Is Cephalus?" *Political Theory* 24: 172–199.
Stevens, J. 2017. "Introduction," in B. Lawrance and J. Stevens (eds.), *Citizenship in Question: Evidentiary Birthright and Statelessness.* Durham, NC, Duke University Press, 1–24.
1999. *Reproducing the State.* Princeton University Press.
Stewart, A. 1995. "Imag(in)ing the Other: Amazons and Ethnicity in Fifth-Century Athens," *Poetics Today* 16/4: 571–597.
Strauss, L. 1978. *The City and Man* (1964). University of Chicago Press.
Tarnopolsky, C. 2009. "Plato's Mimetic *Republic*: A Preliminary Treatment of Plato's Preliminary Treatment of the *Gennaion Pseudos*." Paper Presented at the Annual Meeting of the American Political Science Association, Toronto, Canada.
Taylor, C. 2016. "Social Dynamics in Fourth-Century Athens: Poverty and Standards of Living," in C. Tiersch (ed.), *Die athenische Demokratie im 4. Jh.* Stuttgart, Steiner, 261–277.
2015. "Social Networks and Social Mobility in Fourth-Century Athens," in C. Taylor and K. Vlassopoulos (eds.), *Communities and Networks in the Ancient Greek World.* Oxford University Press, 35–53.
Thucydides 1919–1923. *History of the Peloponnesian War*, 4 vols. Trans. C. F. Smith. Cambridge, MA, Harvard University Press.
Trevett, J. C. 1992. *Apollodorus the Son of Pasion.* Oxford University Press.

Tzelepis, E. and Athanasiou, A. (eds.) 2010. *Rewriting Difference: Luce Irigaray and "The Greeks."* Albany, State University of New York Press.

Usher, S. 1999. *Greek Oratory: Tradition and Originality.* Oxford University Press.

Vardoulakis, D. 2013. *Sovereignty and Its Other: Toward the Dejustification of Violence.* New York, Fordham University Press.

Vernant, J. 1991. "The Birth of Images," in J. Vernant, *Mortals and Immortals: Collected Essays*, ed. F. I. Zeitlin. Princeton University Press, 164–185.

Vidal-Naquet, P. 1999. "Foreword," in M. Detienne, *The Masters of Truth in Archaic Greece*, trans. J. Lloyd. New York, Zone Books, 7–14.

1995. *Politics Ancient and Modern.* Trans. J. Lloyd. Cambridge, Polity.

1988. "Oedipus between Two Cities: An Essay on *Oedipus at Colonus*," in J. Vernant and P. Vidal-Naquet, *Myth and Tragedy in Ancient Greece*, trans. J. Lloyd. New York, Zone Books, 329–359.

1986. *The Black Hunter: Forms of Thought and Forms of Society in the Greek World.* Trans. A. Szegedy-Maszak. Baltimore, MD, Johns Hopkins University Press.

Villa, D. 2001. *Socratic Citizenship.* Princeton University Press.

Vlassopoulos, K. 2007. "Free Spaces: Identity, Experience, and Democracy in Classical Athens," *Classical Quarterly* 57/1: 33–52.

Vlastos, G. 1991. *Socrates: Ironist and Moral Philosopher.* Ithaca, NY, Cornell University Press.

Voegelin, E. 2000. *Plato (1957).* Columbia and London, University of Missouri Press.

Von Reden, S. 1998. "The Well-Ordered Polis: Topographies of Civic Space," in P. Cartledge, P. Millett, and S. Von Reden (eds.), *Kosmos: Essays in Order, Conflict and Community in Classical Athens.* Cambridge University Press, 170–190.

1995. "The Piraeus—A World Apart," *Greece & Rome* 42/1: 24–37.

Wallach, J. 2001. *The Platonic Political Art: A Study of Critical Reason and Democracy.* University Park, Pennsylvania State University Press.

Walsh, G. B. 1978. "The Rhetoric of Birthright and Race in Euripides' *Ion*," *Hermes* 106/2: 301–315.

Walzer, M. 1983. *Spheres of Justice: A Defense of Pluralism and Equality.* New York, Basic Books.

Watson, J. 2010. "The Origin of the Metic Status at Athens," *Cambridge Classical Journal: Proceedings of the Cambridge Philological Society* 56: 259–278.

White, H. 1987. *The Content of the Form: Narrative Discourse and Historical Representation.* Baltimore, MD, Johns Hopkins University Press.

Whitehead, D. 1986. *The Demes of Attica, 508/7–ca.250 B.C.: A Political and Social Study.* Princeton University Press.

1977. *The Ideology of the Athenian Metic.* Cambridge: Cambridge Philological Society.

1975. "Aristotle the Metic," *Proceedings of the Cambridge Philological Society* 21: 94–99.

Wijma, S. M. 2014. *Embracing the Immigrant: The Participation of Metics in Athenian Polis Religion (5th–4th Century BC)*. Stuttgart, Franz Steiner Verlag.

Winkler, J. 1990. "Laying Down the Law: The Oversight of Men's Sexual Behavior in Athens," in D. Halperin, J. Winkler, and F. I. Zeitlin (eds.), *Before Sexuality: The Construction of Erotic Experience in the Ancient Greek World*. Princeton University Press, 171–209.

Wohl, V. 2015. *Euripides and the Politics of Form*. Princeton University Press.

2010. *Law's Cosmos: Juridical Discourse in Athenian Forensic Oratory*. Cambridge University Press.

2002. *Love among the Ruins: The Erotics of Democracy in Classical Athens*. Princeton University Press.

Wolin, S. 2016. *Fugitive Democracy: And Other Essays*, ed. N. Xenos. Princeton University Press.

Wolpert, A. 2002. *Remembering Defeat: Civil War and Civic Memory in Ancient Athens*. Baltimore, MD, Johns Hopkins University Press.

Wood, E. M. 1988. *Peasant-Citizen and Slave: The Foundations of Athenian Democracy*. London and New York, Verso.

Worman, N. 2014. "Mapping Literary Styles in Aristophanes' *Frogs*," in K. Gilhuly and N. Worman (eds.), *Space, Place, and Landscape in Ancient Greek Literature and Culture*. Cambridge University Press, 200–239.

2008. *Abusive Mouths in Classical Athens*. Cambridge University Press.

2001. *Making Silence Speak: Women's Voices in Greek Literature and Society*. Princeton University Press.

Xenophon. 1968. *Scripta Minora*. Trans. G. W. Bowersock. Cambridge, MA, Harvard University Press.

Yoshikawa, H. 2011. *Immigrants Raising Citizens: Undocumented Parents and Their Young Children*. New York, The Russell Sage Foundation.

Zacharia, K. 2003. *Converging Truths: Euripides'* Ion *and the Athenian Quest for Self-Definition*. Leiden and Boston, Brill.

Zeitlin, F. I. 1996. *Playing the Other: Gender and Society in Classical Greek Literature*. University of Chicago Press.

1989. "Mysteries of Identity and Designs of the Self in Euripides' *Ion*," *Proceedings of the Cambridge Philological Society* 35: 144–196.

Zerilli, L. M. G. 1994. *Signifying Woman: Culture and Chaos in Rousseau, Burke, and Mill*. Ithaca, NY, Cornell University Press.

Zuckert, C. H. 1996. *Postmodern Platos: Nietzsche, Heidegger, Gadamer, Strauss, Derrida*. University of Chicago Press.

Index

Page numbers with "n" are notes.